THE REAL BUSINESS 101

LESSONS FROM THE TRENCHES

BY JIM SOBECK

What People Saying About
The Real Business 101: Lessons From The Trenches.

Jim's book passes on lessons learned over 40 years as a serial entrepreneur and teaches a lot of things you won't learn at most business schools. It isn't just a book on business to be read once but a reference guide you'll use over and over.

> -**Verne Harnish** is the Founder of Entrepreneurs' Organization and author of *Mastering the Rockefeller Habits* and a Fortune Magazine columnist

Jim Sobeck is one of the brightest people I know. He not only has had a lifetime of exposure to the business world, he is an outstanding student and possesses a great thirst for knowledge.

The Real Business 101 reads just like Sobeck communicates, straightforward and direct. Sobeck doesn't pull any punches as he shares with the reader the lessons he has learned from his roots as a sales representative to the present as the CEO of a highly successful chain of distribution businesses.

There's really very little that Jim Sobeck has not done in the business world and he has done an excellent job of documenting almost every aspect of managing a business. I've read literally hundreds of business books and I've never seen a book as thorough and as comprehensive as The Real Business 101. The book covers everything a general manager needs to know to run a business from sales to asset management to people management to purchasing to hiring to how to ensure profitability and so much more.

If you buy this book, it will become like a business manual you'll refer to often as you negotiate your way through the real world of business management.

> -**Bill Lee** is author of Gross Margin: 26 Factors Affecting Your Bottom Line and 30 Ways Managers Shoot Themselves in the Foot.

Having consulted with hundreds of distribution businesses over the last 30+ years I have found that practical and easy to understand business advice is sorely needed in most small to medium sized businesses today. Jim dispenses advice learned over a 40 year successful career as a serial entrepreneur in an engaging and easy to understand way. I think this book is an indispensable part of any small business owner's library.

> -**Bruce Merrifield** is President of The Merrifield Consulting Group and author of: Electric Commerce for Distribution Channels, Supply Chain Math Management for Distributors, and High Performance Distribution Ideas for All.

Having played rugby with Jim in Dallas in the 80's for the Dallas Harlequins and winning a National Championship together, I wasn't surprised to see that he brings the same intense, competitive drive to business that he did on the rugby pitch. He is one of the greatest men I have had the pleasure to meet in my intense life. *The Real Business 101: Lessons From the Trenches* is a must-read for any business owner. Instead of the dry, analytical instruction found in most business textbooks, Jim's book is a fun read, packed with real world examples learned over his successful 40 year business career. I highly recommend it for any entrepreneur or wanna be entrepreneur."

> -**Edouard "Spyk" Gheur** Former professional rugby player, stuntman, actor and now author of... *A Naughty Thing Called Life* and *Life's Bad Hand* by Papa Spyk

This book is dedicated to my many mentors, especially my Dad, E. J. "Jim" Sobeck, Jr., Clarence Bauknight, Lanny Moore, Sr., Bill Lee, Michael Johnson, Bud Stoner, and Bruce Merrifield. There are several more mentors who taught me many great lessons and I apologize in advance to anyone whose name I didn't mention here in the interest of saving space. I also want to thank my wife, Cindy, and our children, Jimmy, Thomas, and Jillian who have been very supportive as I have pursued my career. I also want to apologize to them for the birthdays and anniversaries I missed while traveling on business over the years. This is the downside of being an entrepreneur and my biggest regret.

TABLE OF CONTENTS

FOREWORD

You've probably heard the old saying, "Business is easy. You buy something at one price and you sell it at a higher price. That's all there is to it... except for a million details." The mission of this book is to identify as many of those million details as possible and share solutions I've learned (mostly the hard way) in my almost 40 year career in business.

CHAPTER 1
HIRING

The first chapter is about hiring because nothing is more important in business than having a great team. You can do everything yourself when you have a paper route or if you're a life insurance salesperson, but if you have, or want to have, a business that services customers, there is nothing more important than having great people on your team.

I don't care how great your facilities, furnishings, and delivery vehicles are, or how spectacular your inventory assortment is, mediocre people will ensure that you fail. On the other hand, you can have mediocre facilities, secondhand furnishings, and used delivery vehicles, but if you have a great team of self-motivated people you will win, and win big.

So, how do you find great people? Here are some ways that have worked for me:

- Word-of-mouth referrals. When several people you respect tell you about a superstar, you need to hire him/her. Remember, it's never the wrong time to hire the right person. I don't care how bad the economy is, superstars always find a way to pay for themselves... and then some.

- Postings on a web-based service such as CareerBuilder. We only run help wanted ads on the web, never in the newspaper anymore. Why? First, you get a better grade of candidate over the web versus newspaper ads because your applicants have to be at least a little bit computer literate to find your job posting on a site such as CareerBuilder. Any person with a sixth-grade education can find your ad in the newspaper. We've found that people who respond to a posting on the web are a cut above people who respond to newspaper ads. Another thing we like about CareerBuilder is they have "screener questions" that give us a score for every person responding to our ad. Below 70 is a failing grade in school and it is with us. If someone doesn't get a score of over 70 (and preferably over 90) I don't even bother reading their resume.

- Ask your customers. Ask them who they deal with from other companies that impress them. Don't send them an e-mail, pick up the phone and call them. Most people are so busy they will either delete your e-mail or respond that they don't know anyone, but when you get them on the phone and engage them in conversation you invariably will get a few names. Better yet take them to lunch. I guarantee you they'll come up with a few names over lunch.

- Networking. Be active in business groups and trade associations and you invariably will meet people that impress you. Plus, if you've known them for a while through a trade group you're not hiring a total stranger. Hiring total strangers is a crapshoot. Increase your odds of success by hiring known entities.

- Always be looking. When you meet someone with "the right stuff", you know it. Herb Kelleher, one of the founders of Southwest Airlines, a legendary airline with a market cap more than all of the other airlines in the world combined, says that, at Southwest, they hire a type of person rather than a person with certain experience. He says that when you meet someone with a great attitude and a magnetic personality you can teach them everything else they need to know but no amount of training can fix a bad attitude. In my career I have hired waitresses with great personalities and made them inside salespeople, I have promoted truck drivers into outside sales because of their attitude and their drive, and I have made people with just a high school education an officer in my company because of their absolute unwillingness to cut corners, their integrity, and their commitment to excellence.

CHAPTER 2
INTERVIEWING TIPS

Once you have candidates for your open positions how do you proceed with the interview process? The first thing I do is always a 30 minute or so telephone interview as the first step. Why a telephone interview? There are two main reasons. First, so much business is done over the telephone these days I like to see what sort of impression a candidate makes over the phone. Does he/she come across as positive and upbeat, does he/she speak clearly and understandably, does he/she answer my questions or duck them, are his/her answers concise, or long and rambling, and, my pet peeve, do they let me finish my questions or do they interrupt me and start answering before I have even finished asking the question? I use a telephone interview form so that I am sure to ask the same questions of each candidate and I grade each phone interview on an A-F basis as soon as I am done, while my impressions are fresh in my mind.

The second reason for the initial interview being done over the telephone is that it saves the candidate and me the time of the personal interview. If someone is driving several hours to meet me I feel bad only giving them 30 minutes. I don't feel bad only giving someone 30 minutes over the phone. Plus I do a lot of the telephone interviews at night and over the weekend because it's normally easier for both parties to do then versus during the work week, especially if the candidate is employed.

After the round of telephone interviews I cut the field to two or three candidates and have them in for a personal interview. My time allotment for a personal interview is normally about two hours or even longer for senior positions, preferably including a meal so I can observe his/her manners, how they treat servers, and how they engage in small talk. Again, I use a standardized list of questions to ensure that I ask the same questions to each candidate, and again I grade each candidate on an A-F basis.

After the personal interview round I have the leading candidate come back to interview with several other people in our organization. It's helpful to get the perspective of other people and if the consensus is that this person will fit in our organization, then, if their background check and reference checks are good, we make a written job offer. We always make our job offers in writing so as to avoid any misunderstandings as to exactly what the compensation package entails.

CHAPTER 3

PRE-EMPLOYMENT TESTING, REFERENCE CHECKS, AND BACKGROUND CHECKS

The area of pre-employment testing, reference checks, and background checks is where I find that most companies either come up short in the hiring process or, as incredible as it may sound, don't do anything at all. When I talk to other CEOs I find that only a very small percentage do any pre-employment testing whatsoever and most don't do reference checks or background checks. I think that doing these three things, and doing them thoroughly, is absolutely critical to successful hiring. I hear many managers say that they are lucky if one in three or one in four of their hires work out. Our batting average is more like three out of four. The difference between batting .250 and .750 in baseball would be millions of dollars a year and a guaranteed spot in the Hall of Fame. I submit to you that the same kinds of dollars are at stake in business. What is the cost of a bad hire? If you are hiring to replace a salesperson who was selling $2 million a year at a 30% gross margin you're talking about $600,000 in gross profit that needs to be replaced. How long does it take a new salesperson to sell the same amount as the successful salesperson he or she replaces? My experience tells me that it's about three years before a new salesperson is generating the volume of his or her predecessor. So, if you hire hastily and the new hire washes out after a year and only generates $100,000 in gross profit during that year, your company just lost $500,000. If you make another hasty hire and that person fails as well you could easily lose $1 million in a two-year period. Doesn't that merit spending a few hundred dollars on pre-employment testing, a thorough background check, and an hour or two of your time checking references? Let's look at each of the three steps mentioned above.

In terms of pre-employment testing we use the Wonderlic personnel test to give us a rough idea of the intelligence level of the candidate. You may be familiar with this test if you're a football fan because the NFL has used it in "The Combine" for years. If you aren't familiar with the combine, it is an event held by the NFL where promising college football stars go to a city for a few days of extensive physical testing, intelligence testing, and interviews. Even in the NFL, talent, experience, and strength isn't enough...intelligence matters. A lot. When NY Giants Super Bowl winning quarterback Eli Manning of Ole Miss went to the combine he got a 43 on the Wonderlic test. That same year Vince Young of The University of Texas scored a seven. Seven is borderline functional and 43 is genius level. Guess who was drafted first and got more money? In our building materials distribution company we look for at least a score of 15 for truck drivers, 20 for sales, 25 for management, and preferably 30 or higher for senior management. The Wonderlic tests are not expensive; you can get volume discounts that bring the price down to only a few dollars per test. To learn more about this test click here.

We also use the Kolbe Conative index (www.kolbe.com), the DISC (www.discprofile.com), and the Athene Quotient assessment (www.atheneinc.com) to give us a better understanding of each candidate and what makes them tick . We obtain the preceding three assessments, as well as help with interpreting them, from Lee Resources International. Click here to see their website.

Regarding background checks, there are several reasons to do a thorough background check. One of the most important is for liability reasons, both for your company and you. If you hire a person without doing a background check and it turns out this person is a violent felon who rapes and kills one of your employees, you are exposing your company, and you personally, to millions of dollars of liability, not to mention the guilt you would feel for hiring such a person. In this Internet age you can get a background check in a matter of minutes for less than $100. Isn't that worth it? There are a lot of good background checking services but the one we use is www.backgroundchecks.com.

We check criminal records, motor vehicle records, and credit reports. I've already explained why we check criminal records but you may be wondering why we check motor vehicle records and credit reports. We check motor vehicle records because most of our employees will drive on company business at some point. Obviously outside salespeople drive all the time, but even people in our accounting office go to the bank and post office on company business and should they have an accident while driving on company business we could be liable. If it turns out that we hired a person who has a suspended license or has had multiple accidents and/or tickets we could be convicted of gross negligence.

Why do we check credit reports? There are some obvious and less obvious reasons. One of the obvious reasons is we are worried about theft. Studies have shown that the vast majority of business theft is from within, not from shoplifters or burglars. If we hire someone with terrible credit they may succumb to the urge to steal to try to get them out of their financial bind. Also, one of the most important ingredients in a good hire is judgment. Show me someone with terrible credit and almost always they will have terrible judgment.

The last thing we check once a candidate clears the above hurdles are references. Ten to 20 years ago it was hard to get references because I would call a company for reference and be connected to the human resources department who would almost always tell me that they can only give out the date my candidate started, the day they left, and their position. That isn't much help. Now in the age of mobile phones I ask candidates to give me the cell phone number for each of their references. That way you circumvent the HR department and get right to the person you need to talk to. I ask candidates for 3 to 5 personal as well as business references. That way I generally can talk to at least three personal references and three former supervisors or coworkers. To put the person giving the reference at ease I state that I have made the provisional decision to hire the person I'm checking on and I just want some input on how to help them achieve their potential. Once you get a reference talking most of them will tell you anything you need to know. The hard part is to get them talking. That's why I put them at ease at the outset.

I use a standard reference check form so that I don't forget to ask any important things and so that I ask the same questions to each reference. I have never finished doing a round of reference checks where I didn't think it was time very well spent. I invariably know the candidate much better and have a clearer hire/don't hire decision by the time I'm done with reference checks.

One last thing about reference checks — — do them yourself. Don't delegate them to your HR department and never delegate them to a headhunter. You want to hear the comments the references make with your own ears and sometimes an HR person just wants to close out the search so they can move on to another one and they will shade the reference a little more positive than it actually was. Headhunters are nothing more than salesmen and I found out the hard way early in my career that you never get a bad reference when you have the search firm representative do it for you as they just want their commission, except in rare instances.

The above may sound time-consuming and expensive. It isn't. To do all of the things above shouldn't take you more than two or three hours and $200-$300. If that saves you $500,000-$1,000,000, isn't worth it?

CHAPTER 4
MONTHLY MEETINGS

Former Intel CEO and legendary businessman Andy Grove said in his book *High Output Management*, that if he had only one management tool available to him it would be the monthly meeting. If you manage people I can't stress enough the importance of monthly meetings. In today's fast-paced business climate with most communication via e-mail and the occasional phone call, face-to-face meetings are much rarer than in the past. A lot of miscommunication or misinterpretation can happen via e-mail so a monthly meeting of an hour or so can be very helpful.

Throughout the month put notes or e-mails in a file about things you want to discuss with those who report to you that aren't important enough to merit an immediate meeting. Prior to each monthly meeting review the items in the file and, if you're like me, you'll end up not discussing most of the items because with the benefit of a little time you'll find most really weren't that important.

The format of the meeting goes like this. The person you're meeting with begins the meeting by reviewing action items assigned at the last meeting and the status of each. You then bring up new items and they are discussed. The items that are discussed and not resolved go on the action item list for the next meeting. The list is then sent to you after the meeting so you can verify that the tasks assigned were properly understood.

Also, take time at the end of the meeting to discuss personal issues if the person you're meeting with is comfortable doing so with you. Remember, people don't care how much you know until they know how much you care.

CHAPTER 5

THE CREDIT PROCESS

Part One - The Credit Application

In most B2B businesses the extension of trade credit is required as most, if not all, of your competition is extending credit, so you will have to as well. Other than embezzling there is nothing that will take your business down faster than weak credit procedures. I have seen the third and fourth generation businesses file bankruptcy due to excessive bad debts, especially near the end of a downturn like we are presently experiencing. Why do businesses fail at the end of the downtown and not as often in the beginning or the middle? Normally it's because that's when weak businesses finally run out of cash. A lot of businesses rob Peter to pay Paul; i.e. they get cut off from supplier A and go on to supplier B, and then supplier C, and so on until they finally run out of suppliers who will extend credit. It's like a game of musical chairs and you don't want to be the one left standing when your customer runs out of cash.

Effective credit procedures began with a comprehensive credit application. Your credit application should contain at a minimum:

1. **A personal guarantee.** A lot of customers don't want to sign a personal guarantee because they don't want to have to pay you if their Corporation fails. Without a personal guarantee you can't pierce the corporate veil and if your customer's Corporation fails you can't collect from them personally unless you have a personal guarantee. Do we always get one? No. Public companies will never give you one nor will large companies with excellent credit. However, if a company has less than stellar credit we insist on a personal guarantee unless we can get credit insurance on them. More on credit insurance in my next post.

2. **An agreement for the customer to pay your legal fees if you have to file suit to get paid.** Without this, you'll have to pay your own legal fees if you have to sue your customer to get paid. You don't want to have to do this for obvious reasons. Plus, more than one customer has paid us when we have pointed out that if we have to sue them, and we win, that they will have to pay our legal fees. We point out that we use very expensive lawyers!

3. **Finance charges.** Unless your credit application spells out the interest rate your customer has to pay for late payment, most states won't let you charge **any** finance charge. I always suggest that your agreement include the highest interest rate allowed in your state. It's not that you want to collect on your finance charges, you want them to be a deterrent to late payment, and a high rate is a great deterrent in most cases.

4. **The terms and conditions of sale.** Make sure that all of your terms and conditions of sale are spelled out in your credit agreement and not just on the back of your invoice. Most judges will rule that the customer doesn't look at the back of the invoice. Also, include in your terms and conditions things such as if no one is there to sign for a delivery, and you leave it at the customer's request, but it gets stolen, that the customer is still liable for payment. We used to have customers tell us to leave a delivery at a job site even if no one was there and then refuse to pay and tell us that the materials were stolen over-night. Having this situation covered in your credit agreement can save you a lot of money.

These are some of the key points of a good credit application but there are many more. To see our credit application it is on the home page of our website, www.newsouthsupply.com.

CHAPTER 6

THE CREDIT PROCESS:
PART TWO - CREDIT INSURANCE

Most people I talk to don't know that you can purchase insurance on your accounts receivable. When you think about it, you insure your property, inventory, trucks, and office equipment, so why not your accounts receivable? In many companies accounts receivable is one of your largest assets yet it is almost always totally uninsured.

I think that your receivables are more likely to go bad at the end of a downturn versus during the beginning or middle of a recession. This is because many customers get put on COD, go to another supplier, and keep going around the horn until they run out of suppliers who will extend them credit. If your customers have 5-10, or even more vendors they can buy your products from, this process can take well over a year before they run out of people that will extend credit to them. If you have credit insurance you won't be the company left standing when this game of musical chairs ends.

The credit insurance process works like this. The insurer is sent your accounts receivable aging statement. They review it, and as you might expect, spend a lot of time looking at past due accounts to see who they are and how much they owe you. All credit insurers have large databases of information about all types of customers. If they see that certain of your customers own money to multiple companies that is significantly past-due they will exclude these accounts from the coverage. In our case, we only had five out of over 2500 customers excluded from coverage.

What is the cost of credit insurance? Without getting into the specifics of our premium I will say that it was significantly less than I expected and it was less than the YTD bad debts we had already incurred at the time of getting the coverage. I am now sleeping better at night knowing that the vast majority of our customers' receivables are now insured and we will get reimbursed if they don't pay us. What is that kind of peace of mind worth?

CHAPTER 7

THE CREDIT PROCESS:
PART THREE -
THE CREDIT APPROVAL PROCESS

Once you have received the credit application back from a prospective customer what do you do then? Well, the first thing to do is to make sure that it has been fully completed. I have found over the years that most customers don't complete the entire application. Sometimes they can't be bothered to take the time to fill out the entire application but other times they are purposely omitting information. You should make sure that they have provided all of the information for which you have asked. Sometimes they won't fill out the entire application and they will attach their own credit information sheet. As long as we get all of the information we need we don't care if it's on an attached form. Most large companies have a credit information form which they attach to credit applications because they are asked for so many. This is fine with me, but we do require that they at least sign our credit application so they are bound by our terms and conditions of sale.

We also require that the credit application be signed by an officer or someone with signing authority. If you accept a credit application signed by a low-level employee it may not hold up in court as the debtor may claim that the person signing the application didn't have the authority to do so. Beyond an officer, we will accept signatures from a controller, a purchasing manager, or project manager, among other titles.

What do you do if a large company refuses to even sign the credit application? We have this happen from time to time and if we check with Dun & Bradstreet (D&B) and they have good credit then we send them a letter with a copy of our terms and conditions attached stating that unless we hear otherwise from them we will assume that they are in agreement with our terms and conditions of sale. Rarely do we ever hear back from the customer after we send such a letter. Our collection attorneys have told us that this will hold up in court as long as the customer doesn't send us back a letter stating that they don't agree with our terms and conditions of sale.

What about credit references? Our credit application asks for five credit references however we don't put a lot of weight on what these credit references say in that most companies handpick a few suppliers to list on their credit applications that they are sure to always pay on time. Sometimes we have even found that credit references were affiliated companies or owned by the applicant's relatives. Therefore we put a lot of stock in what D&B says and what our credit insurer says about the applicant. Also, our customer service manager (we use that title instead of credit manager because it sounds much friendlier to our customers) belongs to the National Association of Credit Managers (NACM) and she goes to regular monthly meetings of the chapter to which we belong to keep up with what is being said about our customers by other companies selling them. NACM has different meetings for different industries so you don't have to go to meetings where customers you don't sell to are being discussed.

As most of our customers are commercial contractors working on jobs with performance bonds, our credit application asks for information about their bonding company. We have found that if you don't get the bonding company information up front it's hard to get it once they owe you money as a contractor never wants you to file against their performance bond because it will either impede their ability to get bonded on future jobs, raise their rates, or both. If you deal with companies that have to provide performance bonds I strongly suggest you get the bonding company information when setting up the customer.

Once a customer clears all of the above hurdles then we send them a welcome letter outlining how we do business and our expectations of them. We also ask them to provide us with any specifics about how to best do business with them. We have found that when we don't get paid on time it's normally because we didn't comply with some regulation our customer has that we didn't know about such as sending all invoices to their main office and not the local office with which we are dealing, or not providing proof of delivery. We only provide proof of delivery upon request but if we know that a customer requires that for us to be paid on time we are happy to provide it.

We only start a customer out with the credit line required for the job for which we have currently quoted them. We will then raise their credit line over time provided that they comply with our payment terms.

CHAPTER 8
THE CREDIT PROCESS: PART FOUR - USING DUN & BRADSTREET

I don't know why all businesses don't use Dun & Bradstreet to get credit and payment information about their current and prospective customers. They are the oldest and largest credit bureau. Some of the reasons for not using them that I hear are, "They are too expensive", or "Their information isn't always timely or accurate". My experience using them for over 30 years is just the opposite. We use their DNBi service (www.dnbi.com) which, for one affordable annual payment of less than an average bad debt, gives us unlimited access to credit reports on our current customers as well as prospective new customers. I have also found that most of the time their information about our customers is both timely and accurate. Yes, there are exceptions, but most of the time we have found their information to be up-to-date.

When we are considering opening up a new account the first step for us is download a full credit report from D&B. The first things we look at are the prospective customer's D&B rating and their PAYDEX score. The PAYDEX score shows how many days past the due date companies pay their bills. In our industry (construction supply) it isn't unusual to see companies that pay their bills 15 days late or so. However, when we see that someone consistently pays their bills 30 days or more beyond terms we avoid selling those types of companies, especially because we pay about 90% of our bills within 10 days to get the prompt pay discount.

The next thing we look at is the public records section of the D&B report. That shows any liens, suits, or items placed for collection. If we see that a prospective new customer has three liens, two pending lawsuits, and four items placed for collection it doesn't take a genius to know that we are asking for trouble if extend credit to this customer. We are especially cautious about federal tax liens. If a company has been withholding taxes from their employees' paychecks and then not remitting the money to the US government, why in the world would we expect to get paid? Not paying withholding taxes to the government shows a business is in desperate straits because federal tax liabilities aren't discharged in bankruptcy. Very few companies that do this ever survives. My advice is to steer away from any company that hasn't been paying Uncle Sam.

Most companies don't give a financial statement to D&B, but if they do that can be very helpful as well. If we see that a company has $5 million dollars of cash on hand and total current assets of $8 million against total current liabilities of only $3 million, and has little or no debt, and several million dollars in net worth, they are a good credit risk. However, one caveat: D&B will print just about anything you give them. In my career, on a few occasions, I have seen people give fraudulent financial statements to D&B only to find out the hard way that they were fabricated. So, don't place total faith in the financial statements a business provides to D&B, but also look closely at their vendor payment record and the public record section of their D&B report.

One way you can help D&B have more timely and accurate information is to send your Accounts Receivable aging to them each month, if you are a D&B subscriber. We simply e-mail a spreadsheet with all of our AR aging to them every month and they import it into their vast database. The more companies that do that, the more current information they have about each account they track. Plus, by our sharing this information with D&B it gets on their credit report and may keep another company from extending more credit to a company that's already in over their heads. If you use D&B and don't submit your AR aging monthly, talk to your D&B rep about how to do so. It will help you and every other D&B subscriber rate

One last plug for D&B. They also have a very affordable collection service which we like to use because we know it will show on their D&B report that an item has been placed for collection if we turn the past due account over to them to collect. We also have found that a collection call or letter from D&B carries a lot more weight than a call from a local or even regional collection firm.

Smart credit decisions begin with amassing as much good information as you can about each customer. In my over 35 years in business I have yet to find anyone with more good credit information about our customer base than D&B.

CHAPTER 9

THE CREDIT PROCESS: PART FIVE COLLECTING SERIOUSLY DELINQUENT RECEIVABLES

Most receivables get paid within 60 or 90 days as most customers aren't deadbeats but some go through cash flow problems from time to time. I'm not going to talk about how to collect regular receivables because most people know that. This post is about how to collect seriously delinquent receivables. By seriously delinquent receivables, I mean receivables more than 90 days old.

Once a receivable gets to 90 days old we take any and all measures to collect it as we have seen too many people not take aggressive action at 90 days, only to regret it later. In most states you lose your lien rights if you don't file a lien within 90 days from the date of the last shipment to the job. If you don't exercise your lien rights within that timeframe, you lose your lien rights. That can be a very expensive mistake.

Also, if the job is covered by a performance bond, in most states, you have to file a notice with the bonding company within 90 days of your last shipment to that job or you lose your rights under the performance bond as well.

If you don't have bond or lien rights then if the amount due is less than the small claims court limit in the state where the service was performed, or the products were sold, then we file in small claims court. Small claims court is a lot less expensive than normal litigation in that you normally only have a small filing fee of less than $100 and you don't need to hire a lawyer to represent you in court. The vast majority of the times we sue in small claims court we are awarded a default judgment as the other party rarely shows up for the hearing.

If the amount owed is more than the small claims court limit then we engage a proven collections attorney. Don't hire just any attorney but ask a number of people you respect for a referral to a good collections attorney. Chances are if you hear the same name multiple times that's the right person to use.

Our collections attorneys vary by state in that you need to use an attorney licensed to do business in that state. I prefer to use one who is totally up to speed on the laws in the state where the litigation will be brought so that the attorney is familiar with the various judges that hear cases in that state and is totally up to date on that state's collection laws.

We instruct our attorney to file a complaint as soon as possible and to ask for interest at the maximum allowed by law from the date the debt was incurred as well as attorney's fees. You can only ask for interest and attorney's fees if your credit agreement calls for this and the customer assigned it.

We provide our attorney with a copy of the credit application signed by the debtor as well as copies of all unpaid invoices and signed delivery tickets proving that the unpaid merchandise was in fact delivered.

Most of the time the judge finds for us and we get a judgment. That's when the fun begins. Getting a judgment is one thing, collecting on it is another. A lot of debtors submit false financial statements to the judge showing that have no assets. When that happens we ask the judge for a court order that we can send to all banks in a 60 mile radius of where the debtor resides asking if the debtor has any funds in their bank. Most of the time we find some hidden bank accounts which weren't disclosed to the judge and the bank has to wire those funds to us immediately.

When we don't find any funds we perfect the judgment. Sometimes several years down the road the debtor contacts us because he can't get credit or can't sell an asset because of our judgment, so they have to pay us so that we will remove our claim against that asset.

If, after exhausting all avenues, we can't collect on a bad debt then we write it off and send the debtor a 1099. How can we send the debtor a 1099? Simply stated, forgiveness of debt is imputed income and the IRS views that as a taxable event. We may not get paid but we get the last laugh when the debtor has to pay taxes on the amount we wrote off.

CHAPTER 10
GIVING CREDITS AND REFUNDS TO CUSTOMERS

One of my many pet peeves is when you have to force someone you've done business with to give you a refund or credit when you're not happy. When people are that shortsighted they obviously aren't looking at the lifetime value of a customer. I have made it a practice to give credits and refunds quickly, and pleasantly. It aggravates me when someone finally agrees to give me a credit or refund but then they do it begrudgingly. If you're going to do it that way you should hang on to the money because you're going to lose the customer anyhow if you aren't pleasant when you issue the credit or refund.

I had a situation a couple of years ago where a customer called me and said that we had sent the wrong materials to his job site. I apologized profusely, told the customer I would look into it immediately, and would be back in touch with him within an hour. When I talked to our branch that was involved in the sale they e-mailed me a copy of the purchase order showing that we gave the customer exactly what the project manager had ordered. As I dug into it further I found that the project manager was probably practicing a little CYA. Rather than the project manager admitting he made a mistake, he blamed it on us.

I then had a choice to make. I could send the owner of the company a copy of the purchase order showing that we delivered exactly what his project manager ordered, in which case I would win the battle, but lose the war. If I did that, surely the project manager would never buy from us again, that is if he still was employed by this contractor.

As discretion is the better part of valor, I called the owner of the construction company and told him that indeed we had made an error and that we were going to pick up the wrong product, issue a full credit, and we would pay the air freight expense to get the correct product to the jobsite the next day. I asked the owner if that would be sufficient and he assured me that would make him happy.

A few days later I got a call from the project manager who told me he knew what I did and that he appreciated that I covered for him. He then let me know that he was going to be giving us a purchase order for $72,000 later that week. The credit I issued and the cost of the air freight was a total of $2400. Do you think we would have gotten that $72,000 order if I had stood on principle and embarrassed the project manager by showing the owner the original purchase order that proved we didn't make a mistake? That $2400 credit was one of the best investments I ever made in that I now have a loyal, long-term customer.

Think about this story the next time you're confronted with a similar situation.

CHAPTER 11

LAYOFF TIPS

One of the worst parts of being a manager is occasionally having to lay people off. While I have no problem terminating people who have done something to deserve it, after almost 40 years in business, I still lose sleep over laying off good people who we simply can't afford during a downturn. Fortunately I've only had to do this four times in 40 years, but it's never easy. However, not doing it when needed results in far worse consequences. **Over the years I have seen too many companies go out of business because management was too goodhearted**. Instead of some people in the company losing their jobs, everyone lost their jobs, and in some cases the owner lost his home and everything else he had worked for over the years. Which scenario is sadder? As an entrepreneur I won't hesitate to tell you that the latter scenario is much more disconcerting to me.

When do you lay people off? Most people do it later instead of sooner. Why is this? Well, from first-hand experience, I know that aside from the humanitarian reasons for not wanting to do a layoff, one of the other main reasons is those of us who own businesses spend a lot of time interviewing, hiring, and training people. Therefore, we are all loath to lay off people in whom we have made a big investment. I do like to wait at least two or three months from the beginning of a downturn to ensure that the decrease in sales is a trend and not just a blip. To lay people off after just one bad month is too reactive, but to wait six months or more is too long. I've generally waited to do layoffs until we've had three consecutive bad months, and when industry forecasters say it's not going to get better anytime soon.

Another reason to lay people off is that most of us who own businesses have bank loans. With bank loans come loan covenants, which are rules that, if broken, can cause the bank to call your loan. I will admit to having broken loan covenants in my career but when I have done so I have quickly met with my lender to explain what happened and how I am going to get back in compliance with the covenants. Bankers don't want to see pie in the sky projections of sales increases getting you back in compliance with covenants. Sales increases may or may not happen. During a downturn, they probably won't happen. However, overhead reductions are guaranteed. **Nothing makes a banker feel more comfortable about waiving a covenant violation or re-doing your covenants like a definitive plan to lower overhead enough to get back in compliance with covenants.**

Who do you layoff? Well, unless your business is unionized, I recommend that you don't do it by seniority. We lay off people based on the following criteria:

Hiring mistakes. We all make hiring mistakes that we rationalize during good times. When I begin to make a layoff list the first group of people I look at are people that, after having been on board awhile, I wish we had never hired. This is your opportunity to rectify hiring mistakes. Don't let it pass.

People with bad attitudes. I don't think any of us in management knowingly hire people with bad attitudes but some people who fool you during the interview process surface rather quickly after coming on board. Bad attitudes rub off on everyone else in the company to varying degrees. People with bad attitudes can be dangerous to your business in good times but I submit to you that they can be lethal in bad times.

Poor performers. Some people never come up to speed the way you hope they will when you first hire them, and some people have their performance degrade over time for a variety of reasons. You can't afford poor performers in good times and you really can't afford them during bad times. Here is your opportunity to let them find a new career.

New people who have not yet come up to speed. Laying off people in this category can be hard because sometimes you are convinced that they are really going to be top performers in one - three years. However, during bad times you simply can't afford the luxury of letting them come up to speed. However, this is the first group of people I call back when business improves.

How do you lay people off? Many years ago a mentor of mine told me that you should do all of your layouts at once, similar to pulling a Band-Aid off all at once instead of one hair at a time. When you lay off people one at a time over a period of months, everyone is nervous and looking over their shoulders and not doing their job. Even worse your best performers start to look for a new job while they are still employed. I have found it to be best to cut deeper than you think will be necessary and to do it all at once. Then hold a company meeting or, if you have multiple locations, do a conference call immediately thereafter, and let everyone know that you don't envision the other shoe dropping. Let them know that you have laid off all the people that you think you will need to cut to get through the downturn. I have even, in some cases, given a 5 or 10% raise to the remaining associates, out of the savings from the layoff, to compensate them for having to do more work. Nothing tells an associate that their job is not in jeopardy like giving them a raise right after a layoff.

What day of the week is best to lay people off? This is also hotly debated. I have found that it's better to lay people off at the beginning or middle of the week that the end of the week. If you lay people off then they can immediately start looking for a job but if you lay people off on a Friday they generally can't start networking and interviewing until at least the next week. Instead, they stew over the weekend and become even bitterer.

Should you provide severance and/or outplacement counseling? Unless your business is in such poor shape that you simply can't afford severance, I think that severance should always be given for humanitarian reasons. How much severance to give is a matter of what you can afford and how long each person has been with you and how high up they were in your organization. The higher someone's income, the longer it takes him or her to find a new job so I tend to give more severance to people at higher levels and people who have been working with me for the longest period of time. I almost always also give outplacement assistance to people who were higher up in the organization because, again, it is harder for them to find a similar job. Outplacement counseling generally isn't outrageously expensive and nothing helps to salvage a relationship with the person you've laid off than helping him or her find a new, and in some cases, better, job in the shortest time possible.

Also, your remaining associates look at how you treat the people you lay off. If you treat them fairly and humanely it sends a strong signal to your remaining associates that you didn't take this action lightly or cavalierly.

Should you give reference letters to the people you lay off? If people are laid off rather than terminated for cause, I have no problem providing a reference letter, upon request. If that will help the laid off person get a new job sooner, rather than later, I am happy to do so.

In summary, layoffs are never fun but not laying people off when times call for it is even worse. My advice is to do it quickly but humanely, and the impact on the morale of your remaining associates will be minimal. And remember, you're not taking advantage of a small percentage of your workforce; you are protecting the jobs of the majority of your workforce. Failure to do a layoff has had disastrous consequences for many people I have known over the years. Don't let it happen to you.

Chapter 12
Purchasing Tips

While I am firmly convinced that more money is made on the sell side than the buy side there are still certain purchasing disciplines which must be adhered to, to maximize profitability. Some of the things I've learned about the purchasing side of the business over the last 35+ years include:

- **Always issue a purchase order for all purchases over $100.** It isn't always practical to issue a purchase order for a purchase less than this because many times under $100 purchases are done at the spur of the moment and out of necessity. However, all purchases for inventory and all larger purchases such as a set of truck tires should be done via a purchase order. Why? Simply stated, unless your business is tiny and you have a photographic memory you can't just look at a vendor invoice and remember if that was the price you were quoted when placing the order. And, without needing a price to put a purchase order, a lot of people don't even ask the price for things they buy. Especially if it's not their money. **Over 20 years ago I read a study that showed that companies that always issue purchase orders made almost 5% more pretax profit than companies that rarely or never issue purchase orders.** That's a lot of profit to leave on the table due to a lack of discipline.

- **Pay off of your purchase order not your vendor's invoice.** Why? Aside from the obvious reason that you don't want to pay a penny more than was on your purchase order another good reason is you don't want to pay for more items than you ordered. Many times a supplier will ship you a quantity that is convenient for them to ship versus what you ordered. For example, if you ordered 278 widgets but they come in boxes of 50, most suppliers will just send you six boxes. You end up with 22 more widgets than you ordered. That might be acceptable to you if this was a stock order but if it was a special order and you don't normally sell that particular widget what's going to happen to the 22 extras you got but didn't order? Answer- -they will sit around for years until they are thrown away, donated to a charity, or deeply discounted. When a supplier ships us more than we ordered we only pay for what was on the purchase order and tell them that they can pick up the overage or we can ship it back to them at their expense. Most of the time they just tell us to keep the extras. That's why we almost always have an inventory gain when we take our year-end inventory instead of having to take an inventory write-down.

- **Pay off of invoices but reconcile vendor statements at least quarterly.** Most of our suppliers don't provide monthly statements anymore unless they are requested. We request them at least quarterly. If you don't get a statement it's easy to overlook credits which have been issued to you but not taken. This is another profit leak that needs to be plugged.

- **Have a new vendor negotiation checklist and use it.** The time to ask for marketing allowances, rebates, extended payment terms, extra discounts on opening orders, sponsorships for golf tournaments and other customer events, etc. is when you are in the initial negotiations with the new vendor. At that point they want to land a new account and have a hard time saying no. Once you're already doing business with them it's much easier for them to say they don't have the budget for such things. We have a checklist and we use it religiously as we negotiate with each new vendor.

- **Mean a lot to a few instead of a little bit to everyone.** My father taught me this when I was working for him in high school in his commercial roofing business. You don't want to put all your eggs in one basket but, on the other hand, you don't want to buy from so many vendors that you dilute your purchasing clout. We like to have a main vendor and two secondary vendors. Keeping each product category to a maximum of three vendors cuts down on inventory, increases inventory turns, and you end up meeting with less vendors. Who among us wouldn't like more time?

- **Join a buying group.** A lot of buyers like to think that they buy better than anyone but unless you're the head of purchasing for Home Depot, guess what, you don't! If you are part of a buying group you take advantage of the collective purchasing clout of hundreds, if not thousands, of members. Plus the buying group has professional buyers who do nothing but negotiate and who have more purchasing power than you do. If you think you are buying better than them you're kidding yourself.

What other purchasing tips do you have? I'd like to hear from you.

Chapter 13

Benchmarking

One of the business practices that has been very helpful to me over the years is benchmarking. If you're not familiar with benchmarking, it is simply a fancy term for visiting with a similar company to yours that is located far enough away from you that both parties feel comfortable divulging confidential information about their business. Many years ago, a mentor of mine said, "Somewhere, someone has figured out the answer to every problem". The question is, "How do you find those people?"

I find those people by networking through trade groups and other business organizations. When I meet someone with a similar business and they appear to be successful and intelligent I asked them if I, and some of my key Associates, can spend a day with them comparing notes. The vast majority of the time the answer is yes.

Once another company agrees to benchmark with you the first step is to create a list of items that you want to see when you visit the other company. That way you don't show up at their business and just shoot the breeze. If you send a list of items and topics that you want to discuss on your benchmarking visit the other party should be relatively well-prepared for you, and have most, if not all of those things available for your visit. **One caveat: don't ask for anything that you're not willing to share about your business.**

We have a standard list that we modify for each visit, based upon the type of company we are visiting, where they are located, and the particular challenges of their market. This way you don't have to create the list from scratch for each visit. This makes preparing for the visit much easier for both companies. We don't have to reinvent the wheel for every visit and the company we are visiting knows exactly what we want to learn during our visit.

When we arrive at the other company's location we begin with a general session with the management teams of both companies. Each CEO does a broad overview of their company to kick things off. Then we break into functional groups; i.e. the purchasing people from each company go to one breakout room, sales does the same, accounting, IT, HR, etc. We get back together at the end of the day and compare notes. We usually go to dinner as well, and often times we learn more over dinner and a few drinks than we did back at the office. (It must the drinks that loosen people up!)

We have never done a benchmarking visit that wasn't highly beneficial. You generally get a lot of new ideas as well as validation of things that both companies are doing successfully. Invariably, you also hear some horror stories of things that were tried that didn't work as envisioned. Those types of stories can save you from some expensive learning experiences.

The company we benchmark with almost always then visits with us at a later date, and sometimes we have ended up making annual visits to each other's companies. Both companies benefit from these visits. If you've never tried a benchmarking visit, give it a try and let me know how it goes. If you have benchmarked other companies in the past and it went well or poorly I'd like to hear about that too.

CHAPTER 14

BENCHMARKING QUESTIONS

Here are some of the questions we ask most often when benchmarking with another company:

- Approximately how many sales orders do you process a day?
- How many people handle this function?
- If more than one, how are the jobs split?
- What do you do with open PO's and sales orders at month end, if anything?
- Who handles direct shipments, accounting or sales personnel?
- Do your sales orders automatically create a PO or does this have to be done by Accounting?
- How do you handle credits, is this a manual function or done systematically?
- Do you process credit card payments?
- If so, does this fall under Receivables function or Payables function?
- How many people process vendor payments and what function does this fall under?
- Do you have to coordinate payments received from a credit card company?
- Approximately how many payables invoices are processed a week?
- How many people handle this function?
- Do you have a set limit that a PO and Invoice can be out without checking with your location managers?
- How are payables reviewed prior to payment and by whom?
- Is any payroll processed in house?
- If processed outside, what functions are handled in house, if any?
- Do you perform background checks and testing on new em-

ployees or is this outsourced?

- How many people are in your credit department?
- What functions do they perform, dunning letters, setting credit limits, liens, credit applications, references?
- Who handles financial reporting, bank reconciliations, bank reconciliations, audits (tax, internal, W/C, Premium)?
- Is Cash Management handled here, if so, under what position?
- Are deposits done and if so, by whom?
- Do you support IT problems in house, if so, which function handles this?
- Is system training for new locations handled by someone here?
- Do you have more than one location?
- If so, who handles problems created in inventory by incorrect receipts, transfers, etc.?
- What is your sales compensation plan?
- When are commissions paid?
- Do you pay commissions based on when the sale is made or when the money is collected?
- Do you take back commissions if a sale is uncollectible?
- Do you take back commissions if invoices are paid late?
- Do you have central purchasing?
- If so does the purchasing department do all of the buying?
- If not all, what is bought centrally and what is bought locally?
- Do you do cycle counts?
- What is your average inventory shrink %?
- How many inventory turns are you getting?
- Do you belong to a buying group?
- What is your DSO?
- What percent of sales was written off last year?
- At what point do you put a customer on COD?
- Do you assess a late payment fee?
- What percent of the late payment fees you collect?

These are just some of the questions that we ask on a benchmarking visit. Do you have any other questions that you ask that you don't see here? If so, let me know.

CHAPTER 15
CASH FLOW MANAGEMENT

Cash flow management is always important, but never as important as it is during an economic downturn such as the one we are currently in. You've probably heard the old saying, "Buy low, sell high, collect early and pay late". That's a simplistic view of cash flow management. Here are some of the things that we do:

- **Take all prompt pay discounts.** We ask our vendors for a prompt pay discount and if they will give us one we discount our invoices as the cost of borrowing is usually less than the value of the discount. If we don't get a prompt pay discount we pay in 45 days. Most of our vendors go along with that. Those extra 15 days beyond the net 30 terms we usually get from suppliers who don't offer a prompt pay discount is worth a lot to us over the course of a year.

- **Ask for extended terms from your suppliers.** We also negotiate special terms with our top suppliers. For example, we have terms from some suppliers of 2% 10 days, net 60 instead of net 30. That gives us the flexibility to either take the 2% prompt pay discount, or if cash is tight, pay those vendors in 60 days.

- **Pay your bills with credit cards.** Many of our suppliers accept credit cards. If a supplier accepts a credit card we wait until their payment terms are about to expire and then we pay with a credit card. That gives us an extra 30 days or so, depending upon when we make the charge and when the credit card company's cut off is. Plus we also get rewards points that we use for going to conventions, office supplies, etc. We pay a large number of suppliers with credit cards as well as a many service providers such as telephone companies, ADT alarm systems, dumpster fees, association dues, and may others. Look through all of the invoices your company pays in a month and I bet you find a lot of your suppliers who accept credit cards.

- **Time your purchasing.** When possible, you should also time your purchasing so that you make large purchases right after a vendor's cutoff date. By this I mean, if you have a supplier who gives you terms of 2% 10th prox, net 30, with a 25th of the month cut off, if you make a large purchase on the 26th of September your payment isn't due until the 10th of November. If you are making a large purchase for stock think about the optimal time to make such a large purchase.

- **Accept credit cards.** We also accept most major credit cards. We pay a small discount fee (as low as 1.69%) and then get our money in a matter of a few days instead of the 45 or so most of our customers take to pay us. And, we transfer the credit risk to the credit card company. To me, just offloading the credit risk is well worth the credit card fee. Getting our cash sooner is a bonus.

- **Prepayment.** We have some customers who, to get the best price, or due to credit issues, prepay us before we will deliver their order. We don't have a lot of those customers but we do have some. It just goes to show that if you don't ask, you don't get.

- **Accept checks.** I see a lot of companies that won't accept checks any longer due to negative experience with bad checks in the past. We gladly take checks because we use TeleCheck, and for a very small fee they guarantee payment on checks we get approved by them, in advance. It only takes a few seconds to run a check through their machine and get an approval or denial.

Chapter 16
Outsourcing

These days we hear a lot about outsourcing. Not all of it is good. I am not in favor of outsourcing any sales functions because I can always tell when someone is reading from a script when they call me. However, there are a lot of other functions within a business that can be outsourced, and if you choose the right outsourcing partners, it can be done without any negative effect on your business. Some of the things that we have outsourced include:

- **Billing.** We used to have two people that did nothing but billing. They would print the invoice, stuff the invoices in envelopes, seal the envelopes, apply postage, and mail them. It was a boring job and no one liked it so we had a lot of turnover. We have now outsourced all of our billing to a company that does nothing but that. Every night we transmit a data file to them containing all of our sales for the day. About 38% of our invoices are then transmitted electronically by the billing company to our customers. A few are faxed, but the balance are mailed via US mail. This company is set up to have the right equipment to print the invoice and have a machine inserted it into the window envelope, affix a barcode to get the lowest postage rate, and then mail the invoices for us. They do it for less than we can do it ourselves and we eliminated two positions that had a lot of turnover.

- **E-mail.** We used to have our own e-mail server but that required an investment in hardware, software, maintenance contracts, and part of one person signed to keep it up and running. Now we outsource our e-mail to a hosting company that has redundant data centers around the country and guarantees 99.999% uptime. We no longer have the investment in hardware, software, maintenance, and personnel. We have had one brief service outage in about five years.

- **Web server.** Similar to the e-mail server, why invest in hardware, software, maintenance and support contracts, etc. when you can outsource this to a firm that does nothing but this for a living? We outsourced our Web server years ago and have never once regretted it.

- **Payroll.** This is nothing new. Most businesses outsource their payroll processing but I still meet many business owners who have their payroll processed in-house. This is another boring, tedious job that generally has a lot of turnover. On top of that, there are security concerns and opportunities for fraud. In a prior company where our payroll was done in-house, a payroll clerk left a spreadsheet with the weekly payroll information in the copier once and it caused a lot of hard feelings around the company when it got passed around. Another time, we had a payroll clerk who gave herself a large raise and our controller, who was supposed to review the payroll each week, stopped doing so and this clerk hit us for over $35,000 before being found out. If you outsource your payroll to a payroll processing firm that eliminates all of those problems. And most payroll processing firms can do it for less than you can do it in-house.

- **Human relations.** We have even outsourced our HR department to the same company that does our payroll processing. Their president is a labor lawyer and he is much more up to date on labor laws than any HR manager I could hire, and they do this for us had a fraction of the cost of having our own HR department. This firm also does things for us such as 360° reviews and associate satisfaction surveys. By outsourcing the HR function we have a much more professional HR department and it costs us very little.

- **Delivery.** Last year we only delivered 52% of our sales on our own vehicles. The other 48% was delivered by vendor trucks, UPS, LTL freight lines, and contract haulers. I would never get rid of all of our delivery vehicles because I wouldn't want to be totally at the mercy of outside delivery services, but we have been able to outsource almost half of our deliveries with no problems. Also, during this recession, we have been able to sell some trucks, turn in some leased trucks, and lay off some drivers, thereby saving on overhead, without sacrificing any delivery capabilities.

- **Telephone system**. Like many companies, we have outsourced our telephone system and its maintenance to a local company. They are much more up to speed on the hardware and software, and again, at a fraction of the cost of having someone in-house in charge of our telephone system.

CHAPTER 17

BUDGETING AND STRATEGIC PLANNING

Do you do an annual budget and strategic plan for your business? If you are like most small businesspeople the answer is probably no. It has been written that no one plans to fail, but most fail to plan. I have found this to be very true in my 35+ years in business. I have found that most people just "wing it" and hope for the best. I find this especially strange as most small business owners have personal guarantees with their banks and are betting their homes and their other assets without even having written plans for success.

Early on in my career I was fortunate enough to become a partner in a dynamic company that grew at roughly 20% a year for about 20 years. I never worked harder or had more fun in my life. One of the disciplines that were instilled in me back then was doing an annual budget and a strategic plan. You may be asking, "What is the difference between a budget and a strategic plan?"

A budget is simply a compilation of all revenues and expenses, by profit center, and for the entire company in total. In our company, we do a "bottoms up" budget which means that the people who generate the revenue at each of our branches project what they are going to sell in the upcoming year and at what margins. Management then adds the expenses to the budget based upon the previous year's expenses, an inflation factor, raises, and any new expenses associated with new initiatives at that branch. We also then add corporate expenses to the budget as well. This includes senior management compensation, IT expenses, insurance, debt service, advertising, marketing, legal and accounting expenses, etc. We then spread the corporate expense over all branches so they can see what their profit is after they pay their share of corporate overhead.

Once we have the first cut of the budget we then review it to see if it looks too low or too high. Some branches are sandbaggers who turn in a budget showing only miniscule growth because they don't want to be held accountable to an aggressive budget. Other branches are wildly optimistic and turn in budgets that are pie-in-the-sky. The job of management is to "massage the numbers" until we come up with a budget that is ambitious but achievable.

Why have a budget? Well, if you don't know where you're going, any road will take you there. If you have a budget you have something to measure yourself against, and if you have done the budget properly, coming up short of budget should be cause for examination of the reasons for the shortfall. It may expose substandard performers or an unrealistic plan. To me, going into the New Year without a budget is like playing a football game without keeping score. You have to have something to measure yourself against to know if you are winning.

On the other hand, a strategic plan is a document that begins with a SWOT analysis; i.e., a review of your Strengths, Weaknesses, Opportunities, and Threats to your business. Once you have finished the SWOT analysis then you review your current initiatives and see how you're doing against the goals you set. You look at which ones to continue with, adjust, or drop. Then you look at new initiatives, as well as short term, intermediate, and long-term goals. While a budget is just for one year, most strategic plans that I have seen are for 3-5 years because some goals aren't achievable within one calendar year.

We update our strategic plan quarterly so that we can see how we are doing against our quarterly goals. We also review the intermediate and long-term goals each quarter as well to make sure they're still valid. Nothing makes a strategic plan more worthless than continuing to include goals which are no longer viable.

We use a simple one-page strategic plan that is built on an Excel spreadsheet. If you would like a copy of it send me an e-mail and I will be happy to send you one.

If you have put off doing a budget and/or a strategic plan, this turbulent economy is a good time to make yourself do a budget and a strategic plan. Doing these may very well help get you through the challenging times we are presently experiencing.

CHAPTER 18
OUTSIDE BOARD MEMBERS

The vast majority of entrepreneurs I know have a board of directors which consists of the owner, his wife, and maybe his accountant or lawyer. How much value does a business owner get from a board of directors like that? I would venture to say little or nothing. All you do is breathe your own exhaust. Plus, most entrepreneurs I know don't hold regular board meetings, and if they do have the occasional board meeting they don't write up meeting minutes until they get a notice that they are being audited. Then they scramble like crazy to create a bunch of backdated Board of Directors meeting minutes. Sound familiar?

I am fortunate in that the company in which I became a partner in 1980 did everything by the book and it rubbed off on me. We did budgets, strategic planning, management retreats twice a year, were audited by a top national accounting firm, and we had a board of directors mainly comprised of outsiders who could give their honest opinions and challenge management without fear of retribution. And we did minutes promptly after every board meeting.

What is the benefit of outside board members? Well, as mentioned above, board members who don't work for your company are free to challenge you and disagree with you because they don't count on you for their livelihood. If your board is comprised of you, your wife, and your accountant, how much critical thinking are you really going to get and how beneficial is your board really?

The board of my current company is comprised of me, my partner (who is also our CFO), the top consultant to distribution businesses in North America, the CEO of a manufacturing company who also is the UK version of a CPA, and the former CEO of my company, from whom I purchased it in 2001. All of these people are smarter than me and have no problem disagreeing with me.

Our board reviews and approves budgets and major capital expenditures, and, as we have a compensation committee, even sets my base salary and bonus plan. As my partner and I have outside investors this makes them very comfortable that the company is being run for maximum profitability, not to line our pockets. I get the benefit of unbiased advice from some of the smartest people I know.

We also have an audit committee that meets at least annually with the partner in charge of our account at the accounting firm we use to do our audit. The audit committee meets with this partner without me being present so that he, and they, are all able to speak candidly about any concerns about how our accounting is being done and how the business is being run.

What are they paid for being on the board? They get $1000 for each quarterly meeting and $500 for each committee meeting. We do all of our board meetings telephonically using *Go to Meeting*, and each meeting only takes about two hours, so their hourly rate is actually pretty good.

I get more value out of our board thing you can imagine. If you don't have at least three outside board members who are smarter than you, you are leaving a lot of money on the table.

CHAPTER 19
MORE ON STRATEGIC PLANNING

We use a one page strategic planning form. The developer of this form, Verne Harnish, CEO of Gazelles Inc. has created a new interactive "vook" (video book) that guides you through completing the revised One-Page Strategic Plan. Just click on each box of the interactive plan and a short 30 to 60 second video pops up explaining what is to go into each box. You can also fill it in online and then print a completed copy. Here's a link — expand the "Strategy" section and you'll see the Vook. They're creating vooks for all the other one-page tools as well.

If you have tried to use the form but didn't quite understand each section of it, this should be a big help to you.

CHAPTER 20
HIRING FOR ATTITUDE

When you are hiring what do you look for? When I ask most people this question I generally hear, "Experience in my business". While experience is a good thing to have most hiring managers make the job offer to the person they find that has the most experience in their business. I submit to you that isn't the best way to hire. I know this from experience.

When I was first made a manager and had to hire people, the main thing I looked for was someone with a lot of experience in our business. This caused me to make a lot of bad hires. I ended up hiring a lot of people with experience in our business but many of them didn't work out for various reasons. Lack of people skills, job hoppers, drinking and/or drug problems, excessive tardiness, couldn't get along with coworkers, etc.

I was very frustrated with my poor batting average until I went to a seminar on hiring conducted by Bill Lee of Lee Resources of Greenville, SC. Bill talked about the TEC method of hiring. The T stands for talent, the E stands for experience, and the C stands for chemistry. Bill said that the perfect candidate has the talent, experience, and chemistry you are looking for. So if you find someone that has those three things you should hire that person. However, if you can't find a person that has all three of those things then the first thing you should compromise on is experience. This is because experience can be gained but you can't teach talent or chemistry. So, if you can't find a person that has everything you're looking for. but you can find a person that has talent and with whom you have great chemistry, hire that person because they can get experience.

I have found this to be very true. We have all come across a waitress, an airline ticket agent, or a sales clerk that has a magnetic personality.

When you find someone like that snatch him or her up (unless you are filling a highly technical position) because, especially in sales, people with those types of personalities do extremely well. They do much better than a person with loads of experience but a dour personality.

Further to this point, I was at another conference where the keynote speaker was Herb Kelleher. If you aren't familiar with Herb, he is the cofounder of Southwest Airlines. While most airline companies lose money most years, Southwest has never had a losing year. In fact, their market capitalization is more than every other publicly traded airline combined. Why is that? Well, if you responded that they hedge fuel costs in the futures market and that shelters them from the wild fluctuations in the price of aviation fuel, you would be partially right. But Herb says the main reason for this exemplary track record is because of the great people they hire. Herb said that Southwest Airlines hires for attitude. He said when they interview for open positions the main thing they look for is people with great attitudes. They don't care what their background is; they only care about whether they exhibit a great attitude.

Southwest is a nonunion airline and because of that they are able to have their associates fulfill a wide number of roles such as ticket agent, baggage handler, and gate agent, or whatever needs to be done at the time. People with great attitudes don't care what job they do whereas people with bad attitudes say, "That's not my job". Herb also said that by hiring people with great attitudes who are willing to do a wide variety of jobs they have never been organized by a union. Disgruntled people with bad attitudes are very susceptible to union organizing pitches.

Now, when I interview someone, immediately after the candidate leaves (so my feelings are fresh in my mind) I rate the candidates on a 1-10 scale in terms of:

- Friendliness
- Smile
- Sense of humor

- Personality
- Fun to be around
- Enjoyable to interview
- Charisma
- Aggressiveness
- Preparation for interview (had questions and notes written down for interview)
- Good listener or interrupted a lot?
- Concise answers or long rambling ones?

Hiring based on attitude made a huge difference in my success rate with new hires. If you haven't been hiring for attitude, give it a try and see how it works for you.

Chapter 21
Some Thoughts on Marketing

A lot of people are confused as to the difference between sales and marketing. Earlier in my career, I was too. What cleared up the distinction for me was when I read this definition of marketing: "Everything that takes place before and after the sale". When you think about it, that makes a lot of sense. Marketing is comprised of a lot of things. To name but a few it includes your logo, the signs on your trucks and in your office, promotional literature, your website, branded items such as T-shirts and caps, private label merchandise, advertising, to name but a few.

My current business is construction supplies, mainly for commercial construction. Earlier in my career I was in the residential building materials business where there was a lot more marketing done. For example, when I was with Owens Corning in the 70's they licensed the rights to the Pink Panther and used it in their ads. They even sprayed pink dye into their insulation and then got a trademark on the color pink for building materials.

When I bought my present company and got involved in the commercial side of the building material business I was shocked to see how little marketing was done. As I talked with the manufacturers with whom we do business, most of them told me that they put the majority of their efforts into calling on architects to get their products into the specifications for as many projects as possible. They believe that not much more than that is necessary. I disagree.

The previous owners of my company did almost no advertising or marketing. They were very successful despite this but, not long after buying them out Home Depot started buying up a lot of our competitors, united them under one brand, and started building or leasing superstores, and created a national brand. I felt that, if we didn't respond in kind, we would look like a dinosaur and meet the same fate as the dinosaur. Extinction.

One of the first things we did was engage a branding company to create a new logo and brand image for us. Our old logo was over 25 years old and looked it. The company we used, Brains on Fire, in Greenville SC, came up with a new logo, tagline, website design, and even a style guide so that whenever we did any marketing in the future we could send a link to the style guide to the company with which we were working. That way they could download logos in different sizes and colors, get our exact PMS colors, and ensure that they stuck with the style and image Brains on Fire came up with. This has worked exceedingly well.

When we did the rebranding we decided to do it over a weekend so that not only our customers would be surprised on Monday morning, but our associates would be as well. When our associates arrived for work Monday morning after the rebranding they were shocked. We had new signage on our trucks, on the exteriors of our warehouses, and in our showrooms. We also had new shirts, caps, scratch pads, and other branded items available that Monday morning. It created a lot of buzz and everyone had a lot of fun with it.

Besides branding, what else do we do in terms of marketing? Below are just a few of the things we do:

- **Electronic newsletter**. Then I started in business in the 70s, a lot of companies printed four-color newsletters which, by the time customers received them, were many times out of date. Plus, a printed four-color newsletter is expensive to produce and then you have even more costs to stuff it in the envelope in which it's mailed, and the cost of postage to send it out. We do an electronic newsletter which we send out immediately after it's done, and by sending it via e-mail, we have no postage or handling costs. We spotlight three suppliers in each issue, and we charge the suppliers to be in the newsletter, so we more than recoup our cost to produce it. I also do a president's letter in each issue where I pass on information I have gleaned from a variety of sources about the direction of the industry as well as information about upcoming price increases or decreases. As I travel around and meet with customers one of the first things I hear is how much the customers value the market pricing information and how they use it in their bidding strategies. What started out as a pure marketing piece has also turned into one of the most valuable things we provide to our customers.

- **Golf tournaments.** Many of our customers play golf, especially at the executive level. Golf tournaments give us a lot of time to spend with our customers and, if they are at attractive venues, you will attract a lot of key decision-makers. We, with the help of our suppliers, get hospitality tents at PGA events. We get a set number of tickets for each day and we have never failed to sell out every day. We also have sponsored charity golf tournaments with the Make-A-Wish foundation as the beneficiary. Our customers and suppliers have always been very willing to support the Make-A-Wish foundation as it grants wishes for children with life-threatening illnesses. Everyone has a great time helping out a great cause.

- **Social media**. Things such as Twitter, Facebook, and LinkedIn are all the rage these days. We started a Twitter feed in 2012 and have close to 400 followers at this time. We send out Tweets with links to industry forecasts, information about new products we are stocking, sales we are having, etc. Twitter is free and easy to use and I highly recommend it. It also helps give us a cutting edge image. I know this because I recently spoke to a group of young construction professionals and most of them told me they knew of our company from following us on Twitter. We also have a company profile on LinkedIn and a fan page on Facebook. These social media sites are also free and will add to our image of being a cutting-edge company.

- **Blog**. This book began as a blog (web log). I read that creating a blog allows you to establish a conversation with your customers. I debated what type of blog to do but after several customers and industry friends urged me to share lessons I have learned, mostly the hard way, over my 35+ years in business, I decided to do my *Biz 101* blog. Within two months of launching the blog two industry trade magazines asked for permission to reprint some of my blog postings as columns. How can that not enhance our company's image with our customers? After three years of blogging I compiled my blog posts into this book.

- **Website**. Our website generates a lot of "hits" but more importantly, a lot of leads. We have a lot of things on our site that customers and prospects find helpful. Some of them are; our line card, our full catalog, our credit application, our branch locations and contact info, a photo gallery, links to supplier sites, and much more. Also, we have used Search Engine Optimization (SEO) so when contractors search for sources of the products we sell we turn up most of the time on the first page of the search engine results. And, we don't pay Google or anyone else even a penny for this.

- **Private label merchandise**. When we rebranded it dawned on us that we should promote our "brand" as well as our supplier's brands. We now offer a lot of private label merchandise. It not only makes us look like a bigger company but customers don't have to remember where they bought a certain product when they need more. Plus, a customer can't say, "I can get the exact same thing down the street, only cheaper".

- **T-shirts and caps.** In our business T-shirts and caps are always popular. By purchasing in bulk and sourcing from overseas we are able to get caps for about two dollars and T-shirts for about three dollars. We also get suppliers support for many of these items and our customers never tire of getting them.

- **Press releases.** Whenever we do something of note, take on a major new product line, or win an award, we issue a press release. Most of our industry's trade publications are hungry for news to print and as long as the press release is newsworthy, most of the industry trade publications use information from our press release in their publication. Again, this costs us nothing but enhances our image in our industry.

Chapter 22

Run Your Company like You Are Going to Sell it Tomorrow

I have purchased five companies in my career and most of the sellers didn't get what they should have for their company because they didn't run it like they were going to sell it tomorrow. Most small to medium-sized businesses are run as "lifestyle companies". By that I mean they are run mainly to support the lifestyle of the owner or owners and their families. Most owners have multiple family members on the payroll, even if many of them don't work in the company. Most family members also have company cars, company credit cards, and expense accounts which they use to run almost all of their personal expenses through the company. Many of the family members are overpaid, some grossly so. Many family members use the company to pay for personal purchases that have nothing to do with the family business. I knew of one situation where a car dealer and his wife would go to New York City on shopping trips and have clothing billed to their dealership as auto parts. If the IRS ever audited them they would know from the names of the stores that there is no way they sold auto parts.

When I begin examining the books of a company I am interested in buying many times I am told that the operating expenses of the business were much higher than normal because of family members running personal purchases through the business. The seller always tries to get me to lower the operating expenses by some arbitrary number they pluck out of the air. While I might lower the expenses a little in my pro forma, I never adjust to down as much as seller wants me to. As you generally purchase a company based upon a multiple of earnings, if the earnings would have been much higher without the added expenses from family members, the sellers end up leaving money on the table.

For example, most businesses these days are purchased for a multiple of 6-8 times earnings. So if earnings are understated by $200,000 due to excessive family compensation, when you multiply that by even six, there is $1.2M that is left on the table that sellers don't get it.

What some sellers do is prepare the company for sale by stopping excessive compensation for a period of 1-3 years so that they maximize earnings prior to sale. Alternatively, some keep detailed records of excessive compensation so they can show a buyer exactly how much excessive compensation was paid. Just be sure that those records aren't kept anywhere that the IRS might find them during an audit!

Also, most closely held businesses don't have audited financial statements. Generally, the banks I have dealt with, want audited statements so they can be certain that the earnings of the company are real before they will fund the purchase. Most of the acquisitions I have done have had an adjustment to the purchase price for the sellers to pay for a three-year reverse audit. Having auditors do an audit for the three previous years is both time-consuming and expensive. Therefore you will save both time and money selling your company if you get an audit done every year.

I've also found that most companies I have acquired had little or no annual reviews of employees in their files. When buying a company, it's extremely helpful to the buyer if you can look at multiple years of reviews for each employee of the company being acquired. Not having these reviews on file isn't a deal killer but if you do have multiple years of annual reviews for each of the employees it helps speed the sale of the company as the seller can see who they want to keep and who they may want to let go.

Another important factor when selling your company is having valid, up-to-date, *assignable* non-compete agreements with at least your key employees, if not all employees. No one wants to buy a company if the buyer has to worry about key employees leaving right after the sale and going in competition with them. And, believe me, I have seen it done. I recall one situation where a company I knew acquired a competitor and the day after closing all of the key employees quit and started their own company to compete with a company that had just been acquired. It ended up being a disaster for the acquirer. They basically lost their entire investment of several million dollars. This all could have been avoided if the seller had assignable noncompete agreements that had been assigned to the purchaser at closing.

If you have distribution agreements for product lines that are critical to the profits of your company make sure that all of those vendor agreements are readily accessible and see which ones are assignable to a purchaser of your business. If the agreements are not assignable, try to get your suppliers to amend the agreement to make its assignable. No one wants to buy your business if many of your key vendors will not sell to the purchaser of your business.

You should also check your license agreement with your software vendors. Most software vendors only grant you a license for use of their products for as long as you own your business. Most license agreements aren't transferable to a purchaser of your business unless a new license fee is paid. I have seen a lot of sellers find that out the hard way when I researched their files and pointed that out to them. I make a purchase price adjustment to cover the cost of re-licensing the software to run the business if the license isn't transferrable for free. The time to negotiate for a no fee, transferable software license is when you are negotiating to license the software in the first place. Most software vendors are anxious to get your business and will grant this concession at the time but of the initial sale, but not afterwards as you have no leverage then.

Most savvy buyers also deduct for dead inventory. I generally view inventory to be dead if it hasn't sold in 12 months or more; however, I know some buyers who consider inventory dead if it hasn't sold in six months. A savvy buyer also deducts the value of dead inventory from the purchase price so make sure that you constantly monitor dead inventory and try to get rid of it via auctions, close out sales, eBay, etc. Not only is this good business but it will save you from having a large adjustment made to the selling price of your business if you let dead stock accumulate.

When I buy a business I also like to see how happy the customers are. I don't want to buy a business if most of the customers aren't happy. I have generally gotten the sellers to pay for the cost of a customer satisfaction survey prior to closing. You will benefit from doing this annually anyway, but if you're going to sell your business, having several years of customer satisfaction surveys available that show your customers are happy will help you get a premium price for your company.

CHAPTER 23
NON-COMPETITION AGREEMENTS

Non-Competition Agreements, or "noncompetes" as they are more commonly known are almost always controversial, and in some states, such as California (surprise, surprise), illegal. They are controversial because no employee ever likes to sign one. However, as an employer, I require one from management and both inside and outside sales. I require a noncompete from management because they have intimate knowledge of the inner workings of our business. They know who we buy from, who we sell to, what prices we charge, who our top customers are, and many other trade secrets and confidential supplier deals that would materially damage our business if someone in management left us and went with a competitor.

Most of the same reasons apply as to why we require noncompete agreements from our salespeople. Another major reason why we require noncompetes from our outside salespeople is because we provide liberal expense accounts that our salespeople use to entertain customers. I have always felt that it was unfair for our salespeople to build relationships with their customers using their company expense account and then leave the company and compete with us. Because of the preceding, we get noncompete agreements from management and salespeople 100% of the time. If someone won't sign the agreement then we won't hire them. Many things are negotiable during the hiring process but not this. This is probably the only thing that is sacrosanct to us.

A lot of times you will hear that the noncompetes don't hold up in court. That is true if they aren't written properly based upon the laws of the state in which you do business. For a noncompete to be enforceable in most states it needs to adhere to the following guidelines:

- It cannot be overly broad

- It must be short in duration
- Consideration must be given

Let's examine each of the above points. By overly broad, I mean a noncompete can't state that the employee can't work for any competitor, direct or indirect, anywhere in the United States. Believe it or not, I have seen agreements that state that. Our agreement states that our employees can't work for a direct competitor within a 60 mile radius of where they worked for us. Several courts have upheld our noncompete because the judge found that restricting an employee only from working for a direct competitor, within a 60 mile radius was not overly broad.

Short in duration means no longer than one year. Our agreement calls for our employees to not work for a direct competitor, within a 60 mile radius, within the first year of leaving our employment. Our noncompete also states that our salespeople cannot solicit business from customers to which they were assigned for a period of two years. This has also been upheld in several courts.

Consideration means either a bonus for signing the agreement, or in our case, we condition our job offer upon getting a signed a noncompete. Courts consider the job offer to be consideration provided that the applicant signs the noncompete prior to the first day of employment with us. If a company asks an employee to sign a noncompete agreement after already being employed, then consideration, in the form of a cash bonus, must be paid for the agreement to be valid. Courts feel that if an employee accepted a bonus to sign the agreement, then the agreement should be upheld because consideration was given. As hard as it may be to believe, I have interviewed people who told me they signed a noncompete agreement after being employed as long as 15 years and not only didn't receive consideration, but were threatened with termination if they didn't sign the agreement. As you might imagine, courts view that such an agreement was signed under duress and declare the agreement to be invalid.

The above information is based upon my 35 years of experience, but I am not an attorney so do not rely on my advice for your company. If you are considering using a noncompetition agreement I urge you to find a good labor lawyer in your area and ask him or her to draft the agreement for you.

CHAPTER 24

CUSTOMER SATISFACTION AND NET PROMOTER SCORES

I think most businesspeople are in agreement that high customer satisfaction leads to high profits and low customer satisfaction leads to bankruptcy court. When I bought my current company in 2001 I commissioned a customer satisfaction survey so I would have a baseline to measure whether customer satisfaction increased or decreased on my watch. The Internet was in its infancy then, and the vast majority of our customers didn't use the Internet or e-mail, so I commissioned a market research firm to do a customer satisfaction survey. The survey was conducted via mail with follow-up calls over the phone to people who didn't respond to the mail survey. The survey took a couple of months from conception to completion and cost almost $5000. When we got the results, we were happy with what we saw, but some of the results were open to interpretation. This caused me to want to do a simpler, faster, and less expensive survey. As time passed and more of our customers used the Internet we moved to an Internet-based customer satisfaction survey using www.surveymonkey.com. This was much less expensive as we were able to draft the questions ourselves and send the survey to our customers via e-mail. Survey Monkey compiled the answers and within a week we had the results, and at a fraction of the cost of the old-fashioned way.

About four years ago when we were doing our corporate rebranding, the branding firm we used, Brains on Fire (www.brainsonfire.com), told us about the net promoter score. If you aren't familiar with it, I think it's brilliant in its simplicity. The survey consists of just one question, "Would you recommend our company to a similar company or a colleague"? The theory is that if a high percentage of your customers answer "yes" you have high customer satisfaction and vice versa. Also, when your customers see that the survey consists of only one question that can be answered in 5 seconds or less, you tend to get a higher participation rate versus a survey that takes 15 or 20 minutes to complete.

We now send out this one question survey each quarter and track our results on a spreadsheet so we can compare each score to all our previous scores. Whenever we see our score has dipped we know that we have work to do. There is also an area below this one question for customers to write in any comments or suggestions they may have. Not many of our customers write in comments but the vast majority who do have positive comments or praise for various people within our organization. We see very few complaints.

Our most recent quarterly score was one of our best ever. Ninety three percent of our customers say they would recommend us to a similar company or a colleague. Given that, like everyone else in the construction supply industry, we have done quite a bit of belt tightening, it was gratifying to see such high customer satisfaction. That's quite a testament to our associates, our management, and our corporate culture.

If you would like to learn more about the net promoter score, go to www.netpromoter.com

CHAPTER 25

TIPS ON BUYING A COMPUTER SYSTEM

Buying a computer system for your business is a very complex under-taking and entire books have been written on how to select a computer system, so this is just a list of tips based upon the 15 years I spent in the computer system business and the last nine as a system user.

- **First select the software that fits your business best and *then* select the computer hardware.** It always amazes me to see a company buy the hardware first because they either have a friend working at the hardware company or they had a previous relationship with the hardware vendor. Then the buyer could only choose from software that ran on that particular brand of hardware. Some buyers were precluded from buying software that was best for them because it wasn't compatible with the hardware they had already chosen. This is less of an issue today with the advent of open architecture but buying hardware first can still limit your choices in some cases.

- **Use a consultant.** Most business owners only buy a new computer system every 7-10 years so they aren't exactly experts at this complex task. If you aren't an expert, why not hire one? For a few thousand dollars you get the benefit of a professional who buys software and hardware on a regular basis versus once every 7-10 years. Even though I was in the computer systems business for 15 years, when we bought a new computer system a few years ago, I hired a consultant because, even though I knew what to do, I didn't have the time to do it right.

- **Create a request for proposal (RFP).** Either you or your consultant should create an RFP and send it out to all of the suppliers of computer systems for your industry. It takes a lot of time to create an RFP unless you already have a template created the way a consultant does. The RFP should ask general questions about the computer systems provider as well as very specific questions about the features of each of the modules; i.e., accounts payable, accounts receivable, general ledger, etc. The consultant also knows who should receive the RFP. If you aren't in the market all the time you may not even know all the companies to send it to.

- **Tabulate the responses to the RFP.** Once you receive the responses to your RFP, either you or your consultant needs to tabulate all of the results and see which vendors have most of the features you're looking for. Again, unless you have a lot of time on your hands, it's better to let a consultant tabulate the results.

- **Schedule a meeting with the top 4 respondents.** Once you have found out which vendors come closest to meeting your needs, then and only then, should you invite the top four in for a one-two hour meeting to discuss their answers to your RFP. The software vendor will want to do a demo at this time. Don't let them do it. Some vendors will dazzle you with a slick demo that will affect your judgment as you make the buying decision.

- **Ask for proposals.** After you have met with the four vendors ask each of them to make a proposal to you. Also, ask each vendor to give you the five-year cost of ownership for their system. By this I mean the cost per year for five years of software maintenance and support, and hardware maintenance (if you are buying the computer hardware from them). *I strongly recommend you buy the hardware and software from the same vendor* because otherwise if you have a problem, the software vendor will blame the hardware vendor and vice versa. You don't want to be caught in the middle of that mess.

- **Review the proposals.** You and the consultant (if you are using one) should then review the four proposals, compare them to the RFP responses, and then invite the top two in for (preferably) back-to-back full day demonstrations. Either you or your consultant should write a script that each software vendor must adhere to as they do their demo. The script will spell out which features you want to see demonstrated, and in which order. The software vendors will not want to stick to the script.

Make them. I know from being a software provider that all vendors have a slick demo that highlights their strengths and avoids their weaknesses. This is what they will want to show you. Don't let them. Make them go through the script and show you each feature in the order listed on the script. When I was in the software business I used to hate this for the reasons mentioned above. However, now as a buyer of computer systems, I see the value in it and make the vendors stick to the script.

- **The demos.** When we bought our new system we had one full day demo on a Saturday and another full day demo on Sunday. We did the demos over a weekend because we were simply too busy to give up two full workdays. We rented the computer lab at a local community college and the software vendor loaded their software each day on the main server and each of our associates participating in the demo were able to follow along on their own computer. We had our entire accounting department participate in the demo, along with inside and outside sales as they were the ones who would use the system the most, and their buy-in was crucial to our success. Holding the demo in a computer lab also gave them the opportunity to play around with the software a little bit as each attendee was seated at a PC. We paid only $250 a day for the computer lab and each of the final two vendors reimbursed us for the fee incurred for the day they did their demo.

- **Scoring the demos.** After the demos were done our consultant showed us his score sheet so that we could see how each vendor scored versus the script they were given. In our case, one vendor was clearly head and shoulders over the other vendor but we didn't let either vendor know that because we still needed to negotiate the final cost.

- **Final proposals.** We told each vendor that they were still in the hunt but we needed them to sharpen their pencils and give us their absolute best price. Once we had the revised proposal from our favorite vendor our consultant sat down with them and negotiated the price down a little lower. At that point I got involved and negotiated the price even a little lower. A few points about negotiating for software. Having been in the business, I know that the gross margin on software is in the 95% range, so all software vendors have a lot of room to give, if they want your business badly enough. Most computer systems vendors only make 10-25% on hardware so there isn't as much room to negotiate on the hardware. At this time, also negotiate rates for any custom software that you might need (now or in the future) and also negotiate the price for any optional modules, even if you aren't buying them at this time. Try to get the vendor to lock in those prices for one year or even longer because once you sign the contract the power shifts to the vendor. One last point, if you want the absolute best deal conduct the final negotiation at the end of the month or quarter. That's when systems providers need to "make their numbers" and are most willing to negotiate.

- **Negotiating the license agreement and contract.** The systems provider will try to get you to sign their standard boilerplate software license agreement and contract. Don't. I know from experience that the vendor's standard agreement is tilted strongly towards protecting the rights of the vendor, not you. This is where a consultant really pays for him or herself. A good consultant knows all of the areas where the buyer needs extra protection and generally has dealt with the vendor before and knows where they will give and where they won't. For example, when we bought our new system the vendor's agreement was only three pages long. Our consultant got the systems provider to agree to a 13 page addendum to the contract. Those 13 pages were full of additional protections for us.

- **Installation.** This is where most buyers try to save money by skimping. Don't. The installation process is crucial to the success or failure of your installation. As, in many cases, you will be spending over six figures for your new system (when you consider the cost of software, hardware, data conversion, installation, and training) don't cut corners on installation and training. In our case, we started preparing for the new system seven months before the installation. During that time all of the associates in our company who would be using the new system went through computer-based training for the modules they would be using. Our vendor's computer-based training program included quizzes after each chapter, and a final test.

That way we could see the scores that each of our associates were getting and if any of the scores were substandard we had those associates do the training again. We "went live" on our new system on *exactly* the date we projected seven months earlier and, due to the thorough training prior to the installation we had no hiccups on the "go live" date. In fact, we had paid for three trainers from the vendor to be on-site so that we could dispatch them to any branches experiencing problems during the go live process. I'm happy to report that money was totally wasted as we didn't need to dispatch any of the trainers to any of our locations.

In conclusion, as I stated at the outset, these are just a few tips about how to buy a computer system based on my experience as both a software vendor, and a building products distributor. There is a lot more to buying a computer system. You can either buy some of the many books available on the subject or you can hire a consultant. As I've said many times already, I recommend you save yourself a lot of time and grief and hire the best consultant you can find for your industry.

Chapter 26
Termination Tips

Terminating underperforming employees is one of the most distasteful parts of management. No one likes to do it but not terminating poor performers can lead to the demise of your business. In my 35+ years in business I have terminated a lot more people than I would like to admit. Many of the terminations were my fault in that I never should've hired some of those people in the first place. However, as distasteful as terminations may be, I have found it's not the people you terminate that make your life miserable, it's the ones you don't. In over 35 years in management, I've never terminated someone and regretted it. The only regret I have ever had is that I didn't do it sooner. Years ago I saw a survey that showed that most managers know they have made hiring mistake within the first 30 days but it takes about one year to terminate someone you recognized as a bad hire within the first 30 days.

Why is that? I think there are many reasons. Some of them are below:

- Not wanting to admit to your employees that you made a bad hire.
- Not wanting to have to go through the hiring process again.
- Not wanting to have to meet with the underperforming employee and terminate him/her.
- Not wanting to pay severance.
- Not wanting to worry about a wrongful dismissal suit.

Of all of the reasons mentioned above the most valid one for dragging your heels on terminating someone is worrying about a wrongful dismissal suit. Even if your state is a "right to work" state, which ostensibly gives you the right to hire and fire at will, you still need to worry about wrongful dismissal suits. Especially if the person you're terminating is in a "protected class" (over 40, a female, a minority, or disabled). The worst possible scenario is that the employee is all of the above.

The best way to protect you and your company from a wrongful dismissal suit is to "build a case" prior to terminating the employee. By this I mean taking the following steps:

- Noting in an annual or quarterly review form that the employee's performance is substandard and needs to improve or the employee may be terminated. Be sure the employee signs the form.

- Putting the employee on probation and giving a series of goals that must be met within a reasonable period.

- A series of written warnings signed by the employee.

- Holding counseling sessions with the employee to help him or her meet the goals he or she has been given.

If you terminate someone in a protected class after taking some or most of the above steps your chances of losing a wrongful dismissal suit are much lower than if you don't take the above steps. I also recommend that you consult with a labor lawyer prior to terminating anyone in a protected class. If you terminate someone in a protected class without taking the above steps, in addition to a wrongful dismissal lawsuit, you also have to worry about an EEOC claim. The Equal Employment Opportunity Commission was established to protect the rights of people in protected classes and losing a case brought by the EEOC is no fun. So, no matter how anxious you are to terminate an underperforming employee, if they are in a protected class you need to proceed with extreme caution, and with the benefit of professional advice.

Chapter 27
Wage and Hour Laws

As if have done acquisitions of other companies over the years and as I have served on many boards of directors, one of the most common violations of the law I have seen is in the area of wage and hour laws. Some people don't know they're breaking the law and others have told me that they know they are breaking the law but they are taking their chances on getting caught. One of the most common violations I see is paying salary to employees so avoid paying overtime. What most employers don't know is that if you get caught you are liable for **treble damages**. Now, most employers don't get caught unless a disgruntled employee turns them in, but I have seen it done, and I have seen huge penalties and fines assessed after a government audit. When the government gets a complaint **they generally audit all of your payroll records**, not just the records of the employee who complained. If, for example, the auditor finds that you have been paying 35 people incorrectly for five years, they calculate the amount you should have paid in wages... **and triple it**. That can be a hefty sum at any time, but in this kind of economy, it could break your business.

What are the rules for paying people salary (exempt) versus hourly (non-exempt)? Exempt employees meet one or more of the following three criteria:

- **Professionals.** This includes lawyers, doctors, CPAs, etc. This also includes people who set policy for your company such as a human resources manager, credit manager, and other similar positions.

- **Outside sales.** These sales people must spend over 75% of their time out of the office selling.

- **Managers.** To pay someone salary as a manager they must supervise at least two or more full-time people.

As I said above, a many companies unknowingly break the law in this area, but some knowingly break the law and just take their chances. One company I acquired had every single employee on salary, including the receptionist. They were lucky they never got caught because they were looking at a fine in the mid-six figures.

Here are some of the other common violations I have seen over the years:

- Having people work over 40 hours per week and then giving them "comp time" (extra vacation time or having them work less hours the next week) instead of overtime. That is blatantly illegal. If a non-exempt employee works over 40 hours per week they are entitled to overtime pay. **No exceptions.**

- Making people do work from home and not paying them. I have seen companies make their employees review product information or do other work from home and not pay them. That is begging for trouble.

- Making people run errands for the company and not only not paying them, but not paying them mileage for using their own vehicle. In our company, if we send a non-exempt person to the post office, we pay them for their time and we also reimburse them for their mileage at the IRS approved rate.

- Asking employees to work beyond 40 hours but not record the time over 40 hours. I have seen managers ask their subordinates to not record their time over 40 hours, "Because we are over budget and can't afford it". Some employees do this to be a team player but it is illegal. Even if the employee volunteers to work more than 40 hours you still need to pay them for it. The government views this as coercion because the employee may only "volunteer" to do this because they are afraid they will get fired if they don't.

The above is the result of my experience over the last 35 years but you shouldn't rely on my advice alone. Talk to a good labor lawyer in your area before following any of the above advice.

CHAPTER 28
NEGOTIATION TIPS

Whether you are in a purchasing role in your job or not, we all negotiate in life. You negotiate when buying a car or house, you negotiate when being offered a job, you negotiate for a raise with your employer, you negotiate with your spouse, and the list goes on and on. Here are a few tips that I have learned along the way about negotiations:

- **You don't get what you deserve in life, you get what you negotiate.** A lot of people don't like to negotiate. They think it is beneath them. Those people get taken advantage of in life.

- **Always do more "homework" than the person you'll be negotiating with.** It always amazes me when I go into a negotiation and the other party has done no homework on me or my company, or the transaction at hand. If it's worth negotiating, it's worth preparing for. Try to find out as much as you can about the other party, their company, and what their goals are in the negotiation. This will allow you to craft a negotiating strategy to maximize the outcome for you.

- **Never let your opponent in a negotiation know any of your internal deadlines.** If you do this, a skilled negotiator will drag out the negotiation until your deadline is looming and then you will agree to anything because you have to. On the other hand, if you can find out the other person's deadline you can use this strategy to your advantage.

- **He who appears to care the least wins the negotiation.** If the other side senses that you absolutely have to have the item you are negotiating for, you have lost all your leverage. For example, when buying a house, I always find a lot of things to nitpick over. This puts the other party on the defensive and gives you the leverage. This can be applied to a lot of negotiations.

- **In a negotiation, never give something unless you get something in return.** I learned this early in my career. Professional negotiators never give on a point unless they get something in return. When I negotiate with someone who keeps giving me things I'm asking for without asking for anything in return, I know that I am dealing with an amateur and I use that to my advantage.

- **When dealing with a commissioned salesperson, remember that they believe that "Something, beats nothing, all to hell, every time."** Before most commissioned salespeople will walk away from a transaction and get nothing, they will give on a large number of points, because if they walk away from the transaction they get nothing. If you are negotiating with someone who is paid on commission, keep this in mind.

- **Try to make the other party go first.** In other words, don't be the first one to name a price. In a negotiation, always try to make the other party name the price and terms first. Generally, he who names the price first, loses.

- **Always "flinch" when someone quotes you a price for the first time.** Then remain silent. When the other party caves in and names the price first, always flinch by saying things like, "Are you crazy? I can get it for half that price elsewhere.", or "You are awfully darned proud of that, aren't you?" When you are negotiating with an amateur, the flinch almost always gets them to immediately start negotiating against themselves and give you a lower price or better terms.

- **"You can name the price, if I can name the terms".** When negotiating with someone who is hung up on getting a certain price for whatever they are selling, then negotiate over the terms. Over the years, I have agreed to a lower price than I wanted to sell something for, provided that I got paid in advance, the other party gets no return rights, etc. The terms of the negotiations are every bit as valuable, if not more so, than the price.

- **Once the other party thinks you've agreed on a deal, keep "nibbling" for more.** As soon as the other party thinks they have a deal, especially if, when doing your homework, you have found that they are desperate to sell, start nibbling. Once the seller has emotionally done the transaction in his or her head, they don't like to walk away from the deal. That's when you can ask for a lot of other things that will make the transaction better for you.

- **In a negotiation, never admit to having the final authority. Always defer to someone else. A board, an executive committee, a CFO, etc.** Amateurs like to show off by telling you that they have full negotiation authority. Even with owning my own company I say things like, "I need to run this by my banker", or "I need to run this by my board". I then step out of the room and either I do call someone whose opinion I value and get their ideas on the transaction, or sometimes I just take the time to compose my thoughts further. Amateurs admit to having full authority, professionals do not.

CHAPTER 29
TIME MANAGEMENT TIPS

Time management has probably had more books written about it in any other business related subject. This is probably because almost everyone feels like they can do a better job at managing their time. Time is the only commodity that cannot be replaced. Once you waste 15 minutes, it is wasted forever. I hate it when people tell me, "I couldn't find the time". I am quick to point out that time is not found, it is made.

Here are a few time management tips that I have discovered over the years:

- **Take care of the urgent before the important.** Many of us take care of urgent tasks while important tasks go undone. I have made a spreadsheet with four quadrants which I use as my time planner. On the vertical axis is "important" and "not important" and on the horizontal axis is "urgent" and "not urgent". I spend most of my time in the top left quadrant which is tasks that are both urgent and important. My second priority is tasks which are important but not urgent, my third priority are tasks which are urgent but not important, and my last priority is tasks which are neither urgent nor important. When you focus on mainly the upper left quadrant that's where you get the best results.

- **Use something like the Task function in Microsoft Outlook.** You don't have to use Outlook but use something like it so you can put all of your tasks into it and then you will get reminders when you need to start working on each task. Once I have put a task into Outlook I forget about it because I know Outlook will remind me to do it so that I don't miss the due date.

- **Tackle first things first.** A lot of people are tempted to first knock off a bunch of easy tasks on their daily "to do" list so that they can feel good about seeing a lot of items crossed off. Resist that temptation. You will be much more productive if you attack the toughest tasks first provided they are both urgent and important.

- **One bite at a time.** Tackle big projects one bite at a time. By this I mean if you have a project that is going to take eight hours it won't quite as daunting if you do it in four two-hour increments over one week. Plus you'll end up with a better product work as each time you work on the project you will refine the work you have previously done. It's just like in school; if you cram the night before a test your grade is never as good as if you studied for a week instead of the night before. Plus the task doesn't seem that tough when you break it up this way.

- **Under promise and over deliver.** When you agree to take on a task don't be aggressive in saying when you can have it done. If you think you can have it done in a week, say it will be done in two weeks, and then if you deliver it in 10 days it looks like you delivered on the project early. Obviously, you can only do this when the deadline isn't time sensitive.

- **Don't overcommit yourself.** I am constantly asked to be on boards and committees. The problem is I enjoy doing this but I only have so many hours in the day so I turn down most of them. You have to learn how to say no or you will end up stressed out and doing a lot of things at the last minute; and that is never when you do your best work.

CHAPTER 30
TURNAROUND TIPS

In our currently sluggish economy some businesses that had previously been successful, some for many generations, are now losing money and are in danger of going out of business. Having been in business for over 35 years I have been through three recessions and have had to take steps to ensure the viability of my companies. How do you turn around a business that is losing money?

Here are a few tips for you to consider:

- **Take a good hard look at your overhead and look for ways to lower it.** While you will save a little money by using both sides of copy paper, recycling paper clips, and having printer cartridges refilled instead of buying new ones, the big bucks are in personnel, especially middle management and above. Look at jobs that can be combined such as combining the VP of Sales position with the VP of Marketing position, and let the weaker person go. It's painful doing such things but not only is this where you save the most money but it sends out a message to all of your employees that you have no sacred cows in your company. Generally, for every senior management position you eliminate, you get to keep three or four lower-level people. Yes, you should look at closing unprofitable operations, suspending your 401(k) matching contribution, eliminating bonuses, not holding a Christmas party, etc. but the biggest savings are in the personnel area. However, this is the hardest thing to do therefore many companies put it off until it's too late. Over the years, I have found that it's best to cut deeply and quickly, so the healing can begin. Plus, I've found that I get a lot more support from lower-level employees when they see that I'm willing to cut upper level personnel as well.

- **Make sure you have superstars in the "game breaker" positions.** By this I mean, once you have done your cuts make sure that you have superstars in the critical positions for your company. For example, if you are a financial services firm or bank, you need to make sure that you have superstars in the CFO and chief credit officer positions. If you have a software company you need superstars over sales, product development, and customer support. If you don't have superstars in your key positions it's very hard, if not impossible, to turn your business around. What is the definition of a superstar? A superstar is a person who has the total respect of your organization. If you have a person over sales who brings in a tremendous amount of new business but alienates the other members of your team by cutting corners, encouraging customers to fudge credit applications, etc. that person isn't a superstar because sooner or later his positives are going to be outweighed by his negatives.

- **Nail down the cash.** Make sure that you aren't paying any vendors early. This may sound obvious, but when I have done turnarounds I'm always amazed when I see that many vendors are being paid early. Why? Sometimes people in Accounts Payable believe that payment terms of "upon receipt" means just that and they pay the bill as soon as it's received. I've generally found that as long as you pay a bill with terms of "upon receipt" prior to the next billing cycle the vendor is never going to complain. One example is attorneys. Their invoices almost always say that payment is due upon receipt. Accountants, consultants, utilities, auto repair shops, and the like generally state that their payment terms are upon receipt. Make sure that you aren't paying them upon receipt.

- **Sign Accounts Payable checks yourself.** I sign the Accounts Payable checks myself unless I'm out of town and then I have two trusted associates who also have check signing authority. However, you can count the number of times per year they sign checks on one hand with a few fingers left over. Not only does this ensure that vendors aren't paid early but it helps guard against fraud. Some Accounts Payable people create fictitious companies and fictitious invoices and then issue checks to these fictitious companies. By signing the Accounts Payable checks yourself you will see when there is a check going to a vendor you have never heard of.

- **Ask your suppliers for extended payment terms.** My current company is a building products distributor. Our industry has been in a protracted recession for about three years now and this downturn has taken its toll on our cash flow as many of our customers are hanging on by a thread and are paying us slower than in the past. We asked our vendors for extended terms and the suppliers that comprise about 75% of our payables dollars have agreed to give us extended payment terms. Ask your suppliers for extended terms. All they can say is no.

- **Pay late.** As a last resort, if things get really bad for you, start paying your noncritical suppliers late. By noncritical I mean any suppliers of products you can get from multiple other vendors. If you have a key vendor that supplies a product that you can't get anywhere else then you need to make sure to continue to pay them within terms. However, if you buy commodity items that are provided by numerous companies you can afford to get cut off by one vendor as you can buy from any one of their competitors.

- **Draw down your credit lines.** This is a last resort move. If things are getting really bad and you have lines of credit with one or more banks, draw down the available balance from each bank and deposit the money in a new bank before your banker freezes your account. Your banker won't like that but he or she won't be able to get at the money either and you will have it when you need it. Again, this is a desperation move and should not be done lightly.

- **Monitor cash flow daily.** When I have been involved in turnarounds it has always amazed me when companies I have worked with have no idea how much is available against their credit lines on a daily basis. One of the key reports I can't live without is the daily availability report. On a daily basis I get a report that shows me how much is available against each credit line both before and after checks issued but not cleared are accounted for. It is always comforting for me to have a firm handle on this. It also keeps you from bouncing checks and nothing will destroy morale more than your employees having their payroll checks bounce. If you don't have a report like this, have your CFO create one.

- **Aggressively collect receivables.** In a downturn, and even in good times, some companies take a lackadaisical approach to collecting receivables. Several companies that I have acquired didn't even have a credit manager when I acquired the company. They simply sent out invoices and hoped that they got paid. A good credit manager is necessary in good times but a <u>great</u> credit manager is necessary in tough times. My current credit manager is the best one I've ever been around. In the seven years she has worked with me I have only had two customers call me to complain about her. That's because she knows how to ask for money without destroying the relationship with the customer. Some credit managers are so tactless that they cause more harm than good. What kind of credit manager do you have?

- **Be actively involved in credit.** I chair two credit meetings a month. One is our monthly credit meeting where we review every account over 60 days old, and we review the status of every pending lawsuit. The other monthly credit meeting is to review all accounts over 90 days old. Those are your most critical accounts. Studies have shown that once an account becomes 90 days old your chances of collecting what you are owed diminish rapidly with every passing day. That's why we have a separate meeting just to discuss our strategy for every account over 90 days old. Also, I personally get involved with some of our biggest accounts who have fallen behind on paying their bills. I do this because not only are they our biggest exposures but I want to ensure they are handled with kid gloves so that when business improves they have no malice towards us. Due to the above actions, our DSO is currently 41 in an industry where 45 DSO is considered optimum in good times.

- **Fire toxic customers.** All businesses have toxic customers. How do I define a toxic customer? A toxic customer is someone who constantly haggles over price and then, to top it off, pays late. Another attribute of a toxic customer is that they constantly ask for proof of delivery, want to return materials without paying a restocking fee, and are verbally abusive to your employees. During a turnaround situation you can't afford to do business with toxic customers. I also submit to you that you shouldn't do business with toxic customers during good times as well.

- **Celebrate wins.** During a turnaround look for things to celebrate, no matter how small. Collecting a large overdue receivable, making a large sale, landing a long sought-after customer, etc. needs to be celebrated. During tough times you can't afford large cash bonuses for such things but things such as an extra vacation day, a handwritten note sent to the employee's home, a $25 gift card to a local restaurant, and other such low-cost things can make a big difference in morale. Everyone likes to feel appreciated.

- **Never, ever give up.** During protracted tough times, it's tempting to just give up. However, you can't lose if you don't quit and, just like in sports, you can't lose until the clock runs out. When times are tough, find a way to put more minutes on the clock. That might mean talking a bank into not calling your loan, raising additional capital, or mortgaging your house. The objective is to put enough minutes on the clock so that your business survives until your industry experiences good times again.

CHAPTER 31
KEY REPORTS

One of the greatest benefits of computerization is that you can get more reports than you can possibly read. And, if you find the time to read them all, you rarely have the time to interpret them. Therefore I have come to rely on a handful of reports over the years that help me run our business. These reports include:

- **Daily availability report.** As mentioned in my previous posting, the daily cash availability report is extremely important to me. In over 35 years in business I've never bounced a vendor check or a payroll check but I live in dread of doing so. This report shows me how much is available against our credit line each day both before and after taking into account checks issued but not cleared. As you pay your bills with cash, not profits, I watch cash much more closely than profits.

- **Daily sales register.** This is a report that shows each sale of the day and the gross margin on each. I look at it to see who is buying and what kind of gross margins we are getting.

- **Gross margin exception report.** This report shows sales below preset minimum margins that we have deemed to be acceptable for various types of sales. It also shows sales over $10,000 and gross margins of over 50%. After 35 years I still get excited seeing large sales and high margin sales!

- **Dashboard report.** Every day this report shows our sales for the day versus budget and last year for the day, the month, and the year. I find it helpful to see daily how we are doing against our budget and if sales are up or down versus last year.

- **Stock status report.** This shows a lot of information about each item we stock. We can sort this report a lot of different ways. One thing I like to look at is the month's supply for each item. As we can get most of what we stock in no more than two weeks, when I see more than a four-week supply I'm not happy. When I see several *years'* supply of an item I get extremely unhappy. This report shows turns for each item and also the profitability index. The profitability index is nothing more than turns times margin. We shoot for a profitability index of 1.8 or greater for each sku. How we get to 1.8 I don't care. You can get there with a 30% margin and 6 turns or you can get there with a 20% margin and 9 turns. Again, I don't care how we get to 1.8, as long as we do.

- **Expired/about to expire inventory report.** Some of our inventory items expire, but luckily most of them don't. However, things such as caulking and chemicals have expiration dates and this report shows which items in our inventory are already past their sell by date and which items are getting close to being past their sell by date. This allows us to isolate those items and either transfer them to another of our locations or try to sell them before they expire.

- **Key ratios report.** There are 16 ratios that I monitor to determine the health of our business. These ratios include things such as current ratio, quick ratio, ROI, ROA, inventory turns, debt to equity, etc. It's very helpful to get this report each month and not have to calculate them manually.

- **COD list.** Every two weeks our credit manager sends sales and management a COD list. I review this closely each time it comes out and assign certain accounts for follow-up. Once a month we have a credit committee meeting and the COD list is reviewed in detail. At this meeting we also decide who to turn over for collection, sue, lien, or file against performance bonds.

- **Over 90 report.** This report comes out monthly and shows every account with invoices over 90 days old. As mentioned in past postings, once an invoice gets to 90 days old the likelihood of the successful collection of the invoice starts dropping dramatically. It's extremely important to make aggressive collection efforts for invoices over 90 years old. Generally we file suit on all accounts with invoices over 90 days old.

- **High-risk accounts report.** At a seminar a few years ago a speaker suggested that a business should set up a separate report to track sales to accounts that don't meet your normal criteria for a house account but that I, as CEO, have a good feeling about. Since we started doing this over three years ago we have generated almost $2 million in sales and $500,000 in gross profit from sales to those accounts. During this time our losses have less than $50,000. Since I, and I alone, chose to sell those accounts, I watch them very closely.

- **NSF report**. I get a report once a month of all checks that were returned for non sufficient funds. The report also shows whether we have been reimbursed by the customer or TeleCheck, the service we use to verify checks. If we haven't been reimbursed we take aggressive action, up to and including, the arrest of the person who gave us the bad check.

- **New customers/credit limits.** Once a month I get a report that shows all new customers set up by our credit manager during the past month and the credit limits she assigned to each. I like to look at this to see how many new accounts were opened in the last month and whether I agree with the credit limits given to each.

- **Changed credit limits.** Also monthly, I get a report that shows changes in customer credit limits, whether up or down. Again, I review this to see if I have any concerns that a customer has too high of a credit limit or whether we are limiting our sales by giving a particular customer too low of a credit limit.

- **Open order report.** This is another monthly report. I look at this to see how many open orders each branch has, and if they are over 30 days old, we look into why they haven't been invoiced yet. Sometimes the customer placed an order and then canceled it and someone forgot to take it out of the system. However, in some cases I find that a customer received the merchandise but, for various reasons, the invoice was never generated. Obviously we invoice customers as soon as possible in those instances.

CHAPTER 32

KEY RATIOS

In my last post about the reports I use to run my business I mentioned that one of the reports is the key ratios report. I received several emails asking which ratios I track. The ratios I track and my targets for each follow.

Ratio	Target Range
Current Ratio	2:1 or greater
Quick Ratio	1.5 to 2
Debt/equity	1.5 to .5
Asset turns	2.5 to 4
Inventory turns	5 to 8
DSO	35 to 45
Sales per FTE	$300K to 500K
GP per FTE	$85K to 125K
Profitability Index	1.3 to 1.8
Stock sales/inventory	7 to 9
Sales/payroll	9 to 12
Overall GP %	26 - 30%
Operating profist %	6 - 10%
Return on assets	10 - 20%
Return on equity	15 - 25%
Expenses as a % of sales	18 - 24%

Most of these ratios are pretty standard. The one that isn't is the "profitability index". As I said in my previous post, the profitability index is simply inventory turns times gross margin. Our optimum profitability index goal is 1.8. You can get there with a 30% margin and 6 turns, a 20% margin and 9 turns, etc.

Also, FTE means "Full Time Equivalent". If you have 40 full-time employees and four part-time employees who each work roughly 20 hours per week, that would be the equivalent of 42 full-time employees.

CHAPTER 33
COMPLAINT HANDLING

All companies make mistakes, but how you handle them is what separates the men from the boys. Recently I had an experience with the company that services my home HVAC system that is prompting me to do this posting. This company has been to our home six times in the last two weeks and still hasn't fixed the furnace that heats the addition to our house. Luckily, the main part of the house has heat but our kitchen addition hasn't had heat for two weeks, including through the Christmas holidays. The problem is quite serious in that the furnace was malfunctioning and spewing carbon monoxide into our house. Luckily, or shall I say smartly, we have a carbon monoxide detector that went off in the middle of the night and alerted us to this situation. If it were not for that we might all have died in our sleep. **If you don't have a carbon monoxide detector, get one.**

As this problem has continued to go unresolved, I have gotten more and more frustrated with this company. (By the way we have had a service contract with this company for over 20 years. However, once this problem is fixed we will definitely be switching to another provider.) This episode is replete with broken promises, no shows for appointments, unreturned phone calls, calls dropped when calling in to inquire about what's going on and, worst of all, a dispatcher who keeps interrupting me every time I call and who threatened to hang up on me when I asked her to stop interrupting. I am not exaggerating, this has been a nightmare.

So, how should you handle complaints? Below is what I have learned over the years:

- First, when a customer calls with complaint... listen. Don't interrupt, let the customer completely vent. Then ask, "Is there anything else I should know about this situation before I respond?"

- The next step is to immediately apologize for the incident and ask the customer what he or she would like you to do. Most times the customer just wants to vent and they don't want anything. However, many times the customer will tell you what they want. If it is within reason, agree to the request immediately.

- If the customer asks for little or nothing, I still insist on giving them a credit so that I will exceed their expectations regarding the incident. Henry Kaiser, an early 20th century industrialist once said that, "Problems are opportunities in work clothes". **View every problem or complaint as an opportunity to make a customer for life, not something to dread.** I find that when you exceed a customers' expectations when they have a complaint, you not only solve the problem, but you create a loyal customer who will recommend you to others.

- Once the issue has been resolved make sure that someone calls the customer a week or so later to ask if the problem is still fixed or if any further follow-up is needed. When you do this, you, once again, stand out as a company giving outstanding service. So few companies give outstanding service these days that even mediocre service stands out compared to the lousy service that most people get.

- Another thing to remember is, "No one ever won an argument with a customer". No matter how outrageous the customer is being, **do not argue with the customer**. Years ago, I heard the legendary motivational speaker and sales trainer, Zig Ziglar, say, "The next time you're tempted to tell a customer off, remember that you can feed your ego or you can feed your family, you can't feed them both."

CHAPTER 34
EFFECTIVE COMPLAINING

Most of us don't like to do it, but from time to time anyone involved in business needs to complain to a supplier or vendor about a problem. (Or you need to complain about a personal problem.) How you complain determines how quickly your complaint gets resolved, or if it gets resolved at all. As I mentioned in my previous post, I had a serious problem with my furnace in my home recently and I had to complain to get it repaired. Here are a few tips I've picked up over the years on how to effectively complain:

- **Always be professional.** Not only does ranting and raving rarely work, but is usually counterproductive because the other party digs their heels in because they have the leverage in this situation and you aggravated them.

- **Make note of who you talk to.** Not only does this come in handy if you have to escalate the problem but when you ask the person you're talking to for their name, and you ask them to spell their last name, and you ask them for their direct line and their e-mail address, they know they aren't dealing with an amateur. This alone generally gets me better responsiveness.

- **Escalate the problem.** If the problem doesn't get solved in a reasonable period of time (reasonable varies with how severe the problem is) you should escalate it. I escalate things by calmly asking the person I have been dealing with to transfer me to his or her supervisor. I tell them it appears this problem is beyond their level of authority and I need to speak with a person who has the authority to solve my problem.

- **Put it in writing.** I find that a well-written e-mail (or letter or fax if the company is old-fashioned) lets people know that they aren't dealing with a moron or crackpot. Most of the time I get satisfaction after I put my complaint in writing.

- **When that doesn't work.** I don't always get my problem resolved after I put my complaint in writing and after I have dealt with a supervisor. When those techniques don't work I call back and ask for the e-mail address of the president of the company. Believe it or not, some companies have done such a poor job of training their switchboard operator (who is the face of the company to the outside world and should be a shining star) in customer service that they refuse to give out the president's e-mail address. When that happens I ask the switchboard operator for his or her name. When they ask why I tell them I'm going to mention them by name when I finally do get the president's e-mail address, and I'm going to let the president know that he or she refused to give me his or her e-mail address. That normally gets them to give me the president's e-mail address. When that doesn't work I go to the Internet and search their website for either the president's contact information or for a "Contact Us" button on the website and I enter my complaint into that form.

- **Last ditch efforts.** When the above techniques don't work I call or e-mail the Better Business Bureau and report the company. Also, in this age of social media I go to Twitter and Facebook and express my displeasure with the company via social media.

Do I always get my problems resolved to my satisfaction? Not always, but I would estimate I get my problems resolved to my satisfaction using the above techniques about 95% of the time. Some companies are so pathetic that even when I get to the president I don't get satisfaction, but that is extremely rare. The key to successful complaining is being professional and being persistent. Remember, "If at first you don't succeed, try, try again".

CHAPTER 35
TURN DEAD STOCK INTO CASH

Any business with inventory has a certain percentage of that inventory that is dead stock or obsolete. However, most businesses let the dead stock sit on the shelves gathering dust for years. I prefer to turn dead stock into cash even though that means taking a P&L hit when you do it. I would rather take a loss on the P&L and turn dead stock into cash than hope someone will come in and buy that merchandise one day. Remember, profit is nothing but an accounting term. *You pay your bills with cash, not profit.* In our business, we do a lot of things to turn dead stock into cash. Some of the things we do include:

- **Dead stock list.** We publish a dead stock list every month and send it out to our salespeople. Anyone selling an item, whether they are inside or outside sales, gets 33% of whatever they can sell the item for. In many cases, this is more than our normal commission. Some people think I'm crazy, but I very badly want to dispose of dead inventory and giving the selling salesperson 33% of whatever they sell it for is a strong motivator to sell dead stock.

- **Flyers.** Each branch operations manager produces a flyer at the end of each month listing the top 10 dead items at their branch, in terms of dollar value. Our salespeople are given those flyers to hand out to their customers and we have also started emailing them out to our entire customer base each month.

- **Auctions.** We have found a company that specializes in selling building materials at auction. We have been able to get around half of our cost back when we sell dead stock at auction. That is actually a lot better than we thought we would do when disposing of discontinued or obsolete items at auction.

- **Donations.** We donate dead stock to Habitat for Humanity, local technical colleges, and other charities. We get rid of dead stock and get a tax write-off as well. It is win-win for us and the charity or school.

- **Tent sales**. We have done tent sales, normally in conjunction with a customer open house at one of our branches. We set up a tent in the parking lot and put the discontinued items on tables with each item priced very attractively. We have disposed of items at tent sales that we never thought we could sell.

- **Vendor buybacks.** When you end up with dead stock because of switching product lines, during the negotiation with the new vendor, try to get the new vendor to buy back all of your current stock from the manufacturer being replaced. Many suppliers will do this in return for a significant opening order of their products.

- **Offer it to a competitor.** If you have a competitor that stocks the product line you are trying to get rid of, offer it to your competitor at an extremely lucrative price. When we are offered inventory this way we almost always jump at it. Your competitors probably will as well.

- **Give it away.** When none of the above ideas works, give the dead stock away to your good customers. While this doesn't generate cash, it creates extra space in your showroom or warehouse, and is a goodwill gesture to your customer. This isn't as lucrative as the above ideas but at least you are rid of the dead stock.

CHAPTER 36

PARTICIPATING IN TRADE ASSOCIATIONS

No matter business you are in, there is one or more trade association representing your interests. Are you active in any of the trade associations for your industry? I'm not asking if you *belong* to a trade association, I'm asking if you are *active* in it. There is a big difference between being a member of an association and being active in it. Why should you be active in one or more trade associations?

- **Networking.** None of us has all the answers to the problems we deal with in business every day. However, somewhere out there someone has the answer to a problem you're facing today. How do you find that person? When you're active in trade associations you meet people in the same business from all over the country, or maybe even all over the world, and someone, somewhere has the answer to your question. Being active in a trade association makes it much easier to find that person.

- **Staying abreast of changes in laws and regulations.** Unfortunately, today there are literally thousands of laws and regulations affecting your business. How can you possibly keep up with all of them? Trade associations do that for you. They have professional staffs whose job it is to monitor changes in the laws and regulations governing your business and it's their job to inform you of the changes.

- **Lobbying.** "Lobbyist" has become a dirty word in this country but the fact of the matter is, if you don't have someone lobbying on your behalf in Washington your industry is not going to get the attention it deserves. If you are active in your trade association you will meet with your lobbyists from time to time so you will have an opportunity to let them know what's important to you and how you would like them to represent your interests.

- **Grow your revenues.** Those active in trade groups tend to do business with others in the same group. If you go to the meetings of your trade association you will make contacts with both suppliers and potential customers that will help you increase your sales. Those who are active in associations prefer to do business with others they have come to know and trust through the Association.

- **Education.** Unless you have a very large company you don't have the resources to develop educational programs for your employees. Most associations have very affordable educational programs which will help your employees become more effective, which benefits you and makes them feel more fulfilled.

- **Employee benefits.** Most trade associations pool the collective buying power of its members and are able to offer you more benefits, and at a better cost, then you can obtain on your own. By this I mean health insurance, travel discounts, special deals on shipping, "members only" pricing on vehicles and capital equipment, etc.

- **Fun.** In my 35+ years in business I have been very active in many trade associations, including being on national boards. Not only did I learn and grow a lot from doing this, but my wife and I have had a lot of fun with other members and their wives at some very attractive locations around the globe. Being active in associations isn't all work!

CHAPTER 37

WEASEL WORDS

"Weasel words" are words people use to weasel out of a commitment or to avoid responsibility for something. I first heard this phrase from an attorney we worked with at one of my prior companies. I think it is a very fitting term. Whenever I hear someone use one of the below phrases I think of that name.

Some of the weasel words that bug me the most are:

- **"To be perfectly honest with you"**. I have always hated that phrase. To me it says that the person I'm speaking with has not been honest with me until that point and it doesn't instill confidence in me that they are telling the truth after they use that phrase.

- **"The powers that be"**. This one always drives me nuts. I hear this a lot from people who don't want to take responsibility and hide behind that phrase. Example: "I agree with you but the powers that be won't let me do it".

- **"I haven't found the time"**. I hear this a lot from people who have missed the due date for a project or are late with something else. This phrase also gets under my skin. I tell these people, time is never found, it is made. When someone says, "I haven't found the time", I correct them and say, "You haven't *made* the time".

- **"I'll try"**. This bugs me because it is noncommittal. I don't often quote from the movie, *Star Wars*, but Yoda had a great statement about this. He said, "Do or do not, there is no try". Sean Connery also had a great phrase about "trying" in the movie about Alcatraz, *The Rock,* but I can't quote it here as it's a bit vulgar. If you're interested you can check it out on YouTube.

- **"I have been out of town".** I hear that a lot when people are late responding to an email or are late with a project. That used to be a valid excuse in the 70's when people didn't have cell phones and laptops, but in this age of electronic communication, "I have been out of town" is no longer a valid excuse for being late.

- **"I assumed".** I hear this a lot when someone drops the ball and uses the excuse that they assumed someone else handled something for which they were responsible. Most of us learned in grade school that when you assume you make an *ass* out of *you* and *me*. This is still true today. Don't assume, verify.

- **"To be frank".** This phrase also aggravates me because it insinuates that the speaker has not been frank heretofore. I don't know why people think this phrase is appropriate for any sort of conversation, and it especially has no place being used in a business conversation.

- **"It fell through the cracks".** This phrase makes my skin crawl because any effective person has a follow-up system so that they don't forget to do important things. With tools such as the task function in Microsoft Outlook and other similar things, if you put a task in Outlook you can forget about it because Outlook will remind you when it needs to be done. When I hear this phrase I know I am dealing with an amateur.

- **"I'm sorry I am late, but I was stuck in traffic".** Again, in the age of cell phone there is no excuse for being late without calling and alerting the party you're meeting with that you are going to be late. Even when I started my career in the 70's, if I saw I was going to be late for a meeting I would pull over and use a pay phone to call the person I was about to meet with to let him or her know I was running late. There was no excuse for this then and there is certainly no excuse for it now.

- **"I couldn't find any way to contact him/her".** Despite living in the age of search engines such as Google I still hear this a lot. When I hear it, I normally go right to Google and find a way to contact the person in question in a matter of seconds. When I hear these weasel words I know that the person I'm speaking with didn't even try.

- **"I didn't respond because I was on vacation".** First off, true professionals either respond to calls and emails when on vacation or designate someone to do it for them. It also bugs me when someone uses that excuse but didn't bother to activate the out of office feature in their email system before leaving on vacation and/or putting an out of office message on their cell phone and office phone so people trying to contact them know they are out of the office or on vacation.

- **"That's not my job".** These are the weasel words that aggravate me the most. These words indicate a person who is not committed to his or her job. As I tell my coworkers, "Anything I ask you to do is your job as long as it is legal, ethical, and moral". I also tell people when I interview them that the phrase, "That's not my job" will get them fired in my company.

- **"We've never done it that way".** I don't know about you, but the hair on the back of my neck stands up when someone uses those words with me. The speaker may as well just say, "I have no interest in trying to accommodate your needs. Go away." As I have mentioned before, our company's unofficial motto is, "The answer is yes, now what was the question?" Which would you rather hear?

- **"That's not our policy."** I read a survey many years ago that said that when a customer hears those words they immediately brace for a negative experience. I coach our Associates to avoid using the word, "policy" because of its negative connotations. I have found it's much better to say something like, "That's not our usual *practice*, but we will make an exception for you". That way the customer knows an exception is being made for him or her and that your company values him or her as a customer.

- **"What's your social?"** I don't know about you, but it bugs me when someone (usually a government employee) says this. Is it that much more effort to say, "What's your Social Security *number*?" It seems like people are getting lazier and lazier, even to the point of not being willing to say a complete sentence.

- **"Can you spell that?"** It really bothers me when someone asks for my surname and then says, "Can you spell that?" I reply, "Yes I can." That evokes some interesting responses. Again, is it too much trouble to say, "Would you please spell your surname (or last name) for me, I want to make sure I spell it correctly?"

- **"Hope you are well."** If there is one phrase that has become ubiquitous in e-mails this is it. I think this is the e-mail equivalent of asking, "How are you?" in a face-to-face conversation. In both situations I don't think the person asking really cares. I go out of my way to avoid both of these phrases as they have become meaningless and irritating (at least to me).

- **"Best".** Is it really that hard to type the word "regards" after the word "best"? Are we that busy in our society that we can't take the time to put "Best regards" at the end of an e-mail?

- **"Thx".** This bugs me even more than "Best". To me it is the ultimate in laziness to put "Thx" at the end of an e-mail when it only requires that you type three more keystrokes to say "Thanks", or better yet, "Thank you" at the end of your correspondence.

I guess that since Andy Rooney has passed away I am applying for his position of curmudgeon-in-chief. Am I being too picky? What say you?

CHAPTER 38
DEVELOPING TALENT

I, and many business consultants such as the renowned Peter Drucker, feel that the most important job of a CEO is developing people. In my company I probably spend more time on finding, interviewing, hiring, managing, and in some cases terminating, people than anything else. As mentioned in a prior post, we send out a net promoter survey each quarter and our customers consistently rank us much higher than companies several thousand times our size such as eBay and Costco. How do we do it? One of the key ways not mentioned in prior posts is that we like to develop talent in-house as much as possible rather than hiring from other companies.

There are two main ways that we develop talent in house:

- **MIT program.** MIT stands for Manager in Training. We hire recent college graduates and put them through a fast-paced training program that can result in a young person being a branch operations manager for us in his little as 18 months. How do we do it? Well, we start by posting MIT openings on local college job placement websites. We look for students who have a GPA between 2.0 and 3.0, because if their GPA is below 2.0 they don't have enough intelligence to do the job, or they didn't apply themselves in college, so in either case they likely won't succeed in our company. You might be wondering why we don't look for people with a GPA over 3.0. Our feeling is if they have a GPA over 3.0 and accept a job offer from us they are probably only doing so until they get a better offer. Most people with, say, a 3.8 GPA don't see themselves working in a building supply business as a career.

- Once they get through our battery of tests, and our extensive background check, (which has been described to me as more extensive than a national security clearance), we start them out, literally at the bottom of the company. They start working in the warehouse, learn to drive a forklift, learn to load and unload trucks, and make small deliveries in a truck that doesn't require a commercial driver's license. The next step is getting a permit for commercial driver's license. They then ride with one of our drivers and learn to drive a large truck with air brakes. Over time, they get their CDL and learn to make deliveries. After that, they work in inside sales and learn how to wait on customers, make sales, deal with vendors, use our computer system, place purchase orders, and all of the other tasks that go along with running a branch.

- When they have completed all of the preceding steps to our satisfaction then they are in line for a branch manager position. We had one young man who started with us at 21 and was running one of our bigger branches by the time he was 23. He went through all of the training steps in short order and proved to us that he was eager to learn, a hard worker, intelligent, and could get to work on time... which is hard for some 23-year-olds to do after a long night of partying. He is still with us now and has a very bright future. I don't know many other companies where a young person can go through the ranks and be running their own branch by the age of 23.

- **Intern program.** We also post unpaid internship openings on the job placement websites of local colleges. Many times the young person gets college credit for successfully completing the internship and they also learn some invaluable lessons that are generally more helpful than anything you could ever learn from a textbook. We also get a good look at a person who we may then extend an offer to join our MIT program. It's a win-win situation.

- I have used interns in most of my companies over the last 35+ years and it's very rewarding to see some that are now officers of substantial size companies. Several of them stay in touch with me and tell me how important it was to their careers to have gained on-the-job training as an intern. If your company doesn't offer internships you ought to give it a try.

One of the major benefits of employing people who started off with your company as interns, or in a program like our MIT program, is you don't have to break bad habits that they picked up at other companies.

You can imbue your company's culture in these young people while they are still in their formative years. Over the years I've had to terminate far too many people who came to our company with bad habits learned at other companies and they simply couldn't break the bad habits. When you grow your talent in-house you don't have to break bad habits learned elsewhere.

CHAPTER 39

ASSOCIATE RECOGNITION...
ON A BUDGET

In these times of belt tightening, how do you give recognition to your associates without it busting your budget? Everyone likes to feel appreciated, especially when they are doing more for less. When I was in business school we reviewed a study that showed the number one thing that employees wanted was recognition for a job well done. This was followed by opportunities for advancement, being with a company that is growing, and feeling like their opinions were solicited and appreciated. It was interesting to me that pay came in after all of the above. That's not to say that the pay doesn't matter, it just pointed out to me that money isn't everything. I have known people that have worked for companies that paid very well but worked their employees like slaves and never gave any recognition. The people I know who have worked for companies like this were miserable and only did it for the money. Rarely does that produce high quality work.

Here are some ideas for giving associate recognition on a budget:

- **Birthday cards.** I send a birthday card to all of my associates. I personally sign the card and hand address the envelope. I think that if you use a computer generated label and have your assistant sign the card for you, you're better off not even doing it. I think people resent getting cards like that. I know that I do when I get Christmas cards with an adhesive label on the outside and an engraved signature. That shows me that the person sending me the card didn't make any effort other than telling his or her assistant to get it done.

- **Thank you notes.** It takes less than five minutes to send a handwritten thank you note. I do this for significant achievements. Plus, it scores a lot of points at home when the president sends a handwritten thank you note to an associate's home.

- **E-mail thank you's.** While not as appreciated as a handwritten thank you note, I do send brief congratulations via e-mail almost every night when I review the daily sales register and see which of our salespeople had a big day. I almost always get a response thanking me for taking the time to acknowledge the associate's efforts.

- **Flowers.** Female associates appreciate flowers and I have even sent flowers to a male salesperson's wife after huge month. I thank her and the rest of the family for being supportive of all the time her husband must have spent away from home and family making so many sales. I have gotten thank you notes from wives stating that they have never gotten flowers from their husband's boss before.

- **Gift cards.** I carry a supply of $25 gift cards with me as I make my rounds of our stores. When I hear about someone who has gone the extra mile for a customer or coworker I hand out a gift card. The thought means more than the amount.

- **$100 bills.** While gift cards and thank you notes are appreciated I've always found that a $100 bill speaks louder. Who doesn't like a nice crisp, new $100 bill? I give these out for accomplishments well above what is expected.

- **Dinner for two.** Another thing I do to thank Associates for extraordinary effort is allowing the associate to expense dinner for two, generally with a maximum of $50, but occasionally with a maximum of $100 for a truly outstanding effort. As this award is tax-free it is worth more than its face value as no tax has to be paid on it.

- **A day off with pay.** This really costs you nothing but is generally appreciated a lot, unless the associate is swamped with work and a day off would only add more stress to his or her life. Keep this in mind when giving out such an award.

There are a lot of other low cost things you can do to recognize your associates and keep morale up during tough times. What else has worked for you? I'd like to know.

CHAPTER 40

ACCRUAL ACCOUNTS

One of my early mentors taught me the value of accrual accounts. When you own or run a small business the last thing that you want is for a surprise to destroy your earnings for a month or quarter. The more for which you accrue, the less your earnings volatility. Banks especially like to see steady, not volatile. earnings.

I suggest you set up accrual accounts for most, if not all of the below:

- **Bad debt reserve.** This is very standard. Put a portion of your profits each month into a bad debt reserve and then when you have a bad debt, charge the bad debt off against the reserve instead of against monthly earnings. This way you will have a small earnings hit each month for bad debts instead of a big bad debt expense in the month of the bad debt expense.

- **Inventory reserve.** If you also take a portion of earnings each month and put it into an inventory reserve then you won't have a big charge against earnings in the month when you take your annual inventory, should you have an inventory shortfall. Also, if you do cycle counting then you take any shrinkage from cycle counts and write it off against the reserve, not earnings. This is another very standard reserve account

- **Legal reserve.** Most businesses don't have a regular amount of legal expenses each month. They tend to have the occasional legal bill for a lawsuit or something else. Again, to avoid "lumpy earnings", set up a legal reserve, add to it each month, and write off your legal bills against the reserve, not earnings.

- **Sales tax reserve.** It's never fun to have a state sales tax auditor come in and find out that you did something wrong and owe a large payment, and perhaps penalties, for improperly remitting sales tax. If you set up a reserve, and fund it each month, then you write off these payments against the reserve.

- **Expense account reserve.** If you have associates who travel and get reimbursed for their travel expenses, set up an expense account reserve. Then if you have a lot of people all traveling in one month, say for example, to a convention, your earnings don't get a big hit in that month. You simply write off the large travel bill against your reserve.

- **Insurance reserve.** Sometimes your insurance bills increase dramatically, such as with health insurance. Or you have a deductible to pay for a large claim. If you have an insurance reserve set up you charge these expenses against the reserve.

- **Accounting reserve.** Most businesses pay their accounting expenses on a regular schedule, but sometimes your outside accounting firm sends you a large bill for doing a special project. Again, instead of your earnings being negatively impacted by this surprise large bill, you write it off against the reserve.

Also, if, you have an earnings shortfall at the end of an accounting period, you can review your accrual accounts, and if you are over accrued, you can add the excess amounts back to earnings. You may get a little grief from your auditors about this but I have always stood my ground and pointed out that these over accrued amounts came out of earnings, now they aren't needed to the extent that we thought they would be, so we are adding them back to earnings. I haven't lost that argument yet.

CHAPTER 41

DISASTER PLANNING

I live by the phrase, "Expect the best but plan for the worst." This philosophy has helped me avoid disaster in my 35+ year business career. There are a lot of potential pitfalls in business and in life and you can't avoid all of them but you can avoid most of them with proper planning.

Here are a few things I do to protect against disasters:

- **Property and casualty insurance.** This is no revelation to anyone. Almost all businesses (except those owned by the very foolish for the very broke) have property and casualty insurance. However, you still need to be careful about which carrier you use as I have heard horror stories of people who have filed multimillion dollar property and casualty claims only to find out that their insurer has gone out of business and they are left holding the bag. Remember that when it comes to insurance *good insurance isn't cheap and cheap insurance isn't good.* Be sure to shop around for the best carrier at the best price. Also be wary of buying from friends blindly. My father bought his insurance for his business from his best man at his wedding for over 35 years. When I suggested that my father "shop" him he refused to do it as he was sure that his best man was looking out for him. After my father died suddenly at age 56, my brother got several other quotes and saved over $70,000 a year on insurance for my family's commercial roofing business. As Ronald Reagan used to say, "Trust, but verify".

- **Business interruption insurance.** It amazes me how many businesses don't have this type of insurance, and it's not very expensive. A few years ago we had an ice storm in South Carolina (where we are based) and we had no power at our main office for 10 days. We have a central server for our computer system and it was down for 10 days so all of our branches had to hand write tickets. When our power was restored we had to enter 10 days worth of tickets into our computer system. That caused us to incur a lot of overtime, and our main location was shut down for most of those 10 days. We filed a claim under our business interruption insurance policy and received a check for $56,000. That didn't take all the sting out of a bad situation, but it sure did help.

- **Fidelity bond.** We pay for a fidelity bond for all of our associates. This requires that we do a thorough background check so that we are not hiring people with criminal records or terrible credit. A couple of years ago we had much higher than normal shrink at one of our branches. Our investigation showed our branch manager was either stealing or in collusion with a customer. After terminating him we were able to find records showing that he was letting customers take materials without paying for them. We filed a claim and got reimbursed for $42,000. That will pay our fidelity bond premium for quite some time.

- **Errors and omissions (E&O) insurance.** Even the best people make mistakes and some of them can be costly. When you have errors and omissions insurance it will reimburse you for most of those errors, as long as they weren't related to fraud or gross negligence. Again, the premium for this policy is a small price to pay to be able to sleep at night.

- **Directors and Officers (D&O) insurance.** This policy pays for the legal defense for our officers and our outside directors in the event of a lawsuit against one or all of us. These days you can be sued for anything, whether you have done something wrong or not. Defending yourself can be extremely expensive and D&O insurance protects against disastrous legal bills.

- **IT disaster plan.** Most of us in business rely very heavily on our computer system. How long will it take to replace your computer system in the event of a fire, flood, burglary, vandalism, etc.? If you don't have a written plan (kept off-site with multiple people) it can take you weeks or longer to get a new computer system up and running. Pull together a written plan that describes how and where you will obtain new hardware, copies of the software you use, and anything else related to your computer system.

- **Backups.** Hopefully you make a backup of your computer system data every evening and store it off-site so it isn't destroyed by a fire or stolen by a thief. However, do you verify your backup to make sure that you have a good backup? When I was in the computer systems business I occasionally received a call from a panicked customer who had a disaster and tried to load a backup only to find out that the backup wasn't good and hadn't been done properly for months. *Don't just do a backup, verify it daily!*

- **Backup generator.** After the ice storm mentioned above, I bought a backup generator so that we would never again be down for 10 days. The system runs on propane so it isn't dependent upon electricity. The generator turns itself on once a week for a self test as you don't want to have a disaster and find out your generator doesn't work. (Of course, since buying the backup generator we rarely have had to use it, and never for more than a few hours.)

- **Key person insurance.** What happens if you or one of your officers suddenly dies? If you have a key person insurance policy it won't replace a valuable associate but it will provide you with funds to conduct a thorough search and deal with any loss of income due to the loss of a key person. I also have key person insurance policies on our top sales people. Like any company, the 80/20 rule is in effect at our company. 80% of our sales are made by 20% of our sales people. We insure those key people as the loss of their sales won't be recovered quickly. It's hard to replace a superstar. We have policies for $1 million on each of our key sales people and some of the policies cost as little as $379 per year. Again, a small price to pay for peace of mind.

- **Umbrella policy.** Beyond your regular insurance policy, look into an umbrella policy, if you don't already have one. This policy covers claims above the limits of your regular policies. Should one of our truck drivers run a stop sign and broadside a mom in her minivan with four children, killing or maiming them, you could be looking at a settlement above your normal policy limits. An umbrella policy covers this type of catastrophe and can keep you from losing your business.

- **Disability insurance.** As a business owner what happens if you should suddenly become disabled? Most of us have disability insurance as part of our company insurance plan but generally it is for an amount below the income of most successful business owners. I have a second disability policy that pays out in addition to my company policy. *Tip: pay the premiums for both policies yourself instead of with company funds, that way the disability insurance payments are tax-free to you.* If your company pays the premiums for your disability insurance your payouts will be taxed as ordinary income.

CHAPTER 42
SELLING TIPS

The early part of my part of my career was in sales and, much to my surprise, I excelled immediately. My first sales job was selling roofing materials to distributors in New York. I was 21, fresh out of college, and totally wet behind the ears. I tripled the sales of my territory from $800,000 to over $2.4 million in my first full year selling. It not only gave me an income that exceeded my wildest expectations at that time, but it also got me a lot of attention from upper management who wanted to know what I was doing differently than our other salespeople. I was surprised to see my results because I didn't think I was doing anything special; however, I found that sales is a lot like football. You have to do the basics well before you can do any trick plays.

Here are what I consider to be the basics:

- **Show up early for your sales calls.** The legendary football coach, Vince Lombardi, invented "Lombardi Time", which meant that if you weren't 15 minutes early for practice, you were late. I found, especially driving around New York, that traffic delays were the rule, not the exception. By planning to be at my appointments 15 minutes early, if I got hung up in traffic, I still didn't arrive late. It never ceases to amaze me how many salespeople arrive late for appointments with me and don't even apologize. It seems they think it is acceptable to be late to an appointment. It is not. At least not with me.

- **Take notes.** I'm also amazed by the number of salespeople who sometimes even fly in from another state to meet with me and don't even take notes during our meeting. When I see that I realize I'm dealing with an amateur and I normally end the meeting as quickly as I can. How can I expect someone to follow up on the things I ask of them in a meeting if they don't even take notes?

- **Send a thank you.** After any significant sales call I used to send a handwritten thank you note. Even now, when I ride along with one of our salespeople on a customer call I send a thank you e-mail for a routine call and a handwritten thank you note if the customer does something extraordinary like insisting on paying for lunch, or if we got an exceptionally large order. Amateurs never do this, but pros always do. Which are you?

- **Follow up.** After each sales call I would review my notes and follow up as quickly as possible. Sometimes I would leave the customer's office and look for the nearest pay phone (there weren't cell phones in the 70s) and I would call my office immediately. If the customer had requested samples or literature I would have my office send them out, preferably that day. I quickly gained a reputation among my customers as the salesperson who called on them that followed up the quickest after every call. That alone got me a lot of orders.

- **Under promise and over deliver.** Most salespeople deservedly get a reputation for promising more than they can deliver. I did too at first. However, I quickly learned to under promise and over deliver. If I told the customer that the samples would arrive on Friday and they arrived two days early on a Wednesday, I look like a hero. However if I told the same customer the samples would arrive on Wednesday and they arrived on Friday, I look like a goat. In both scenarios the samples arrived on the same day but due to the expectation level you set you can look like either a hero or goat. Learn to under promise and over deliver. Also, if something happens beyond your control, that extra buffer may still cause you to deliver on the day that you promised.

- **The MacKay 66.** Harvey MacKay wrote a book, "Swim with the Sharks without Getting Eaten Alive". I read it early in my career and picked up a lot of great tips. One of them was a list he called the MacKay 66. It is a list of 66 questions to ask your customers so that you got to know them better than your competition. You don't ask all 66 questions on one sales call as it would be too obvious as to what you are doing. However, over the course of a year I would get all 66 questions answered.

I would end up knowing much more about my customers than did my competition. This gave me another leg up in my quest to take orders away from my competitors. To see the MacKay 66, go to www.harveymackay,com/pdfs/mackay66.pdf.

- **Holiday cards and gifts.** I receive a lot of holiday cards in December of each year. Most of them, with an engraved signature inside and a computer-generated label on the outside. When I see those types of cards I immediately throw them in the trash. However, when I get a card with a hand addressed envelope and a personal signature inside I appreciate the card. When I was in sales I made it a point to send handwritten holiday cards as well as small gifts for the birth of a baby, a death in the family, and other significant events in my customer's lives. Again, most of my competition never did that. Once again I stood out.

- **Articles of interest.** Back in the 70s I would look for articles in trade journals that I thought would be of interest to my customers. I would clip out the articles, make copies, and mail them to customers so that I would once again stand out versus my competition. Today it is much easier in that you can electronically forward an article to your customers with a lot less effort than it used to take me. If you're in sales and aren't doing this, why aren't you?

- **Entertaining.** When I was first out of college I didn't have much money and I quickly learned that if I took a customer out for a meal or to a ballgame I could go for free, as I could expense it. I made it a point to find out what my customers liked to do (see MacKay 66) and where they liked to eat and I did a lot of entertaining. Not only did I have a great time for free but I built close relationships with my customers, which led to increased purchases. Remember, all things considered, people buy from people they like, not necessarily the person with the lowest price.

- **Solve problems.** Instead of always pitching my products I would sometimes ask customers what problems they were having, even if they weren't related to what I sold. Many times when a customer would share a problem with me I would ask other customers if they had faced the same problem, and how they solved it. I would then share the solution with my customer on a future call. More than once this resulted in a large order.

- **Go the extra mile.** It's very true that there is no traffic jam on the extra mile. Most people take the path of least resistance in life and don't go out of their way to do more than that which is expected of them. When my customers asked me to do things that were above and beyond what should have been expected of me I leapt at the opportunity. I did weekend clinics on how to apply roofing, I helped my customers staff booths at home shows over weekends, I adjusted their complaints quickly and cheerfully, and quickly developed a reputation for doing the things that my competitors avoided doing. Again, more orders followed.

- **Network.** When I first started out in sales, I joined every trade association I could find in my territory as well as some national associations. I found out that customers who are active in trade associations make it a point to buy from suppliers who are also active in the same trade association. Plus, I got to spend more time around my customers, usually without my competition present, and again, guess who they bought from when they needed something?

CHAPTER 43

HOW TO GET AHEAD IN YOUR CAREER

Over the years I have had many people ask me how to get ahead in their career. Just like my selling tips in my last post, it isn't rocket science, but it does take above-average effort.

Here are a few of my tips:

- **Arrive early and stay late.** When my son, Thomas, was going to work for a large corporation he asked me for some tips on getting ahead in a big company. The first thing I told him was to arrive early and stay late. Your supervisor notes if you arrive before the appointed hour and stay past the end of the normal workday. *People who do this are generally among the last to be laid off.* Conversely, it will hurt your career if you consistently arrive late and leave early.

- **Volunteer for dirty jobs.** Early in my career I noted that, when in a meeting, and a dirty job needed to be done and volunteers were asked for, most people would drop their pen, tie their shoes, or anything else to avoid eye contact with the boss. If, instead of doing this, you raise your hand and volunteer take on a dirty task, that is also remembered by upper management.

- **Catch up on work over the weekend.** When I was first starting out in business I noticed that when I drove by our office on a Saturday the only cars in the parking lot were of upper management. I asked one of them why he worked on Saturdays and was told that you can get a lot more done on Saturday as the phone isn't ringing and people aren't walking in and out of your office all day. I started going in the office on Saturday mornings and not only did it give me a jump on the upcoming week but the senior officers noted that I was in the office and many times asked me to go to lunch with them when they knocked off around noon. This gave me valuable time with people who could help my career. And they did. Now, with laptops and email it may not be necessary to go to the office on a Saturday but if you spend a few hours over the weekend catching up on email and working on projects or reports it will be noticed and will give you a jump on the upcoming week.

- **Read trade journals.** I noticed that the senior partners in our firm all had trade journals in their offices. I asked one of them if I could borrow some of them and I pulled out subscription cards and subscribed to several. Not only did this give me greater insight into our industry but I would reference stories from various trade journals in my conversations with upper management and customers. This also helped accelerate my career.

- **Take someone in upper management to lunch.** I made it a point to ask various people from upper management to lunch a couple of times a month. Over these lunches I would pick their brains about how they got ahead, solicit their advice on what I could do to get ahead, and developed genuine friendships. I would always try to pay since I asked them to lunch but I quickly found that senior level management would never let me pay.

- **Sharpen your ax.** Anyone who has read Stephen Covey's, *The Seven Habits of Highly Effective People* knows what I mean by this (and, if you haven't read this, you should). If a wood cutter doesn't take time periodically to sharpen his ax his productivity declines. However, many people are so busy with their job they don't take time to sharpen their ax. I made it a point to read self-help books, listen to tapes (now CDs), and go to seminars that would help me become more effective in my job, and thus, more valuable to my employer.

- **Multiply the "we's" and divide the "I's".** When I was about 24 I drafted a business letter and asked the VP over my area to review the letter before I sent it. It came back with every "I" and "my" circled in red and "we" and "us" substituted. It was a lesson I have never forgotten. It sounds egotistical to constantly say "I" and "my" and it sounds much stronger to say "we" and "us".

- **Be slow to claim credit and be quick to take the blame.** Most people try to take the credit anytime something they are even remotely involved with works well. Conversely, when something goes wrong most people try to disassociate themselves from the failure as quick as possible. I found that by being slow to claim credit and quick to take the blame I also stood out. Always remember what Ronald Reagan used to say, "It's amazing what you can get done when you don't care who gets the credit."

- **Under promise and over deliver.** Just as in sales, get in the habit of under promising and over delivering. If your supervisor assigns a project to you, give it a lot of thought, and then say that you can have it done about a week longer than you really think it will take. Then if you deliver the project a week early, you look like a hero. Or, get the project done and then spend the extra week polishing it to perfection.

- **Stay in shape.** If you are overweight and out of shape you will have to work much harder to get promoted. Right or wrong, most bosses assume that obese people lack discipline and conversely most think that athletic people have drive and determination. I know some overweight people who are successful...but not many.

- **Improve on your weaknesses**. When I first started in business, having been a political science major in college, I couldn't even read a financial statement. I knew I needed to learn how to do this so I spent some time with our controller and I also enrolled in *Finance and Accounting for Non-Financial Executives*, a course produced by the American Management Association. I took one of my weaknesses and made it one of my strengths. This did not go unnoticed by upper management.

- **Learn to play golf.** If you don't already play golf, take it up. When my wife and I went with our oldest son to orientation at Georgia Tech that was one of the first tips shared with the incoming freshmen. A lot of business is done on the golf course and if you don't play (and you don't have to be great, as long as you learn golf etiquette, and play fast) you will miss out on a lot, in most companies.

CHAPTER 44
TELEPHONE TIPS

The telephone is a vital business tool but most people don't put a lot of thought into how they use the telephone. Here are a few tips about how to use the telephone in business.

- **Leaving a message.** One of my biggest pet peeves is when someone calls me and leaves a message but I can't make out his name because he mumbles it. Also, I can't return many calls because the caller says her phone number so quickly that even a Yankee like me can't figure out what she said. Also, many of the messages I get from someone I don't know who is trying to get an appointment with me doesn't even mention their company's name. When I leave a message I speak slowly and clearly and I spell my last name after I say it. I also repeat my phone number and my company name twice. *I also leave my e-mail address because many people like me prefer e-mail over the telephone.* Not surprisingly, most of my calls are returned.

- **Securing an appointment.** When I try to get an appointment with someone I don't know over the telephone I always try to mention the name of a mutual acquaintance as that improves your chances of a call back significantly. I also say why I am calling so that the person I have called knows what it is I want. *I also give some times I will be available for a return call. That helps avoid the dreaded game of "phone tag".*

- **Prospecting over the phone.** Back when I was in sales I did a lot of prospecting over the telephone as I didn't want to waste time calling on what might turn out to be a poor prospect. These days not as many executives have secretaries as when I was starting out in the 70s but you still sometimes have to get past the secretary, especially if prospecting at the senior executive level. When I called someone who was having his calls screened by a secretary I would turn on the charm and try to make the secretary my friend. More than one secretary be-

friended me and either put me through to the person I was trying to reach or gave me advice on how to get to the person I
was trying to reach. If I couldn't befriend the secretary then I
would *call very early or very late as most executives come in early and/or
stay late and secretaries are normally not working overtime.* Most executives will answer their own phone when you call them early or
late. If they have a direct number and you don't know what it
is, when you call early or late the receptionist is normally not
on duty either and most phone systems these days give you the
opportunity to select the person you want from a directory.

- **When someone returns your call.** I almost always give my
cell phone number when trying to reach someone so that they
can get me anytime of the day or night when they attempt to
return my call. You wouldn't believe how many people whose
cell phones I call have inappropriate greetings, rap music while
on hold, or an out of date greeting. I have sometimes called
people only to have their voice mail pick up and tell me that
they are on vacation and that they are returning on a date that
is already two weeks in the past. *Make sure your greetings are professional and up-to-date.*

- **Returning calls promptly.** Another pet peeve of mine is
when someone returns my call two or three days after I called.
As mentioned in a previous posting, in the age of cell phones,
there is no excuse for not returning all phone calls within 24 hours. If
you are on vacation and won't be returning phone calls make
sure that your phone greeting states that and names an alter-
nate person who is taking your calls. Also be sure to give that
person's phone number. That might seem awfully obvious but
you wouldn't believe the number of times I have called someone and gotten their voicemail and been told that "John
Smith" is taking their calls while they're on vacation but then
they don't leave John's phone number. Really.

- **Not leaving a message.** I have a lot of people call me and not leave me a message when they can't get through to me. I see a lot of missed calls on my phone but I never call the person back unless they leave me a message. This is especially prevalent with people under 30. My 21 year old daughter tells me that it's understood between young people that you are to call the person back if you see a missed call from them. That may be the unwritten rule for people under 30, *but in business if you want to call back, leave a message.*

CHAPTER 45

TOXIC CUSTOMERS
AND SUPPLIERS

What do I mean by a toxic customer or a toxic supplier? Let's examine toxic customers first. Most of us who own businesses grew up hearing that the customer is always right. While that is correct most of the time there are exceptions. Do you have customers that are always "shopping" you against your competitors for a better price? Have you found that almost always those same customers pay late? And they constantly want you to give them credit on returned products, even when they aren't in like new shape. On top of that they demand immediate service and want you to drop everything you are doing to meet their needs.

Early in my career I felt like I needed to meet the needs of every customer, no matter how demanding. As I have gotten older I have found that toxic customers aren't worth the revenue you get from them. Also, by ridding yourself of toxic customers you have more time to take care of your best customers, most of whom don't buy everything from you that they possibly can. By spending more time with your best customers your sales and profits will increase dramatically.

One of my mentors had the guts to do something that I am still trying to work up the nerve to do. He decided that he wanted to only do business with a small group of customers who appreciated the great service his company gives, was willing to pay a little bit more for it, and paid their bills on time ,or even early, to take advantage of a prompt pay discount.

Most of us know the 80/20 rule, or as it's more accurately known, The Pareto Principle. In 1906, Italian economist, Vilfredo Pareto published a paper pointing out that in business and in almost everything in life, 20% of the participants produce 80% of the output. In business it's uncanny that, with very little variation, generally, 20% of your customers will produce 80% of your revenue and almost 100% of your profit.

This friend closed the accounts of about 80% of his customers and sent them a letter stating that he wasn't staffed to be able to take care of their needs so he was closing their accounts so they could buy elsewhere. He and his team devoted all of their efforts to the other 20% of their customer base. This resulted in their sales and profits more than tripling. They even created a waiting list of customers who wanted to buy from this company that gave this legendary service. When one of their customers retired, died, or went out of business they would invite the customer at the top of the waiting list in for an interview with their management team. If the management team didn't think the customer at the top of the list was a good fit for them, they would invite the next person on the list to come in. I dream of being able to do something like this once this recession ends.

Toxic suppliers are similar. Do you do business with companies that constantly ship late and/or ship more or less than you ordered, causing you problems with your customers? Do you have suppliers who consistently ship poor quality products that result in complaints from your customers and takes up your time resolving these complaints? Believe it or not, some people buy from companies like this for years and years. When I ask why, they give me various reasons such as they always have bought from them, they have friends within the company that they don't want to alienate by taking their business elsewhere, the toxic company has great prices, their customers ask for it by name, it is specified on a lot of jobs, and many other reasons.

We have one supplier that we wish we didn't have to buy from but they have a very broad product line and no one else we deal with can replace all of their products. However, we are lucky that we only have one supplier like that. We have replaced all of our other toxic suppliers since I bought this company in 2001. By doing so my life, and the life of my associates, is much more pleasant and very few of our customers have ever asked why we dropped certain suppliers.

I don't believe in reincarnation, so if you are like me, why put up with toxic customers and toxic suppliers? Life is too short to deal with people who make you miserable. Get rid of your toxic customers and toxic suppliers. I bet you don't regret it.

CHAPTER 46

DO YOU REALLY KNOW WHO YOUR MOST PROFITABLE CUSTOMERS ARE?

Most businesses evaluate their customers by looking at a ranking of who buys the most from them. Some, more enlightened businesses look at a ranking of who generates the most gross profit among their customers. While I agree that it's more important to evaluate your customers on gross profit than revenue, neither is the best way to ascertain who your *most profitable* customers are.

Most computer software programs used by businesses generate a customer ranking report, generally based on volume, and sometimes also based on gross profit. However, we have an internally created custom report which ranks our customers based on PBIT (Profit Before Interest and Taxes). This is a concept I learned from the top distribution industry consultant, Bruce Merrifield (www.merrifield.com), one of our board members. More information about PBIT is on Bruce's website, but the concept is simple but powerful. You simply evaluate your customers by looking at the number of transactions per year with each customer, the average gross profit generated from each transaction, and subtract from that the cost of each transaction, which then yields the PBIT for each customer.

To calculate the cost of each transaction we look at the total cost to operate our accounting office each year and divide that by the number of transaction. To calculate the total cost to operate our accounting department we look at the salaries and benefits for everyone in the accounting department, total bad debt amount, cost of collections (lawyer's fees, collection agency commissions, small claims court filing costs, bond and lien filing costs, and anything else associated with collecting past due accounts), computer system costs, the cost to send invoices to our customers (invoice cost, the cost of the envelopes, and postage), the cost of our credit insurance, a portion of my salary and benefits as I am involved in collecting significant past due accounts, the salary and benefits of our Controller/IT manager, and any other miscellaneous costs involved in running our accounting office. We then subtract the average cost of each transaction from the average gross profit per transaction for each customer. The results can be very surprising. The first time we ran this report we saw that our fourth largest customer (in terms of revenue) was generating losses, not prof-its for us. This particular customer had over 4000 transactions per year with us because his employees did almost no advance planning and called us for additional materials, sometimes as many as ten times per day. Sometimes we had to make deliveries to their job sites but most of the time they came to our branch and picked up the materials them-selves. A lot of our team members were aware that this customer did multiple transactions per day with us, but because we didn't have to deliver most of their purchases, the assumption was that they were still a valuable account. No one had ever looked at the cost per transaction for each of these many transactions per day. When we had the infor-mation to see what it was costing us to service this account it shocked a lot of people.

What did we do about it? I met with the customer, along with the salesperson servicing his account. Our salesperson was terrified that the customer would stop buying from him when we showed him that he was an unprofitable customer, as our salesperson was afraid he would lose over $30,000 a year in commissions he was generating from this account. However, when we met with the customer and showed him that we were losing money on him he quickly pointed out that we were also an unprofitable supplier to him for not having pointed this out. He wasn't aware that his employees were leaving the job site so many times per day to come pick up more materials. He also pointed out that his bookkeeper had to enter over 4000 invoices into their ac-counts payable system, which was extremely labor-intensive for her. The mutually agreed-upon solution to the problem was that he would create a dispatcher position and each of his project managers would think about what materials were going to be needed for their job the next day and call or email the dispatcher each evening with materials requirements for the next day. The dispatcher would then aggregate all of these needs and place an order with us first thing in the morning each day, for each job. This simple solution reduced the number of invoices sent to that customer by almost 75% over the next 12 months and this change made the customer a money maker for us, instead of a money pit.

In summary, don't fall into the trap of evaluating your customers solely on revenue or gross profit. If your computer systems provider doesn't provide a PBIT report or something similar, see if they have a custom programming department that can create it for you. Or, if your software works with Crystal Reports hire your own programmer to create this report for you. Yes, you can make this report even more detailed by also subtracting from gross profit the amount of credits you had to issue each customer, restocking expenses, average days to pay, delivery expense, etc., but we have found the cost to create and maintain a report capturing all that additional data isn't worth the expense. We get 90% of what we need from the simple report outlined above and that is more than enough to see which customers are profit drains.

CHAPTER 47

THE SMALL ORDER PROBLEM

Following up on my previous post on customer profitability, just as many business owners and managers don't know that some customers are unprofitable because of too many transactions, many aren't aware that small orders are eating them alive. By this I mean that most businesses have a large number of small orders that generate less gross profit than the cost of processing the order. As I mentioned in my previous post, if you calculate the cost to process an invoice (see previous post for details on how to do this) and, to use round numbers, your cost to process an invoice is $100, then any transaction with gross profit under $100 is an unprofitable transaction. If you have thousands of unprofitable transactions over the course of a year this can seriously erode your profits.

For example, I was visiting one of our stores recently and it got busy so I waited on a customer. The customer got two items for total of $11. I told him to just take the items for free because it was more profitable for me to give him those items than to bill him for them. Our gross profit on that transaction was only about four dollars and our cost per transaction was well in excess of that, so why would I want to bill him? On top of that, he might not pay us and it would take time for our credit manager to pursue him for payment. The people in our store thought I was crazy to just give him the materials for free but once I explained why I did that, they understood.

Now, I'm not saying that you should give your customers products for free every time their purchase generates less gross profit than the cost of processing the transaction because if you did that too often some wily customers would always only pick up one or two items. The best solution to the problem is to train your salespeople to do **"related item selling"** so that when a customer attempts to make a small purchase the salesperson asks questions and then suggests related items that go with the items the customer initially wanted to purchase.

In my 35+ years in business I have found that most salespeople resist related item selling as they feel they are being pushy. I constantly have to point out that, in most cases, they're doing the customer a favor by suggesting related items. By this I mean, if a customer gets home and finds out that she didn't purchase everything she needed to get the job done and she has to make another trip back to your store, is she happier then? No! A professional salesperson can do related items selling while sounding like a consultant, not pushy salesperson. A good salesperson can ask the right questions about the purchase in such a way that the customer isn't offended and the size of the sale grows, sometimes significantly.

Another problem with small orders that is even worse occurs when a customer phones in a small order and wants it delivered for free. In my business, which is building supplies, we regularly have customers call in an order for less than $100 and want us to deliver it 30 miles away. That is a 60 mile round-trip and when you add in the driver's pay, fuel, and wear and tear on the truck, that sale is a huge loser for us. If we can't get the customer to increase the order size, we mitigate this problem by charging an "expedited order charge" starting at $25 and going up from there based upon how far the order has to be delivered. If the customer balks at the expedited order charge we tell the customer that if he is in no rush we will deliver it without the expedited order charge the next time we have a truck going in his direction. Sometimes the customer will decide to wait on the delivery to avoid the charge and other times the customer will say that he needs it right away and he will pay this charge.

A couple of points about this: **never call it a delivery fee; call it an expedited order charge.** In our industry free delivery is the standard and customers refuse to pay a delivery fee. However, if you train your salespeople to call it an expedited order fee, and properly explain it, you will be surprised how much you will collect in fees over the course of a year. The other point is you may need to waive this charge for your best customers. For example, a customer who buys over $300,000 a year from us wanted us to deliver two hard hats to a job about 60 miles from one of our branches. When we couldn't get him to add more to the order we did it as a goodwill gesture. While that sale was a huge money loser for us we scored a lot of points with a key customer.

In summary, attacking your small order problem can have a significantly positive impact on your bottom line but don't throw out the baby with the bathwater. Be willing to waive the expedited order charge for your best customers or be willing to lose a lot of business. **There are no "one-size-fits-all" solutions to business problems and there is also no substitute for good judgment.**

CHAPTER 48
TERMINATIONS

One of the dirtiest tasks that any manager has to do is terminating someone who reports to him or her. Most managers do anything to avoid a termination because they find it so unpleasant. I, on the other hand, dread layoffs. Laying off a good person due to a slowdown in business that is not their fault is the task I find most unpleasant. After 35 years in business, terminating people who deserve to be terminated doesn't bother me at all. Years ago, a mentor of mine told me, "It's not the people you fire who make your life miserable, it's the ones you don't." That is so true. *Have you ever terminated someone and then regretted it? I never have.* The only thing I've ever regretted about terminations is that I didn't work up the nerve to do it sooner.

I saw a survey many years ago that showed that most managers terminated a substandard employee *over one year after they should have.* Why is that? Well, as mentioned above, it is a distasteful task and it takes some people a year or more to work up the nerve to do it. Another reason is that finding a replacement is time-consuming and, in most companies, 50 to 75% of new hires don't work out due to the lack of a proper selection process. (See my previous post on how we recruit and select new associates.)

It takes a lot of time to post an ad, sort through tons of resumes (most of them not even vaguely relevant to the job you posted), interview the candidates that appear to be the best, do background checks, check references, and then train the new hire. To hire properly is a tiring, time-consuming process and most managers dread it, especially in times like these when most managers are already doing the work of several people. The thought of adding to their workload causes most managers to put up with a poor employee for a long time.

Once you finally decided to terminate a poor performer how you do it? And more importantly, how you do it without getting sued? Even if you are in a so-called "right to work state" such as we are here in South Carolina, employers can still get sued for wrongful dismissal, age or sex discrimination, sexual harassment, and a raft of other reasons that a crafty lawyer being paid on contingency can come up with.

What we do when we decide to terminate someone is called "building a case". How do you build a case for a legal termination? The first step is meeting with the substandard employee for a coaching session. You need to clearly state what the employee is doing wrong and what they need to do differently. I also recommend giving up to five specific goals for the employee to meet during the next 90 days. You need to give the employee a reasonable period of time to improve their behavior so, if you end up in court, a judge won't feel that only giving an employee a week, or even a month, to improve was a reasonable period of time. I have found that judges feel that 90 days is the minimum amount of time you should give an employee to improve. After the meeting be sure to document what was said and the goals that were given, either by email and ask for an e-mail response, or put it in writing and have the employee sign it.

At the end of 90 days if the employee's performance still hasn't improved you should terminate the employee immediately. Don't wait another 60 or 90 days as that could be used against you in court. The judge may ask you if his or her performance was so poor why didn't you terminate this employee at the end of the 90 day probationary period?

When you decide to terminate anyone I recommend that you do it in private and have a witness present, preferably someone from human resources. I also recommend you get right to the point when the employee walks in the room. *I have heard of terminations that began with jovial chitchat and ended up in such a way that the person being terminated didn't even know they were terminated and came to work the next day. You want to avoid that!*

I prefer to hire slowly and terminate quickly. When I terminate someone, the length of the termination meeting is generally less than five minutes. When the person being terminated walks in the room my first words are, "Effective immediately you are being terminated." I refuse to engage in a long debate about it. I simply state the reason for the termination as briefly as possible, and then if human resources or an outplacement firm is present, I then leave the room and let them explain the outplacement process, COBRA, severance, and any other relevant information. Either HR or I accompany the terminated person to their desk, watch as they gather their belongings, and escort them out of the building. *This process may seem cruel and heartless but I think it is much more cruel and heartless to drag out the termination.*

To avoid messy terminations, spend a lot of time in the candidate selection process, give the people that report to you honest and timely feedback, and when you've made a mistake, admit it and cut your losses quickly. *I was recently reading Warren Buffett's annual letter to his shareholders and he stated his philosophy as, "Hire well and manage little."* I couldn't agree more. It is my practice to take my time in the hiring process, give the people that report to me a clear set of responsibilities and goals, and then get out of the way and let them do their job.

CHAPTER 49
HOW TO COMPENSATE SALES PEOPLE

Since graduating from college in 1976 and immediately going into outside sales selling roofing products in the state of New York, and then moving into sales management in 1979, I have seen a wide variety of sales compensation plans. I have seen an even wider variety of theories about compensating salespeople published in trade journals and newsletters published by consultants and at conventions. This topic never ceases to draw an audience, all looking for the "magic bullet" that will get salespeople to perform at optimum levels.

Generally speaking, there are two schools of thought about compensating salespeople. There are people who believe in paying salary, but they are in the minority. The vast majority believe in compensating salespeople via commission or a salary plus bonus. When it comes to compensating salespeople via a commission plan there is a lot of argument here as well. Some people believe in paying commission on sales and others believe in paying commission on gross profit generation. Some people believe in not giving salespeople the ability to negotiate prices with their customers and others believe in giving their salespeople pricing authority.

Who is right? The answer is I don't know. I know that sounds like a copout but *sales compensation is not a one-size-fits-all issue.* The main thing I can tell you is that *you will get what you pay for.* If you pay solely on sales generation, regardless of profit, you will get a lot of sales volume, but generally speaking, you won't like the gross profit margin. If you pay on gross profit margin you may sacrifice some volume which you may need to hit vendor rebate levels or to generate cash flow. *The only compensation plan that I am totally against is paying salespeople a straight salary.* Some companies do this, but not many. One of the most notable companies that paid their sales-people solely on salary was Digital Equipment Company, or DEC ("DECK"), as they were known in the industry. Their founder, Ken Olsen, strongly believed in only paying salespeople a salary. The salary varied by tenure more than results and that may explain why DEC isn't around anymore. They were swallowed up by Hewlett-Packard several years ago.

When I was in the computer systems business I knew quite a few DEC salespeople. The one common characteristic most of them exhibited was that they were laid back and came across more as consultants than salespeople. That's not all bad, *but I have always believed that sales-people need to be hungry to produce optimum results.* Not so hungry that they will break the law or cut corners, but hungry enough that they will work long hours and get creative to close sales.

When I bought my present company in 2001 I found that the inside and outside salespeople were at odds with each other. I was riding with an outside salesperson shortly after buying the company and I listened to him calling into our local branch. He asked an inside salesperson to do something for him and I could hear from his reaction that his in-side counterpart wasn't being cooperative. When he got off the phone I asked him what happened. He told me that the inside salesperson flatly refused to do what he asked him to do. I asked him if his inside counterpart got a commission on his sales. He told me that he didn't. That explained why the inside salesperson wouldn't help our outside rep.

One of the first changes I made was giving the inside salespeople an override on what the outside salespeople sold. Within a week the in-side salespeople were cooperating with outside sales and sales in-creased more than enough to cover the additional compensation and the bickering between inside and outside salespeople ended.

When I was in business school I read a case study from the *Harvard Business Review* entitled, "The Folly of Expecting A while Rewarding B". The premise was that you will get what you pay for, so be sure your sales compensation plan rewards that which you want. For example, I once saw a compensation plan that paid a monthly bonus to a credit manager for reducing the company's average number of collection days. The credit manager did what she was paid to do and rapidly reduced her company's DSO. However, she did this by coming down hard on their customers, even threatening to sue some. *This resulted in a drastic reduction in DSO… and also in a drastic reduction in sales in the ensuing months.* So, be careful what you incentivize people to do. Generally speaking, you will get it.

In my present company we pay outside salespeople a draw against 20% of gross profit. That is a rich percentage of gross profit and I rarely hear of anyone paying a higher percentage. However, my father always used to say that *when you pay peanuts, you get monkeys.* While our compensation plan is rich, it allows us to attract, and more importantly, retain, some of the best salespeople in our industry. Until the recent construction downturn we regularly had salespeople earning over $200,000 per year. I had no problem with that because they were getting 20% of the gross profit they generated and the company was getting the other 80%. An 80/20 split seems fair to me.

Another approach I have seen that works is to pay a base salary plus a bonus for achieving one or more objectives. When I worked at Owens Corning they paid a base salary commensurate with results and tenure, and the bonus plan was tied to hitting your sales budget as well as some other objectives such as getting a new product launched, landing some target accounts, and getting back a customer that had been lost to competition. A plan like that can be effective as well.

A more drastic approach is the compensation plan I had with Fry Roofing (later acquired by Owens Corning) when I first got out of college. Fry paid a monthly salary that was barely enough to pay for my meager fixed expenses. However, Fry was known for paying very large bonuses to its superstars. By very large I mean up to a year's salary or even more. After graduating from college in May of 1976, I started with Fry in June, and at Christmas time of that year I got a bonus of six months' salary. That got my attention. *The next year I worked my tail off and got a bonus of 28 months' salary.* You can imagine how excited that got me. The only problem with this type of plan is that not many people will work for a salary that is barely above the poverty level.

In summary, *sales compensation is an art not a science*. The most important thing to keep in mind is that you will get what you pay for. If your current compensation plan isn't getting the results you need, take a long look at it and see if the compensation plan is aligned with your goals. If you aren't achieving your goals your compensation plan probably isn't aligned with your objectives, so come up with a new plan that is.

CHAPTER 50

YOUR ASSOCIATES DON'T LISTEN TO WHAT YOU SAY, THEY WATCH WHAT YOU DO

As I type this my wife and 21-year-old daughter are in Vienna, Austria and I am in my office working. Our daughter is doing a semester abroad in Prague and my wife is visiting her for spring break and they are doing a three day trip to Vienna. You may be wondering why I am sharing this with you as I doubt you care for a status report about my wife and daughter. The reason I am telling you this is I would rather be with them but our company has been going through a three-year downturn in our construction supply business and I know it would look terrible to my associates if I were in Europe with them. Given that we have laid off about 50% of our associates and my remaining associates are absorbing pay cuts and doing the work of 2-3 people, it would look terrible that I am in Europe while they are working so hard. Some of you may be wondering why I care how it looks. Well, I learned a long time ago, that when you're a leader, people don't listen to what you say, they watch what you do. If I were preaching austerity and teamwork via email from Vienna I don't think I would have much support. In fact, I think I would destroy our already battered morale. My dad (a Marine who went ashore in the first wave at Iwo Jima and Okinawa) used to say, "You can't lead from the rear." I agree.

During my career I have never understood why owners treat themselves differently than the rest of their associates and then wonder why their associates hate them. I first learned to care about setting the right example when I was working as a welder at a mobile home plant while going to college. Mobile home sales had fallen significantly and the company did a layoff and cut everyone's pay. However, a few weeks later the owner and his wife (who only worked part time but drew a full time salary) both got new Cadillac's which they parked in their reserved parking spaces under carports erected solely for their use. You could imagine the impact this had on morale. For months the new Cadillac's were all that my coworkers talked about during our two 15 minute breaks and one 30 minute lunch period per day. I noticed that graffiti (some threatening physical harm) denigrating the owners quickly covered the restroom walls and even the break room. The final act of defiance was when another coworker with a large family and an ill wife got laid off. As he was leaving he keyed both of their cars. This lesson has never been lost on me.

During my career in management and as an owner, I have gone out of my way to not treat myself any better than my associates. My wife and I are on the same benefit plan, pay our own deductibles, and I don't allow anyone to call me Mr. I clean up the restroom when it's messy and I clean my own office. I don't have an assistant and I answer my own phone and record my own voicemail greetings. I don't know about you, but I find it extremely pretentious when I call for someone at a customer or supplier's office and get a voicemail greeting recorded by their secretary. I think this looks self-important during good times and utterly ridiculous during bad times. I also have an office that is about 8' X 10' which barely has room for a visitor. If we are busy and a customer needs a delivery in a hurry it's not beneath me to jump in a truck and take the materials to our customer. (My wife has too even thought she doesn't work in our business.) In fact, when customers see me making a delivery they are surprised but also impressed that I don't think I'm too important to make a delivery. You can preach all you want and note on your website about how customer focused you are, but nothing gets the customer commitment message across like a CEO making a delivery to a muddy job site on a sweltering day in July, in the South.

I drive a Nissan Murano and when I'm on the road I stay at Hampton Inn's. I know a lot of owners that drive a Mercedes, have a reserved parking spot at their office, and leave early on Friday and come in late on Monday because they were at their beach house over the weekend. I learned from my father to not drive a flashy car and to not have facilities and a personal office that looks too expensive. Your customers and associates have enough to talk about regarding you and your family without your giving them more ammunition.

I'm not saying that owners and managers aren't entitled to nice things. That's why most of us work 70-100 hour weeks, or even more. But, I am saying that you need to be discreet about the trappings of wealth, especially during tough times.

CHAPTER 51
READING LIST

I got an email recently from a young man who graduated from college recently and is working in his family's building supply business. He said that despite the construction downturn he really enjoys the business and wants to make this industry his career. He went on to say that he was disappointed to find out that most of what he learned in college hasn't prepared him for being involved in a small, family-owned business. I, too, have noticed that over the years. I have found that very little of what I learned in school helped me in my business career, and even less prepared me to be an entrepreneur. I have been fortunate to have some great mentors who taught me much more about business than I ever learned in school, but I have also learned a lot by being an incessant reader. I mentioned this to this young man and he asked me to provide him with a reading list that would help him in his business career.

This list is by no means all-inclusive, it is just a start. So, having said that, here are some great books that have been immensely helpful in my career:

- Think and Grow Rich - Napoleon Hill (How to build real wealth using brains, not brawn)

- See You at the Top -Zig Ziglar (Goal setting and planning for success)

- What They Don't Teach You at Harvard Business School - Mark McCormack (Common sense business tips you won't learn at Harvard, or any college)

- Swim With the Sharks Without Being Eaten Alive - Harvey Mackay (Street smart business tips)

- The Effective Executive - Peter Drucker (The definitive book on management by the greatest business consultant of all time.)

- Built to Last - Jim Collins (How to build a company that will last)

- Good to Great - Jim Collins (How to make a "good " company "great")

- The Seven Habits of Highly Effective People - Stephen Covey (The habits that set highly effective people apart from the merely average)

- First Things First-Stephen Covey (Time management)

- The Purple Cow - Seth Godin (New age marketing)

- Small Is The New Big-Seth Godin (Follow up to The Purple Cow)

- Crossing the Chasm - Geoffrey Moore (How to take a company from start up to maturity)

- How To Master The Art of Selling - Tom Hopkins (The "Bible" of selling)

- The 22 Immutable Laws of Marketing - Jack Reis and all Al Trout (Must do's for successful marketing)

- Buy Low, Sell High, Collect Early, and Pay Late - Dick Levin (A primer on running a small business)

- Half Luck and Half Brains - Kemmons Wilson (Biography of the founder of Holiday Inn)

- Jack-Straight From the Gut-Jack Welch (Lessons on business from the undisputed #1 CEO of the 20th century)

- First, Break All the Rules-Marcus Buckingham and Curt Coffman (Tips on breaking the conventional rules of business in pursuit of unconventional profits)

- Guerrilla Marketing -Jay Conrad Levinson (Tips on champagne marketing on a beer budget)

As I said, this is not an all-inclusive list but it will get you started or add to your knowledge if you've already read some or most of these books.

CHAPTER 52

WHICH MEDIUM TO USE FOR COMMUNICATION AND WHEN

Business has changed a lot since I got my first full-time job after graduating from college in 1976. When I got my first real job there were basically three ways of communicating with our customers: in person, over the phone, and believe it or not youngsters, via letter. In today's digital world there are a lot more ways to communicate with customers but some modes of communication aren't appropriate for certain situations. For example, I see too many instances of people who don't want to tell me bad news doing it via e-mail. That tells me that they are spineless and don't have the guts to tell me in person or at least over the telephone. Below I look at the various means of communication and share with you my opinion on when it's appropriate to use each.

- **In person.** As I said above bad news should be communicated in person. If that's impossible due to geographic separation or time constraints then, and only then, will the telephone suffice. Also, when closing a sale, it's much more effective to do it in person. It's much easier to say no to someone over the phone, and even easier to say no via e-mail. Whenever I am trying to close a big deal I press for an appointment even if the customer tells me to just send my proposal. When you present a proposal in person not only is it harder for the person you're meeting with to say no but you can think of other arguments to make while you are with the prospect that may end up salvaging the deal. You also can read someone's body language when you're meeting face-to-face and you certainly can't do that via e-mail.

- **Telephone.** The telephone is good for routine communication and things such as prospecting, qualifying prospects, and asking for an appointment. Smart salespeople learn to qualify prospects over the telephone, after doing preliminary qualification

143

over the Internet and networking, rather than waste time driving to and from a prospect site only to find out that he or she won't meet with you. Don't use the telephone for bad news and don't use the telephone for things that are better done in writing.

- **E-mail**. E-mail is good for transmitting specifications, pictures, and routine communications. It's also extremely good for confirming appointments instead of calling and disturbing the person you're going to be meeting with. I saw a survey a few months ago that showed that e-mail was the preferred mode of routine communication by 43% of the respondents, more than any other mode of communication. Everyone is busy these days and even the most routine of phone calls takes 15 minutes after you talk about the weather, last night's ballgame, and the like. E-mail is unobtrusive and can be responded to late at night, early in the morning, and at other times when a phone call would be inappropriate.

- **Fax.** Yes, some people still use fax machines. Fax machines are good when you have a paper document that didn't come to you in digital form and you need to share it with someone else. It's also good for communicating with older clients who aren't up to date with using the latest technology. In our construction supply business I am still amazed about the number of faxes that we get every day. It isn't yet time to throw your fax machine in the dumpster.

- **Text messages.** Text messages are the preferred mode of communication for most people under 30. Our 21-year-old daughter sends and receives over 2000 text messages every month. I learned this the hard way when I put her phone on a family share plan that gave each family member 500 text messages per month on the plan. Much to my dismay, I was hit with an overage charge of $86 the first month she was on my plan. I looked at the bill and saw that the phone company said she sent and received over 2800 text messages that month. I was certain that had to be a mistake so I called her and she informed me that it was likely correct as most of her friends text her instead of calling or e-mailing. Even in our construction supply business we get quite a few text messages, especially from our younger customers. Text messages are fine for routine communication but never for anything of great importance.

- **Instant messaging**. We use instant messaging in our business so that our associates can communicate with each other while they are typing or reading an e-mail, reading a spreadsheet, entering a purchase order, etc. Rather than wait for a coworker to finish a task and go back to reading e-mail, if you need an immediate answer and the person you're trying to reach isn't answering the phone, an instant message can be very effective.

- **Two-way radio.** Most contractors use Nextel phones because of the two-way radio function. All day, every day, I hear our inside and outside sales people getting messages from customers and suppliers via two-way radio. This also is all right for routine communications such as asking if a delivery is going to be on time and or to let someone know that you're running late for lunch but, in my mind, that's the extent of it.

CHAPTER 53

PREPARING FOR A RECOVERY

Most businesses are beginning to recover from "The Great Recession". However, how many business owners are proactively planning for the recovery? "Plan for a recovery?", you may ask. Don't you just need to get through the downturn and when things get better the ship rights itself automatically? Sometimes that's the case but in some situations a recovery can lead to a business failing. By now you're probably quite confused so let me explain.

When a company has been through a prolonged recession such as the one we are just now emerging from head counts have been reduced, training has been suspended, inventories have been lowered, investment in technology has been postponed, maintenance may have been delayed on capital equipment and vehicles, and sometimes even more drastic measures have been taken such a closing one or more locations. When sales revenue start to rise again holes can appear in the business to where your business looks like Swiss cheese.

Like a scuba diver that comes up too fast and gets the bends, a business can recover too fast and experience significant problems. Here are a few tips to ease the pain of recovery.

- **Do a thorough cash flow analysis.** Either you or you and your CFO/controller should forecast various sales increase levels, as at some levels you may be exceeding your available credit. If you sit down with your banker now and share those projections with him or her your banker ought to be impressed with your foresight. This should help in getting an increased credit line. Bankers like planners and if they can take your business plan to their credit committee and show them that you are more on top of things than their average customer, this can significantly help your chances of getting an increased credit line.

- **Plan to increase your staff.** Post openings with local colleges, community colleges, trade schools, and the like and begin gathering resumes. You may also want to post job openings with Internet-based job sites such as Career Builder and Monster. Even if you aren't ready to hire just yet you should at least begin building your bench by posting openings and weeding out resumes that don't meet your requirements and keeping those that do. Then when you're ready to start hiring you're several steps ahead of the game.

- **Review your use of technology.** Are you one or more releases behind on the software you use in your business because you stopped spending money on software upgrades during the recession? Did you stop software support and enhancement contracts? Is your operating system out of date? Is your computer hardware held together with glue and string? All of the above needs to be reviewed and a timetable established to bring your use of technology current. You don't want to have business pickup and your systems start failing you.

- **Review the condition of the vehicles used in your business.** If your business uses delivery trucks, company cars, forklifts, and the like, a thorough review of all of the preceding should be done. If you're like most businesses you probably stopped buying new vehicles and made do with what you had. Now is the time to review all of your vehicles and come up with a plan to replace or perform maintenance on all of your vehicles over the next year or two. Your business can be significantly hurt if, when business picks up, you don't regularly deliver on time because your vehicles are breaking down.

- **Review your business premises.** Did you stop painting your buildings, did you let your landscaping go, does the interior of your business need a fresh coat of paint, new carpet or flooring, etc. Again, most businesses stopped spending money on cosmetics and your business may be looking a little worse for wear. Put together a plan to spruce up the interior and exterior of your business over the next six months to a year.

- **Training.** One of the first things to fall under the budget ax is training. However, if you forgo training for your staff for too long a period of time you may be penny wise and pound foolish. I've always thought that the axiom, "If you think training is expensive, try ignorance", was very true. Review all of your associates and come up with a list of who needs what training and get that scheduled over the next year or so.

- **Insurance coverage.** Did you cut back your coverage to save money during the recession? Do you need to let your insurance broker know that your sales and inventories are increasing so that you are properly insured? Did you drop some coverage such as business interruption insurance and errors and omission insurance? Did the value of your property drop but you are still paying for insurance at the old value? Ask your insurance broker to meet with you to review your full portfolio of insurance and make sure that all of your policies are up to date and reflect your current revenues and inventory levels.

- **Employee benefits.** Did you cut back or eliminate benefits during the downturn? Most businesses did. Now is the time to review your entire portfolio of benefits so that you have a competitive offering as you begin hiring again. We were in a buyer's market when it came to hiring over the last several years but that's about to change. Not having a competitive package of benefits may keep you from hiring stars that can make a major difference in your business.

As I said at the beginning, like the hull of a ship that hasn't undergone regular maintenance and then gets sent back to sea to run a heavy schedule, holes can emerge in your business that can be fatal. These problems can be avoided with proper planning and now is the time to start if you haven't already

CHAPTER 54

OVERCOMING PRICE OBJECTIONS

Every business has to charge for their products and services. Some businesses such as doctors and hospitals rarely have their prices challenged. However, other businesses such as car dealers, contractors, and building material distributors (the business I am in) constantly have their prices challenged. This post deals with how to overcome price objections.

Since I got out of college and started in sales over 35 years ago I have pretty much negotiated prices, either on the buy side or the sell side, every business day for my entire career. When I first started out, like most rookie salespeople, I used price to try to sell. I would ask a potential customer what they were paying for the product I was selling and then I would try to get my boss to approve a lower price. I quickly found out that trying to sell on price would result in my having a brief career in sales.

The first company I worked for after college was a roofing manufacturer with 24 plants across the United States. The owner of the company was 85 years old and was still the CEO. He reviewed each salesperson's call reports and expense reports each week and we all lived in fear of the comments he would write on each with a thick red pen. The first time I told him that I needed a lower price than my competitors to be able to sell he told me that if he wanted to sell on price the first thing he would do would be to fire all of our salespeople. Then he would hire helicopters to drop flyers over major cities advertising low prices. I never asked him for a better price again.

Also, a lot of salespeople confuse quoting with selling. As my friend, the noted consultant, Bill Lee, is fond of saying, "Quoting ain't selling". It has never been easier to send out quotes. Anyone with a PC can send out hundreds of quotes a day. However, they won't get many orders. Astute buyers don't buy on price alone. Over the years, I have found that when a buyer says your price is high, he is really saying I have a better relationship with one of your competitors. If someone really wants to buy from you they will give you "last look". If they don't want to buy from you they will tell you your prices are high.

There are several things you can do to avoid selling on price alone. Some of them are:

- **Superior product knowledge.** When I was selling roofing shingles, very few, if any, salespeople I competed with knew more about roofing shingles than I did. I knew how many pounds of tensile strength the mat was that each competitor of mine built their shingles on versus ours, I knew what type of asphalt they used and whether it was pure asphalt or had fillers in it, and I knew whether they used dyed or ceramic granules. I knew whether our competitor's warranty was labor only or labor and materials. I knew all of this and more, and it came across to my customers. People like to buy from salespeople who are professionals, not amateurs.

- **Know your market**. A lot of salespeople fall for buyers telling them they have been quoted a ridiculously low price. If you know your market and talk to multiple people in your industry every day you should know what the market price is for your products. That doesn't mean that, on occasion, a competitor won't dump excess inventory, seconds, closeouts, or something else at a ridiculous price, but those are the exceptions, not the rule. The more you know your market the less likely you will be preyed upon by an unscrupulous customer.

- **Know how to overcome price objections.** Amateur salespeople immediately bite on any competitive price told to them by a buyer. Professionals know to say things like, "You've got to be kidding me, I sell several hundred thousand dollars worth of this product every month at the price I just quoted you", or, "Will you let me see my competitor's quote or one of their invoices so I can see if the quote is apples-to-apples"? Learn to answer a question with a question. For example, if a customer asks you why your prices are so high you should respond with, "What have you been hearing about my competitor's prices"?

- **Build relationships.** The more time you invest in getting to know your customers the less likely they are to lie to you. Be active in trade associations, forward interesting articles to them, spend time entertaining them, and they are more likely to give you last look. Buyers buy from people they know, like, and trust. They only buy from people they don't like as a last resort.

- **Price, service, quality: pick any two.** When a customer tells me my prices high I ask them if they agree that there are really only three things a supplier can give a customer, price, service, and quality. When they agree I then state that if you have the best price, the best service and the best quality you can't stay in business long. Most buyers nod their heads in agreement. I then tell them that if they are hung up on the price they want me to give them, which thing they prefer me to cut back on, service or quality? Of course, almost no one wants to compromise on service or quality so that brings us back to price. More often than not I then get him to buy at the price I originally quoted.

- **Develop pricing fortitude.** Don't automatically agree to match any and all prices that are told to you by your customers. Walk away from some orders. If you are being told by a customer that they can buy something at a ridiculous price, call their bluff occasionally and tell them that you simply can't meet that price. Sometimes you will find they give you the order anyway as they were just testing you to see if you would bite. One of my first mentors told me, "It's okay to lose an order, but it's never okay to lose a customer". When you decide to pass on an order make sure that you are just losing an order and not a customer.

- **Know your competition.** When I was selling shingles I knew more about most of my competitor's products than their own salespeople did. When I had a customer ask me about a competitor's product they had been quoted at a low price I would spout off so much product knowledge about the flaws of their product that I overcame the low price they had been quoted most of the time.

- **Don't give unless you get.** That was another axiom taught to me by one of my mentors. Sometimes I will agree to a lower price than normal if I can get paid soon sooner than normal. Other times I ask for something even as trivial as a reference letter so that I get something in return for a price concession. Remember, never give unless you get.

- **Don't waste your time on customers with bad credit.** Over my career I have noticed that most people who beat me up on price also pay slowly. Spend your time cultivating customers who buy a lot and pay their bills on time. There aren't a lot of those but those are the ones that can make your career.

CHAPTER 55
THE 5 P'S

I first heard of "the 5 P's" from one of my college football coaches. If you haven't heard of this before, it stands for proper preparation prevents poor performance. In my 35+ year business career I never cease to be amazed by people who go into negotiations or presentations for multimillion dollar deals and just wing it. It has been my experience that most people wing it and hope for the best. Most of those people don't get the deal and then wonder why not, or complain about the company that got the deal knowing someone, doing something underhanded to get it, or some similar type of excuse making.

I'm lucky that when I was in my mid 20s I had the experience to work with Clarence Bauknight who was then the CEO of Builder Marts of America in Greenville, South Carolina. When I was in my formative years he drilled it into me that you never went into a negotiation or a large sales presentation (or even a small one for that matter) without being significantly more prepared than the other party. We would do all sorts of research on the people with whom we would be meeting with and then we would rehearse repeatedly so that when we actually got into the negotiation or presentation we were prepared for any eventuality. How about you? Do you do this? If you do, my hat is off to you, but I bet most of you reading this don't over prepare for meetings and negotiations. How does one over prepare? Here is a short list:

- **Get a Dun & Bradstreet report on the company you are meeting with.** Read it closely. Look at their sales and profits, if they give them to D&B. Many companies don't give D&B an income statement; however, some companies provide just a balance sheet and you can learn a lot from their balance sheet, especially if there is a comparison of the most recent year to the prior year. Did their cash on hand go up or down? What about inventories and receivables? Did they go up or down?

One of the most important things to look at is stockholder's equity. If it went down that generally means the company you are studying lost money over the last year. How much money? A little or a lot? If you are meeting with a company because you want to acquire them, and you can ascertain that they lost several million dollars over the last year, you will know that you are dealing with a company that is negotiating from a position of weakness. Use this to your advantage.

- **Google the company and people with whom you will be meeting.** It is absolutely amazing, and a bit horrifying, when you see what you can find out about people via Google. I never go into an important negotiation without doing a Google search on the people with whom I will be meeting, as well as their company. I almost always find out some very interesting information that gives me the upper hand. Information is power and the Internet has made it easier than ever to gather information prior to an important meeting. Also, do a Google search on yourself and your company. You will probably be shocked with what you see. If you see a lot of negative things you may want to engage a company like Reputation Defender to clean up what is available about you and your company on the Internet.

- **Do a PowerPoint presentation.** This is very important if you are doing the selling. Remember the old adage, "A picture is worth a thousand words"? It is still true today, maybe even more so than in the past. I recently had a meeting with our bank and blew away our banker with a 45 slide presentation on our past, present, and future plans. At the end of the presentation I asked the banker if he had any questions. He sat there in stunned silence for a while and then said, "No, you anticipated everything I was going to ask, plus a whole lot more." He went on to tell me that it was the best presentation he had ever seen from a company of any size. If you impress your banker, he or she is much more willing to go out on a limb for you in front of his or her bank's credit committee. A PowerPoint presentation isn't appropriate for all types of meetings but more often than not it is. When I started in business having slides made was a time-consuming and expensive proposition. I would have get hand drawings to our advertising agency about a month before the meeting so they could turn the drawings into 35mm slides. I would then have to drag a projector along to my presentation and hope that the bulb didn't burn out. Having PowerPoint on my laptop makes this process much quicker. More than once I have revised my slides in the lobby of the company I was about to meet with to include the most up-to-date information.

- **Practice.** Before going into an important negotiation or a sales presentation for a large order, practice with everyone from your team who will be in the meeting. Once you feel you have your presentation down pat, then film it. I bet you that when you watch yourself on film you will wince. It's like the first time I watched my golf swing on film. I wanted to throw up. I found out I had two golf swings. The one in my head that was silky smooth and the one I saw on film that was jerky, off balance, and overall, pathetic. The same goes for presentations. The first time I ever reviewed a practice run of an important presentation on film I wanted to cry. I couldn't get over how many times I said "a" and "ya know". The next time you have an important presentation film a dry run of it. If you aren't horrified by what you see you are amazing.

- **The "Wow" factor.** If you are selling, think about what you can do to "wow" the people you are calling on. One time I rented a billboard across the street from a company I was trying to get to make a very large purchase from me. The billboard had a picture of all of my associates in the parking lot of our building. The headline said, "Our entire team is committed to your total satisfaction." Was that more than a little bit hokey? Yes. But did it impress the company I was pitching? Yes, again. Did I get the deal? You betcha.

In summary, the preparation for every important negotiation or sales presentation should be started several weeks ahead of time, you should do as much as research as possible on the company and people you're meeting with, you should rehearse and film the presentation, and then think of what you can do to "wow" them. Do all of the above and I guarantee your success rate will radically improve.

CHAPTER 56

THOUGHTS ON STAFFING AND COMPENSATION

Over the years I have seen many different staffing and compensation philosophies. The three main philosophies on staffing and compensation appear to be:

- **Pay poorly and expect turnover.** Throughout my career I have seen many companies that hire people for the least amount of money they can possibly pay. People employing this philosophy seem to feel that they can make more money by paying the lowest amount of money possible for each position and when they get turnover they just hire more low-paid people. I would venture a guess that about 30 -40% of employers adhere to this philosophy. I have a major customer that constantly is having turnover. I have even stopped adding his employees to my Contacts in Outlook because they don't stay long enough to be worth the time it takes me to enter their information. Because of the type of employees they hire we see a lot of errors from their accounting department (including a lot of double payment of invoices), shoddy work in the field, poor managers, and we hear a lot of complaints from their customers. One of our competitors also seems to employ this philosophy and we hear the same complaints about them.

- **Pay average salaries and expect average turnover.** I think that the majority of companies employ this philosophy. They pay market averages and they get average people. The problem with average people is, as Jim Collins says in *Good to Great*, "Good enough never is." He also says that good is the enemy of great. I agree. One of the biggest fallacies of this philosophy, and the first one noted above, is that you have turnover ranging from 15-50% per year. When you employ these two philosophies you are constantly interviewing, hiring, and training. What does it cost you to replace an employee? I think that it

157

costs you about 1X their annual salary. Why do I say this? Well, experience has taught me that new employees don't perform their jobs at optimal levels until at least one year in their position. There are some exceptions to this such as truck driver or accounting clerk, but sales and management positions take even longer for new employees to come up to speed. My experience has shown me that salespeople don't achieve their highest productivity levels until at least three years in their territory. Not only do they have to gain product knowledge but they also have to gain the trust of their customers. I have found this generally takes about three years.

- **Pay 150% of the market average and expect almost no turnover.** A mentor of mine told me a long time ago that when you pay peanuts you get monkeys. That is so true. Conversely, when you pay 150% of the market rate you get the absolute best people available. I've also found that a person who is worth 150% of the market rate doesn't do the job of 1.5 people. These types of people tend to do the work of about three people. Therefore, by paying 150% of the market rate I get 300% productivity... and almost no turnover because most of my associates cannot make more money elsewhere. Most don't even try to find other jobs because they know what the going rate is for their job and when they know they are being paid well above that rate, why even look for another job? There are a lot of benefits to very low turnover. First off, you don't spend much time interviewing, hiring, and training. And who really likes to do those tasks? I feel I do them well but they aren't my favorite things to do. Also, our inside and outside salespeople tend to sell more than double our industry average. A big part of that is due to the strong relationships that are built when you have salespeople calling on the same customers for up to 40 years, as in the case of our most tenured salesperson. And, you pay benefits and FICA on about 1/3 the normal number of people for a like company.

CHAPTER 57
GETTING APPOINTMENTS

There is an axiom in baseball that you miss 100% of the pitches you don't swing at. It's similar in business. You miss 100% of the sales you don't get to propose. Most underperforming salespeople don't even get to bat because they can't get an appointment with the person making the buying decision. How do you get a meeting with someone who doesn't want to see you? Below are a few tips that have worked for me over the years.

- **Befriend the receptionist or secretary.** With larger companies salespeople need to first get past the receptionist and then get past the secretary to the decision-maker. Many salespeople make the mistake of talking down to receptionists and secretaries. When I was still in sales I made it a point to turn on the charm with these gatekeepers. If you can't get past them you don't stand a chance of getting an order. How do you get these important people on your side? First off, be friendly and respectful towards them. Don't talk down to them. Try to learn personal information about them and mention it during subsequent attempts to get with the decision-maker. Over the years I have gotten many receptionists and secretaries to get the decision-maker to give me 15 minutes. If I could get 15 minutes with the decision-maker my close rate was over 75%.

- **Get a mutual friend to ask the decision-maker to see you.** When I couldn't get the receptionist or secretary to help me I would start asking around my group of industry contacts to see who might know the person I was trying to get to and who would vouch for me. Again, if a friend could get the decision-maker to see me I would take it from there with great success.

- **Get creative.** In the early 1980s I was unable to get an appointment with a key prospect in my sales territory. Finally, out of desperation, I handed the receptionist an envelope with ten

$100 bills in it. I asked her to hand the envelope and the note to the person I was trying to get to. The note said, "I know that time is money so if you'll give me just 15 minutes of your time you can keep the money if you think I have wasted your time". It worked, I ended up spending over two hours with the prospect, including lunch at his club, and went on to sell him several million dollars a year for many years. I'm not in his industry anymore but we are still friends. He loves telling people the story of how we met. I do too.

- **Cold call early or late.** Decision-makers are usually extremely busy and come in early and stay late. I have found that by cold calling (either in person, or over the phone) early in the morning or late in the afternoon I have been able to avoid the secretarial screen and get to the decision-maker. My elevator pitch was polished enough that if I could get the decision-maker on the phone, I could get an appointment most of the time.

- **Use social media.** In the Internet age use social media such as LinkedIn, Twitter, and Facebook to get to key decision-makers. LinkedIn is especially effective because you can see any mutual friends that you may share with your prospect. One word from a mutual friend can get you in the door. The rest is up to you.

- **Send a bulky package.** I have also had success sending a bulky package to a prospect with a request for an appointment inside. Why send a bulky package? If you are like me, I get tons of junk mail every day. Most I throw away without opening it. However, when I get a bulky package my curiosity gets the best of me and I open it. What do you put in the package? A pen, a stress ball, a keychain, and a lot of other similar items with your company logo on them that put enough of a lump in the package that you will get it opened most of the time. Then it's up to you to have a compelling enough written request for an appointment that you succeed in getting a few minutes with your prospect. I have always had a lot of success saying, "If you'll just give me 15 minutes I will leave promptly at the end of the allotted time unless you ask me to stay, and I will never darken your door again." Most asked me to stay.

- **Never, ever quit, with one exception.** A big part of success is never, ever quitting until you get an appointment with your prospect. There is one exception, however. When you get arrested for criminal trespass, you can quit trying to get to the prospect. I say this, because back in the early 80s I was unsuccessful at getting to a major prospect in St. Louis, no matter what I tried. So, out of desperation, I went to his office, ask again for an appointment, was told to leave, and didn't. Finally the police came and arrested me for trespass after notice. Then, and only then, did I give up.

CHAPTER 58

THE NINE MOST COMMON HIRING MISTAKES

During the last 32 years of my career I have been in management and that has required me to hire people. Hiring is arguably the most important, and hardest, part of being a manager. Doing it correctly makes you a hero and doing it wrong can get you fired. What are the most common hiring mistakes I have observed (sometimes through my own errors) over the last 30 years?

1. **Hiring the first person that you interview**. No manager likes to go through the hiring process because hiring someone requires you to spend even more time on the job, and most managers already work well over 40 hours. When you're already swamped it's very tempting to hire the first even remotely qualified candidate that you meet. This is usually a huge mistake. Unless you get real lucky, most of the people that you hire in haste will fail, and you'll have to do the process all over again... if you don't get fired for having made a hiring error. Take the time to do it correctly and you will not only save time in the long run, but possibly you will save your job as well.

2. **Not using the same list of interview questions with every candidate.** Many interviewers don't use a standard list of questions and just ask whatever questions come into their mind during the interview. Not only do you ask better questions if they are written down ahead of time but this will ensure that you ask the same questions of every candidate. Not only does that keep you from getting in trouble by asking an illegal question, but you can evaluate the answers of every candidate versus the same set of questions.

3. **Selling your company instead of questioning the candidate.** When I first became a manager and had to hire I spent most of the interview selling our company instead of quizzing

162

the candidate on their qualifications. Have a list of open-ended questions, and after asking them, stop talking and listen closely to the answers, while taking notes. Better yet, tape-record each interview so that you can practice active listening instead of half listening while taking notes.

4. **Not having a position specification or job description to measure the candidates against.** Not only do candidates like to see a list of their principal duties but having a position specification or job description allows you to tailor your questions so that you can ascertain if the candidate has the proper background to be able to meet the key responsibilities of the job.

5. **Not doing background checks.** Due to the proliferation of the internet we are now able to get a complete background check on most candidates instantaneously. In 70's and 80's we had to wait two weeks or longer to get the results of a background check. Sometimes there were so many alligators nipping at my heels that I would hire people without a background check. I almost always regretted this. Have candidates sign a background check release form and checking their criminal record, credit history, and driving record not only will this keep you from hiring mistakes but, as managers have the responsibility for creating a safe workplace, it may keep you from being sued or, worse yet, going to jail. Imagine the cost to you and your company if you hired someone without a background check and they went on a killing spree in your office. Not only would you have to live with guilt (if you survived the shooting spree) but the financial liability could break you.

6. **Not checking references.** I always ask for a minimum of three business references and three personal references. Yes, candidates tend to give you only good references but some people don't get references that are as good as they think they will be. Plus I can tell when someone is damning a candidate with faint praise. I always have a much clearer picture of a candidate after I talk to at least six references.

7. **Not using testing.** As I have said before, we use a variety of intelligence and psychological tests to ensure that we are trying to put a square peg in a round hole. To see a complete list of the tests and assessments we use, see my blog post of 8.23.10.

8. **Hiring friends.** I have said many times that you never really know a friend until they report to you. I have found out, mostly the hard way, that some people that were great friends ended up being some of the worst co-workers. Not only did I have to fire them, but I also lost a friend in the process. Talk about lose-lose.

9. **Hiring relatives.** This can be even worse than hiring friends as you can avoid friends that you have fired but you can't avoid your relatives. There are exceptions to this rule, but they are rare. In my case, my oldest son works with me and I don't know what I would do without him. However, before hiring him, he and I met with an industrial psychologist and talked about what each of us didn't like that the other person did. We had two follow up sessions after my son began working with me, but after the two initial sessions we agreed we didn't need any more. I once read that nepotism is great... provided you have smart relatives. In my case, I have a son who is smarter than me and who works harder than me. I am very fortunate because he is the rare exception.

CHAPTER 59

USING CREDIT AS A SALES TOOL

Most companies have the credit manager report to the controller or CFO. With very few exceptions, controllers and CFOs have never been in sales. In many companies they are rightly known as the "sales prevention team". In our company the credit manager reports directly to me, the CEO. As nothing happens in any company until the cash register rings I like to be directly involved in the credit process so that we can prudently sell as much as possible.

Many credit departments view the customer as guilty until proven innocent. In our company we try to find a way to sell everyone, even people with bad credit. However, we take a lot of steps to mitigate our risk and we have never had bad debts exceed .5% of sales in the almost 10 years I have owned my current company, and most years we are under .25%.

We recognize that most customers are not trying to steal from us. My experience has shown me that most late payments are due to errors on our end. Errors such as invoices sent to the wrong address, no purchase order number as required by the customer, items billed at a higher price than on the customer's purchase order, billing for items that haven't yet shipped, quality problems with products we sold them, etc. We have found only a small percentage of our past due invoices are because the customer can't or won't pay us. Now, when we find that a customer can't or won't pay us we take aggressive action as I have detailed in previous postings.

How do we sell people with dubious credit while also limiting or risk? Below are a few of the things we do:

- **Personal guarantees.** When a customer will give us a personal guarantee I am much more comfortable then when a customer will not sign the personal guarantee. When I see that a customer won't sign the PG I know that he won't pay us if times get tough as he can hide behind the corporate veil and not legally have to pay us. That raises a red flag. However, when a customer will share the risk with me by giving me a PG I generally will take a risk on him or her.

- **Personal credit check.** In addition to running credit checks on companies and corporations we ask customers with dubious business credit if we can also run a personal credit check on them. If they say no that tells me they have bad credit. If they say yes, or better yet, hell yes, that tells me a lot too. If I see that the owner of a startup company has excellent personal credit I have found that his personal credit habits tend to extend to his company as well.

- **Joint check agreement.** In our case, about two thirds of our business is to subcontractors. If a subcontractor has shaky credit but the general contractor he or she is working for has solid credit, then we will sell the subcontractor as long as the general contractor will sign a joint check agreement along with the sub. This way, the sub can't get paid by the GC and not pay us. Again, if a sub won't agree to a joint check agreement that tells me that he or she doesn't intend to pay us. He will pay another supplier or, worse yet, do something like buy a boat instead of paying us. Did you know that the most popular name of boats in the United States is *First Draw*? It's true. I saw a story in the Wall Street Journal that stated that. Many contractors, when they get their first draw, buy a boat instead of paying their supplier. I don't want to be one of those suppliers. One last tip, make sure that the joint check agreement requires the GC to pay you, as long as the sub did the work contracted for. I have seen many joint check agreements that aren't worth the paper they are written on. A lot of companies accept these agreements without even reading them, or if they read them, there is verbiage in them that they think protects them when it really doesn't. If you want a copy of our joint check agreement, let me know.

- **Credit card on file.** We will sometimes sell a customer with shaky credit provided they give us a credit card number that we can keep on file, and sign an agreement that allows us to charge their card if they don't pay us. Yes, sometimes a credit card isn't any good either, but it's another form of protection for us. Sometimes it works, and sometimes it doesn't.

- **1/3, 1/3, and 1/3.** Another way we sell people with dubious credit is 1/3 down, 1/3 before we ship the materials, and the final 1/3 thirty days after delivery. This way we have 66% of our money before we even ship the customer. As we generally get a higher than normal gross margin from people with shaky credit, we generally have all of our cost recouped prior to shipment. If we don't get the final payment we at least haven't lost any money. Tip: When you sell someone with less than stellar credit you should insist upon a much higher than normal gross margin to compensate you for taking the risk. If we are going to take a higher than normal risk we should get a higher than normal gross profit margin.

- **Character loans.** Early in my career I had a banker loan me more money than the collateral I had to offer. Bankers call the difference between the collateral and the loan an "air ball". Bankers generally don't like to deal with air balls, for good reason. However, this banker had known me for over ten years and properly assessed me as having good character. He made a character loan to me and he never regretted it. I do the same thing on occasion. Sometimes I know of a young person who has been working for one of our customers for a few years and has the itch to go in business. If my experiences with this person lead me to believe he or she has good character I will give them a small credit line to start out and raise their credit line over time, if they pay well. If a more established business is having trouble getting credit I like to meet with the owner, look he or she right in the eye, and ask if we will be paid for the materials we will be shipping. If they hesitate for even more than 15 seconds before answering me I get worried. People with good character tend to respond immediately and tell me that they will pay us come hell or high water. When I get that kind of fast, unflinching response I tend to give them a credit line and I rarely regret it.

- **Set up a high risk credit list.** When our credit manager declines to open a credit line for a customer I immediately am notified and review the credit file. After doing this for over 30 years I have a pretty strong gut feel when I review a credit file and my gut rarely lets me down. If I get a good feeling after reviewing the file our credit manager adds these customers to our high risk credit list. I monitor this list extremely closely because I am taking a chance on these customers, and I also don't want to look stupid to our credit manager. :) For about five years now we have had a high risk credit list and during that time we have generated gross profit of almost $1 million. Our bad debt write-offs to this group is less than $75,000 since the inception of this list. Has this been worth our while? You betcha.

- **Give your credit manager an expense account.** Every business person has situations arise where they have to decide whether they're going to pay one supplier or another if they can't pay them all. If your credit manager has been occasionally taking the accounts payable person for your customers to lunch or happy hour guess who's going to get paid if everyone can't get paid? Also, allow your credit manager to send small baby gifts, wedding presents, etc. to customer accounts payable contacts. If you allow your credit manager to entertain the accounts payable people they deal with the way your salespeople entertain buyers I bet you will see great results.

CHAPTER 60

THE 17 MOST COMMON MARKETING MISTAKES

I have found that most people don't understand the difference between sales and marketing. Most people think that they are the same. They are not. They are very different. The best definition of marketing I ever heard was: "Everything you do before and after the sale." Good marketing inspires customers to buy from you ... and keeps them coming back. Poor marketing drives customers away from you and to your competitors who are good marketers.

What are the most common marketing mistakes? In my experience they are:

1. **Poor company name.** Many of the company names I see make me wince. Most of them don't give you any indication of what the company does. I have seen people name companies after their children, their dogs, their initials, and even their favorite place to vacation. While that may seem cute at the time it doesn't help you build a brand. When I bought my current company its name was New South Supply. It wasn't a terrible name but it gave no indication of what we supplied. People called all the time asking what we supplied. The addition of one word made it very clear as to what we supplied. That word was "construction". We are now New South *Construction* Supply. Now we no longer get phone calls asking what it is we supply. Also, people driving by stop in if they are looking for construction supplies as our name now makes it clear that we sell construction supplies.

2. **Poor or no logo.** Some logos are just block letters. Others scream "1950". Your logo should be done by a professional and employee color and graphics that look up to date and professional. Ours includes the image of a bear wearing a hard hat with a carpenter's pencil tucked behind his ear. The bear im-

plies strength and the hardhat and carpenter's pencil indicate that we serve the construction business. Now, a lot of customers know us as "That company with the bear on the sides of their trucks". At least they remember us.

3. **No tagline.** You should have a tagline under your logo that makes a brand promise to your customers. Under our logo we have our tagline which states: Know How. Can Do. This tells our customers and prospects that we have industry know-how, and a can-do attitude. It also tells our associates that they need to live up to our brand promise. I have had more than one customer tell me that our associates clearly live up to our brand promise.

4. **Bad or no website.** It amazes me that in 2011, when websites are so inexpensive to create, that a lot of companies still do not have a website. Or, they have one that says "Under Construction", or all they have is one static page, unprofessionally done. I don't know about you, but when I hear of a company that we don't do business with that is referred to me, the first thing I do is Google their name and look at their website. If they don't have a website that tells me that they are not a player, and if they have a terrible website I'm not inclined to look any further. Remember the old adage: "You never get a second chance to make a first impression." This applies to your website too.

5. **No use of social media.** Facebook, Twitter, LinkedIn, and other social media sites are no longer just for geeks. They have gone mainstream and if you aren't using them you look behind the times. Every major company, sports figure, newscaster, and Hollywood star has a social media presence. If you don't it says that your company is behind the times. Plus, it is free!

6. **Dirty store or office.** If you have been doing your marketing correctly why fumble the ball on the one yard line when a prospect comes to your store or office and they find it to be dirty, old-fashioned looking, or otherwise unattractive. Make sure that your place of business looks up-to-date and professional. Otherwise, don't waste your time and money getting prospects to come to your store or office.

7. **Dirty vehicles.** If you have delivery trucks and/or company vehicles with your company name and logo on them make sure they are clean. Better yet, make sure they sparkle. A clean vehicle says a lot about your business and so does a dirty vehicle. What do you want your vehicles to say about your business?

8. **No newsletter.** Again, in the Internet age, it is extremely inexpensive as well as easy to create a very professional looking electronic newsletter to send to your customers and prospects. We send out a monthly newsletter to our customers and prospects and we get three suppliers to underwrite the cost of the newsletter in return for featuring their products. We also include information on business-related topics including the outlook for price increases or decreases on our key products. Our customers tell me that they look forward to our newsletter each month and that they use it to help them decide how to price projects. I even get emails asking when the newsletter will be out if it hasn't been published and the end of the month is nearing. To see an example of our newsletter and our website and logo, click here.

9. **No uniforms.** When I see a company that lets their employees dress however they like it doesn't look professional to me. At least not in our business, which is building supplies. If you are a computer programmer, a doctor, an accountant, etc., you don't need to wear a uniform but you should look professional. In our business we provide our truck drivers and our inside sales people with company shirts. Most, but not all of our outside salespeople wear company shirts as well. Every spring and fall we get new shirts for them. This is all part of projecting a professional image.

10. **Sloppily dressed employees.** It doesn't matter how nice the uniforms are that your associates wear if they come to work without showering or shaving, shirt tails hanging out, ketchup stains on their shirts, etc. Coming to work slovenly reflects poorly on your company. Have a dress code and enforce it.

11. **Poor phone etiquette.** I am immediately turned off when I call a company and am greeted unprofessionally and/or rudely. Come up with a standard greeting and phone etiquette guidelines and monitor that all of your associates adhere to it.

12. **Poor business cards.** Business cards also make a good or bad first impression. Spend the money on a professional looking logo and then don't skimp on the cost of your business cards. Use heavy stock paper so they aren't flimsy and don't fall apart. Also, give business cards to every single one of your associates. Everyone who works with you knows other people and can give them their business card if they express an interest in your product or service. Plus, lower-level employees feel important and are more likely to promote your company if they have business cards to hand out. We pay under $100 for 500 very professional business cards.

13. **Poor signage.** When I to go to a business for the first time if I see that their signage is out of date, faded, or, worse yet, hanging crooked by one bolt on the exterior of the building that speaks volumes to me about the quality of the company and their services. Make sure that your signage is replaced periodically so that it always looks fresh and up-to-date.

14. **Poor advertising**. I feel that you're better off not advertising at all if your ads look unprofessional. This applies to print ads as well as TV or radio. Many business owners can't be objective about their own advertising so form an advisory council of key customers and prospects, take them out for dinner in a private room in a good restaurant, and ask them a series of questions about how they perceive your advertising and other questions about your business. It's much cheaper than having an advertising agency put together a focus group and you get the added benefit of spending quality time with your best customers and prospects.

15. **No yellow page ads.** If your competition isn't in the Yellow Pages you don't need to be either. However, if your competition is in the Yellow Pages (either print or online) your ads need to look better than theirs. Your ads don't have to be bigger but they should look better.

16. **Cheap or reused bags and boxes**. If you have a business like ours where people shop in your showroom and take merchandise with them, have first class looking bags for their purchases. If you ship products to your customers make sure you have sharp looking boxes with your logo on them. Also spend a few

extra bucks to put your logo on the packing tape as well. Every little detail adds up and creates an image in the mind of the consumer. If you market your company properly the image created is a great one and adds to your revenues and profits.

17. **No catalog or a poor one.** If your business sells from a catalog don't cut corners on it. We publish a printed catalog, a CD version, and our catalog is also online. We don't put pricing in our catalogs so that they aren't out of date the minute we publish them. We get our suppliers to pay for ads in our catalog so we end up with a very professional looking catalog and it costs us next to nothing due to the support of our suppliers.

I believe that the image your company projects in the mind of your customers and prospects is the sum total of your marketing efforts. What image does your marketing project?

CHAPTER 61

WHICH IS SMARTER: ACQUISITIONS OR STARTUPS?

Recently a business owner emailed me and asked if it is smarter to buy a company or to start one from scratch. The answer is... it depends. I know this sounds like a copout but there are pros and cons to each approach. Here is a brief list of each:

Pro's and Con's of Acquisitions

- If you're buying a company that manufactures what they sell like a power tool company or a software company, many times you can buy the company for less than it would cost to start it. That's because many entrepreneurs underestimate the cost to get their product out the door and by the time they do they are out of cash. If you are patient, you can sometimes buy a company with a great product for a fraction of what was invested in the company.

- You generally get a complete staff; therefore, you don't have to spend all the time and money it takes to assemble a staff. However, don't assume that everyone you are getting is a keeper. In most of my acquisitions I have had to make a lot of changes in key positions. A lot of times it wasn't because the people weren't good; it was because they were outgrown. When an entrepreneur starts a company they become very loyal to the people who were with them from the beginning, sometimes to the point of overlooking their faults when the company has outgrown the individual. Many entrepreneurs get too close to an individual to terminate that person. Sometimes that's why the company got in trouble and you were able to buy it on the cheap.

- You inherit a customer base when you buy a company. Don't underestimate the time it takes to build a customer base. Experience has taught me that it takes generally about three years to get a satisfied customer to switch suppliers. Buying a happy customer base along with the company can save you a lot of time and money.

- You get the company's reputation along with the acquisition. Because of this, make sure, through research and customer interviews, that you're buying a company with a good, not bad reputation. It takes a long time to build a reputation and if you can buy a company with a good one that is invaluable.

- You also inherit the suppliers of the former owners. In industries such as ours (building materials) many suppliers give exclusives and you can't get the product lines that you want if you are starting a business from scratch. However, if your due diligence shows that you are getting a lot of good suppliers with the acquisition that is a huge plus.

- You may get plant, property, and equipment (PP&E) well below replacement cost. When most sellers value a business they value the PP&E at book value, not replacement cost. Most, or at least some, of the PP&E may still be usable but was fully depreciated, so you get it for nothing.

- You also may get a location that is no longer zoned for the business you're getting into. However, by buying the existing business you are generally grandfathered and allowed to do business from a prime location that you wouldn't be able to do business from if you were doing a startup.

Pro's and Con's of a Startup

- You can generally start a company for a fraction of the cost of buying a successful one. If you have the time and capital to start a company from scratch, that's the way to go. However, most entrepreneurs don't have enough capital to wait 3-5 years for a business to become profitable. (Rule of thumb: Do a business plan, then cut the revenue in half and double the expenses. If you still show a projected profit, proceed.)

- You don't assume the liabilities of the company you're buying. Even if you're doing an asset purchase and the seller keeps all liabilities there will be situations where your customers will hold you responsible if the former owners don't, for example, settle a product liability claim to your customer's satisfaction. If the upset customer is a big customer you may find yourself writing a check to settle a claim for which you had no responsibility.

- You can create your own staff. Yes, this is time-consuming but, especially if you have been in business before, you can surround yourself with people that you have chosen and may know well. This can save a lot of time and aggravation, not to mention wrongful dismissal lawsuits.

- You don't inherit old PP&E. While new plant, property, and equipment, is expensive you can generally lease it for a fraction of the cost of buying it and present a modern, up-to-date image to your customers and prospective customers.

- You can pick where to do business. In a building materials business such as ours, when I look to expand into a new market I use mapping software to find where all of our competitors are located. I then open up in other areas in the same metro market. In big cities traffic is a major issue and customers don't want to spend two hours going from one side of town to the other to do business. You can invade the market of an established competitor by offering more convenient locations for customers in different parts of that metro market.

In summary, now I think you can see why there is no pat answer to the question of whether it is better to start a company from scratch or acquire one. I hope I have given you some things to think about that will save you some heartache and money.

CHAPTER 62
DEALING WITH BANKS

If you are in business, unless you are one of the very lucky few with no debt, you have to work with banks and bankers. Here are a few tips to make the process more pleasant and productive:

- **Don't deal with only one bank.** Since childhood most of us have heard that we shouldn't put all our eggs in one basket. Despite most of us hearing that hundreds of times, it never ceases to amaze me how many business owners I come across that are in trouble because they did all of their business with one bank and then that bank called their loan. You should do business with at least two banks, preferably more. This way you're not totally dependent on one bank. These days most banks are bought and sold routinely versus when I was young and most banks were permanent fixtures in their communities. When a bank is sold many times the new management calls a lot of marginal loans and they have no appreciation of past relationships.

- **Keep your bankers informed about your business.** I have lunch with our bankers periodically and once a year I give them a full update on our businesses. Back in February I met with our lead bank and gave a 38 slide presentation on the past, present, and future of our business. At the end of the presentation the banker was blown away. He told me that our handle on our business was the best of any of his clients and that he wished that all of his clients were as financially savvy. This is what you want to hear at the end of the meeting with your banker.

- **Don't surprise your bankers.** It's human nature to not want to deliver bad news. Most red wine gets better with age but bad news doesn't. It only gets worse. If you have a terrible month and post a large loss let your banker know immediately. Don't wait until he sees it when you submit your financials at the end of the next quarter or year. Your banker doesn't want to look incompetent to his boss so if you keep your banker abreast of any negative developments he can pass the news on promptly.

- **Always have a plan.** You should always have a plan, and a contingency plan, but you especially need one when something negative has happened. Don't ever tell your banker bad news without also telling the banker what your plan is to right the ship. This way when your banker tells her boss than bad news she can also share your plan for fixing the problem.

- **Entertain your bankers.** Most businesspeople entertain key customers but not their bankers. Most bankers I know like to play golf, go to sporting events, and go to nice restaurants. Entertain your bankers like they are big customers and they are more likely to go to bat for you when the chips are down. Also include the city executive for your bank. Most city executives have authority to approve loans up to about $5 million and if the city exec is impressed with you and your business he or she can keep you afloat during tough times.

- **Be loyal.** Many business owners switch banks during good times to save as little as 1% on their borrowing rate. That's not very smart. For example, if you have an outstanding loan balance of $2 million and you save 1% per year on your interest rate that's only $20,000. On the other hand, if a few stay with one bank for five or 10 years, or even longer, most bankers appreciate and remember that. We have been with our main bank for six years and our loyalty has been appreciated and rewarded.

- **Be a reference for your banker.** I let my bankers know that if they are trying to close a deal and need a reference they should feel free to give out my name. I have helped bankers close many deals over the years and they are always very appreciative and usually keep that in mind during tough times or renewal negotiations.

- **Try to get a multi-year loan.** Loan renewals are usually lengthy, complicated, and expensive. If you can get a multi-year facility instead of a one year deal it will save you a lot of time and money in the long run.

- **Begin the renewal process early.** Don't wait until your loan is due to start negotiating your renewal. If you wait until the loan is due all the leverage is with your banker as you need to get the renewal done, and done fast. I like to start the renewal process 90 days before the renewal date. That way we are fully prepared for the negotiation and if it's apparent the renewal may have problems you have time to talk with other banks.

CHAPTER 63

M&A TIPS: PART I.
NEGOTIATING THE DEAL

In a recent post I gave the pros and cons of acquiring companies versus starting a company from scratch. As I said, there are times when buying an existing company makes more sense than starting a company. When doing mergers and acquisitions, here are a few things I've learned during the acquisitions I've done:

- **Take your time.** Don't try to rush through the process. There are a lot of steps you must go through to do a successful acquisition and you skip steps at your peril. Also, if you have a motivated seller, the more you drag out the process, the better the deal you'll get. He who cares the most loses.

- **Insist on audited financials.** A lot of business owners don't have audited financials unless their bank has insisted on them. Don't buy a business off of unaudited financials. Try to get the seller to pay for a three-year reverse audit of at least the balance sheet, if not the income statement as well. If you have a motivated seller, they will agree to pay for this. I have gotten sellers to pay for this by saying that even if the deal with me falls through other buyers are going to insist on audited financials so they may as well go ahead and get them done.

- **Walk away from a bad deal.** If the audited financials are significantly worse than the in-house financials you may want to walk away from the deal or at least use this as a reason to get a major price concessions versus what the owners were asking. If there is a major discrepancy between audited and in-house financials that may indicate other problems you won't discover until it's too late. Most good businesses have accurate financials.

- **Make the first offer.** If the seller doesn't indicate a price for the business at the beginning of the negotiations, make the first offer. I realize this is contrary to my standard negotiating advice of always making the other person go first, but when you're buying a company the final purchase price is generally not more than 50% more than the opening offer. Use any negative information you have discovered during due diligence to justify a low offer.

- **Meet with key employees.** When buying a company the key employees are even more important than the top customers. No business runs itself and if the key employees are top notch your chances for a successful acquisition increase exponentially. After meeting the key employees use the pre-employment assessments I mentioned in my post on the hiring process. If the owner won't let you meet with key employees you may want to walk away or, at the very least, use that as justification for lowering the purchase price because you're taking a big gamble by buying a business without meeting the key employees.

- **Do a customer satisfaction survey.** You also don't want to buy a company with a lot of unhappy customers. I have been successful at getting most of the sellers I have dealt with to pay for a customer satisfaction survey prior to closing. The customers don't think anything is amiss because they perceive it as just another normal customer satisfaction survey. When you get the results, if customer satisfaction is terrible, walk away from the deal unless you think you know how to increase customer satisfaction quickly. If, for example, their customers are unhappy because they are required to pay for purchases in 10 days and you are going to offer 30 day terms, then you can increase customer satisfaction quickly.

- **Don't buy dead inventory.** I consider any inventory that hasn't moved in one year to be dead. The seller may protest that there is nothing wrong with that inventory but if it hasn't sold in a year then it is worthless in my books. Who knows if it will ever sell? Also, if the business you are considering buying has inventory with a shelf life associated with it, you obviously don't want to buy any inventory that is beyond the "sell by" date. Eliminating dead and expired inventory from the purchase price will generally reduce the price you are paying for the inventory by 10-20%.

- **Don't buy old receivables.** I generally buy the receivables for two reasons. First, I don't want the seller collecting receivables and coming down hard on customers I'm going to have to deal with in the future. Second, I think I know how to collect receivables effectively so I'm not afraid of it unless the receivables are old. By old I mean over 60 days old. I reduce my purchase price by the amount of receivables over 60 days old. I tell the sellers that they can feel free to try to collect those receivables but I don't want them. (I will take them—at a large discount—as I know a lot of ways to collect even old receivables.)

- **Insist on noncompetition agreements.** If you buy a business and the key employees are free to compete with you, you can potentially be in real trouble. I have seen people buy a company and the key people quit as soon as it is announced and go in competition with the new owner. As the key employees have the customer relationships and you don't, that can be a fatal blow. If you can't get the key employees (and all of the salespeople, both inside and outside), to sign noncompetition agreements, walk away from the deal.

- **Holdback 10% of the purchase price for one year.** During the first year of buying a business you will invariably find problems not disclosed during the due diligence period. If you have a holdback of 10% of the purchase price you can net the problems you find during the first year against the holdback account.

- **Don't overpay.** Sometimes acquirers get what I call "deal fever". They get enamored with the business they are evaluating and end up overpaying. What constitutes overpaying? In a healthy economy a non-high-tech business generally sells for 6-8 times EBITDA. (Earnings Before Interest Taxes Depreciation and Amortization). In a recessionary economy like the one we are in now 4-6 times EBITDA is not uncommon. It depends on whether the seller wants to sell, or needs to sell. If the seller needs to sell, the price could even be less.

CHAPTER 64

M & A TIPS: PART II.
FINANCING THE ACQUISITION

Once you have agreed on the price and terms you need to finance the deal unless you are one of the rare people who has the cash to pay for acquisitions. However, even if you have the cash to pay for an acquisition I recommend that you don't pay 100% cash as your return on investment will be much higher if you leverage the transactions and if you use as much OPM (Other People's Money) as possible.

Below are some of the ways you can finance an acquisition.

- **Equity.** From the 1980s until September of 2008 it was possible to do an LBO (Leveraged Buy Out) with little or no equity. In fact, in the early 80s when I was living in Dallas during the boom years I was part of an investment group that bought ten apartment buildings with no money down. We even got cash back at closing as we got 115% financing. Changes in the tax laws killed real estate tax shelters and getting cash back at closing became a thing of the past. That was a good thing because, when I look back on it now, it seems ridiculous. I did an acquisition in 2001 with 92% debt and 8% equity. Those days are also over. In today's market plan on putting down at least 25% when buying a business, perhaps even more depending on the business, the niche it's in, and its condition. However, equity doesn't have to be all cash out of your pocket. See below for what I mean.

- **Private equity.** There are many private equity firms that will invest in a good deal. However, most will want to have control. That is always a deal killer with me but if you want a deal bad enough you may agree to their (generally onerous) terms. (See previous post about wanting a deal too badly.)

- **Investor financing.** You may know high net worth individuals who invest in private deals. I have found that private investors are generally not interested in control and will be more reasonable with the terms of their investment.

- **Seller financing.** Many times if you can't get enough capital to do the deal and the sellers are motivated they will provide some of the financing, generally at more favorable terms than banks and investors. Get as much seller financing as you can. As banks will require that seller debt be subordinated to them they will view it as equity when computing debt to equity ratios.

- **Mezzanine financing.** Financing that fills the gap between equity and bank debt is known as "mezzanine" debt. Most providers of mezzanine financing will want a higher interest rate (known as a "coupon") than a bank and will also generally want warrants. (A warrant is the right to buy stock at a deep discount in your company at a later date.) Most "mezz" providers want penny warrants. This allows them to buy stock in your company for a penny per share at a later date. Many times this is worth doing if you come up short on the equity required by your bank. Like seller financing, banks will require that mezz debt be subordinated to them so they will view this as equity too.

There are many other ways to finance an acquisition but these are the most common.

CHAPTER 65

M&A TIPS: PART III.
POST ACQUISITION TIPS

Once you have closed on the acquisition there are several steps you need to take to ensure success. Most of these steps need to be done quickly after closing to increase your chances of a successful acquisition.

- **Make headcount reductions quickly.** Don't cut off one finger at a time. Take a long look at who you really need to keep and do one layoff, not several. If you do several everyone will be looking for a new job as they won't be sure who is next.

- **Give raises to those employees you keep.** Nothing says, "Your job is secure" like a raise. From the savings you get from the layoff spread some around to the people you want to keep.

- **Increase selected benefits.** Just like a raise, an increase in benefits also helps morale. Evaluate the benefit package and sometimes even the addition of an inexpensive benefit like vision care helps improve morale after a layoff.

- **Communicate with customers immediately.** You should have a letter ready to go to all of the acquired company's customers on the day you close the deal. You need to stomp out rumors quickly. Nature abhors a vacuum and in the absence of communication from you, your competitors and the rumor mill will put a negative spin on the deal.

- **Meet key customers quickly.** Pareto's Law (aka the 80/20 rule) exists in all industries. See as many of the 20% of the customers who make up 80% of the acquired companies revenues in person as soon as possible after the closing. A personal visit means a lot to most customers and will allay most of their concerns.

- **Meet with key suppliers right after you meet with key customers.** In most businesses suppliers are almost as important as customers. After buying a company you can't afford to lose sales due to the loss of a key supplier. Meet with top suppliers ASAP and share your vision and plans so they know what your goals are for the business.

- **Automate everything that you can.** One of my mentors told me that computers don't get pregnant, they don't ask for raises, and they don't show up for work drunk. Anything that you can computerize will save you money in the long haul.

- **Outsource that which you can't automate.** Other than customer facing people, look for everything that you can outsource such as payroll, human resources, delivery, billing, IT, web hosting, e-mail hosting, and anything else you can think of. This frees you to concentrate on the things that generate sales and profits.

- **Get rid of people with bad attitudes.** Every company I have ever acquired has had some employees that immediately started complaining about any and all changes. The former owners (who they also used to complain about) suddenly become perfect in their eyes. Get rid of these people the way you would get rid of a cancer. Terminate them immediately. That will also make other complainers think twice before they start stirring up trouble.

- **Make other changes slowly.** Once you have made the above changes (and make them quickly) don't make other changes to the business for about a year. You may be surprised you don't have the market cornered on good ideas. Make a show of publicly adopting some ideas from the prior owners so that the acquired employees see that you are open minded. Most of all, never forget that the only people that like change are wet babies. Recognize that change is traumatic for most people so after the initial changes, minimize other changes for about a year unless absolutely critical.

CHAPTER 66

PROTECTING YOUR COMPANY FROM THEFT. PART I: PHYSICAL SECURITY

One of the things that has disappointed me the most over the years is the amount of theft that you need to deal with as a business owner. Even more disheartening is the fact that most of the theft I have had to deal with has been employee theft; either acting alone, or in collusion with a customer or supplier.

Most people who haven't owned or managed a business think of theft as break-ins or shoplifting. My experience is that those types of thefts are the least of your worries. That type of theft normally doesn't add up to a lot of money. Employee theft or collusion can run into the hundreds of thousands of dollars, or even millions.

That doesn't mean that you don't need to guard against break-ins and shoplifting, you do. My experience has taught me that's the easiest type of theft to prevent. Here are a few tips to help stop shoplifting and break-ins:

- **Exterior lighting.** Nothing deters break-ins like a lot of lights. Most criminals avoid businesses that are well lit. Don't skimp on exterior lighting, especially around doors and windows. If a criminal sees that his attempted break-in will be visible to police officers on patrol or neighbors, they will normally move on to an easier target.

- **Security cameras.** I think security cameras are more effective as a crime deterrent than they are for identifying criminals. Again, most criminals case a business before they break-in and if they see a lot of security cameras they tend to move on. Our business has both exterior and interior security cameras....and not all of them are real. You should supplement real cameras with a lot of fake cameras that you can buy at a lot of warehouse stores. The good ones even have blinking red lights so they look real. We have not only used our cameras to find out who stole materials from one of our locations but once we even used a recording to prove to a city where we are located that a city garbage truck backed through one of our fences and the driver got out of the truck, looked around, and took off. When we first asked the city to pay for a new fence they said that we couldn't prove that one of their drivers damaged our fence. A city supervisor came to our store, viewed the recording, and blew his top. We got a new fence for free.

- **Security locks.** It's amazing to me when I visit businesses and see locks that I can open with a credit card. Invest in the best quality security locks you can afford. Don't make it tempting and easy for a criminal to break into your business.

- **Monitored alarm systems.** All of our locations have monitored alarm systems for both break-ins and fire. Most security companies will install an alarm system for free if you'll sign a multiyear monitoring contract. Most contracts are extremely affordable. Tip: have the alarm company put signs all around the exterior of your building and on your windows saying that you have a monitored alarm system. Again, most times criminals will see these signs and look for an easier target.

- **Warning signs.** We have warning signs inside and outside all of our locations in both Spanish and English that let potential criminals know that we prosecute shoplifters to the fullest extent of the law. (You don't want to have too many of these signs as it isn't conducive to a pleasant shopping environment but you need at least a few signs so that thieves get scared off and move on to another business.)

- **Fences.** Depending on the type of business you are in you may or may not want a fence around your business. We are in the building supply business and a lot of our products are stored outside so we have fences around all of our locations. If you are in a particularly bad part of town you may also want to put concertina wire or barbed wire on the top of the fence.

- **Dogs.** If your business is fenced in, and is in a bad part of town, and you may also want to have a couple of security dogs if local laws allow this. Research has proven that one of the biggest fears of criminals is an attack dog. Again, if criminals are casing your business for a possible theft and see that there are two mean looking dogs roaming around your property at night I bet they move on.

- **Gate guards.** For certain types of businesses such as lumber-yards, plumbing wholesalers, electrical wholesalers, and similar businesses where there are a lot of customer pickups as well as deliveries on your own trucks, a gate guard can be a wise in-vestment. Gate guards are an especially effective deterrent against truck drivers who are in collusion with a customer and load extra materials on the truck or hide things such as power tools under or behind truck seats. Being a gate guard is usually a great job for an elderly employee who doesn't want to have all of the stress and pressure of working behind the sales coun-ter anymore. Experienced employees like these know what all of your products look like so they even stop a lot of legitimate mistakes from happening.

- **GPS systems in your trucks.** If you have delivery trucks there are a lot of inexpensive GPS systems available that give you many benefits. Not only can you see the average speed for each truck but you can see if a driver is deviating from his ap-pointed route to drop materials off to a customer with whom he is in collusion. You also can find your truck if it is stolen or if the driver decides to stop for a few beers instead of making a crucial delivery a customer is counting on.

- **Don't leave keys or gas cards in trucks at night.** I learned both of these lessons the hard way. One of our drivers left the keys in one of our big trucks at the end of the day. During the night someone hopped our fence, used the truck mounted forklift to load the truck with materials, and barreled through our front gate. We got the truck back but had to pay for repairs to both the truck and the gate. After that we required that keys be locked in the branch each night but not gas cards. On another recent night someone jumped the fence again, broke into one of our locked trucks, stole the gas card from the glove box and bought gas for everyone he knew. We now lock the gas cards with the keys at night inside the branch.

CHAPTER 67

PROTECTING YOUR COMPANY FROM THEFT. PART II: STOPPING THEFT AND COLLUSION

As I mentioned in my previous post, theft from break-ins and shoplifting is generally a fraction of the losses business owners incur from employee theft and employee collusion with dishonest customers. What steps can you take to minimize your exposure to this type of theft? Here are a few tips:

- **Background checks.** As mentioned in my post about pre-employment screening, the proliferation of the internet has made it inexcusable to not do a background check on all applicants prior to hiring them. Background checks have saved me from hiring embezzlers, burglars, child molesters, drug dealers, and numerous other criminals. Not hiring criminals is the first and most important step in preventing employee theft and collusion.

- **Internal checks and balances.** Do not let only one employee perform financial tasks such as balancing bank statements, issuing checks, transmitting payroll to an outside payroll processor, and other similar tasks. Always have at least one co-worker and one manager review all such work. It is much rarer for three employees to steal than just one.

- **Vacations.** All employees should be required to take at least one week's vacation. Not only does a vacation rejuvenate employees but employees who are stealing generally get discovered when on vacation and someone else is doing their job. Be very wary of an employee in a financial position who resists taking a vacation.

- **Check signing.** I sign almost all checks. Exceptions are petty cash checks written at each of our branches and when I am on vacation. Our petty cash accounts have a maximum balance of $5,000 to limit losses if a branch manager is dishonest. When I am out two other trusted long time employees can also sign checks. We also require two signatures on all checks for $100,000 or more.

- **Bonding employees.** We get fidelity bonds on all of our employees, even truck drivers. If an employee can't be bonded we don't hire the person. In the rare occasion when we have had employee theft our bonding company has reimbursed us. The premium for this policy is a small price to pay for peace of mind.

- **Ship off of invoices, not "pick tickets".** If you ship off of a pick ticket or packing slip a dishonest employee who is colluding with a customer can change the pick ticket after it comes back to the accounting office after a delivery or from the shipping department, before it is converted into an invoice. A dishonest employee can delete items from the pick ticket in return for a cash payment from a crooked customer. Most times your employees will balk at doing this with the excuse that they have to issue too many credits when drivers come back with some of the items that were refused upon delivery. Stand your ground and insist on shipping ONLY off of invoices.

- **Keep track of handwritten invoices.** All businesses need to write handwritten invoices during a power outage unless they have a back-up generator. (A back-up generator is a good idea for this reason as well as many others. We have two.) Be sure your handwritten invoices are in a bound booklet and have carbon copies. Then check the book at least quarterly to ensure that ALL handwritten invoices were converted to computer invoices and mailed. Crooked employees have been known to destroy handwritten invoices in return for a kickback from "buddies".

- **Fraudulent credit cards.** Over the last few years I have gotten about five scam emails a week where a person poses as a contractor from a foreign country looking for materials he can't get in his country. They always say they will pay with a credit card. Many merchants don't know that even if you get an approval code the credit card issuer can "claw back" payments you have received if the card turns out to be fraudulent. When I get these emails I respond by saying we only do business with overseas customers who we don't know if they wire payment to our bank...in advance. I NEVER hear back.

- **Receiving.** A lot of employee theft happens in the receiving area. An employee can be in collusion with a supplier and sign for more material than actually was received in return for a kickback from a dishonest supplier. All inventory receipts should be verified by at least two people and periodic spot checks should be done by someone in management.

- **Hotline.** We have toll-free hotline (provided by the company we use for payroll and HR) where honest employees can anonymously report suspicious behavior. Many employees are wary of "ratting" on a fellow employee to management but are willing to report concerns to an anonymous hotline. If you don't have one set one up.

CHAPTER 68

CLASSIFYING CUSTOMERS: HUNTING WITH A RIFLE INSTEAD OF A SHOTGUN

Most salespeople and managers treat all customers equally. This can be a fatal mistake. Salespeople have a finite number of hours in every day and if they allow low-volume, slow pay customers to take up a lot of their time, the salesperson will fall short of his goals and subsequently, as a business owner or manager you will fall short of your goals.

Growing up in the United States we all hear that, "All men are created equal ", and while that is true it isn't true of customers. Most outside salespeople spend their days careening from one demand on their time to another. Even salespeople who plan their day in advance see the plan fail to materialize because of a large number of phone calls and e-mails that start right after sunup each day. *I have found out the hard way that when you try to be all things to all people you largely end up meaning nothing to no one.*

To be most effective I have found that you should segregate your assigned accounts into three categories: A, B, and C. How do I define the three categories?

An A account is a company that buys a lot of whatever it is you sell, is growing much faster than their peers, and, most importantly, pays their bills on time. The problem with A accounts is that everyone wants to sell them. You have a lot of competition when you try to sell an A account, however, there are not many A accounts.

B accounts are companies with decent volume, a decent pay record, and they probably aren't going anywhere in the near future. They aren't in danger of going out of business but they probably are not growing rapidly. They are most likely just keeping up with their market.

C accounts are slow pay, low volume, and their sales are declining. As a customer of mine from Oklahoma told me many years ago, "They're dead but no one has pushed them over yet ". Also, C accounts generally complain a lot, have a million excuses for not paying on time, request proof of delivery a lot (generally as a stall tactic for not paying on time), and want to be able to return purchases without paying a restocking fee.

How do you deal with three very different types of accounts? Well, first off, you don't deal with them by treating them all equally. If you do that you don't end up with enough time to give A and B accounts the time they need to maximize your sales to them. So, how do you treat each of the above types of accounts?

I tell our salespeople that they are to see their A accounts once a week, their B accounts once a month, and their C accounts, never. This doesn't mean that they are rude to their C accounts. They are to return their calls and e-mails promptly but they are not to make personal sales calls on them nor are they to entertain them. C accounts should mainly be serviced over the phone, both by outside and inside sales.

The theory behind A, B, and C account classification is that this type of account stratification gives you the time to spend with your best customers, your A and B customers. The more time you spend with them the more sales should result. Marketing 101 teaches us that our best prospects for increased purchases are companies that already know and trust us, not new customers.

I first got this idea when listening to Brian Tracy's sales training series back in the late 60's. Brian said that his research showed that it takes six calls for a customer to even remember your name and 12 calls for a customer to trust you enough to even make a small purchase from you. I got to thinking that if it was going to take 12 calls for an A customer to buy from me I could call on that customer once a month and get my first purchase in a year or I could call on that customer once a week and get my first order in three months. I tried this in my second year of selling and tripled my sales over the previous year. I also spent much less time chasing customers for money, approving credits, providing proof of delivery, and other time wasting tasks.

Also, my A accounts didn't tire of seeing me because A accounts are growing so fast they always had lots for me to do when I saw them each week. One customer even gave me an extra office to use when I was there as I was there so much. I used to love the look on the faces of my competitors when they saw me sitting in my own office while they were waiting, hoping for a few minutes with my good customer.

My B accounts were very happy with seeing me once a month and my sales to the B accounts increased as well. A few of the C accounts complained that they didn't see me anymore, but most of the complaints were because they missed the free lunches. I was also much happier because my sales and income went up and the aggravation factor of my job diminished greatly.

If you have never tried anything like this, give it a try for at least six months and if your sales don't increase and your bad debts don't decrease I will be very shocked.

CHAPTER 69
BOB PARSON'S 16 RULES

Bob Parsons, if you don't know him, is the founder of GoDaddy, the website domain registration firm best known for his memorable Super Bowl ads. Parsons is also a serious business leader who has grown his firm to over $1 billion in annual revenue from a start-up in 1997.

Parsons recently sold a stake in GoDaddy to three major private equity firms in late June of this year, one of which participated in the Skype deal with Microsoft (Silver Lake Partners). He remains the largest shareholder. The sale price values GoDaddy at $2.25 billion. Roughly half the purchase price covered his debt and the rest will be used to continue GoDaddy's rapid growth (25% last year alone).

Given Bob's great success I thought you would be interested in reading his 16 rules for success. They follow below.

1. Get and stay out of your comfort zone.
I believe that not much happens of any significance when we're in our comfort zone. I hear people say, "But I'm concerned about security." My response to that is simple: "Security is for cadavers."

2. Never give up.
Almost nothing works the first time it's attempted. Just because what you're doing does not seem to be working, doesn't mean it won't work. It just means that it might not work the way you're doing it. If it was easy, everyone would be doing it, and you wouldn't have an opportunity.

3. When you're ready to quit, you're closer than you think.
There's an old Chinese saying that I just love, and I believe it is so true. It goes like this: "The temptation to quit will be greatest just before you are about to succeed."

4. With regard to whatever worries you, not only accept the worst thing that could happen, but make it a point to quantify what the worst thing could be.

Very seldom will the worst consequence be anywhere near as bad as a cloud of "undefined consequences." My father would tell me early on, when I was struggling and losing my shirt trying to get Parsons Technology going, "Well, Robert, if it doesn't work, they can't eat you."

5. Focus on what you want to have happen.

Remember that old saying, "As you think, so shall you be."

6. Be quick to decide.

Remember what General George S. Patton said: "A good plan violently executed today is far and away better than a perfect plan tomorrow."

7. Always be moving forward.

Never stop investing. Never stop improving. Never stop doing something new. The moment you stop improving your organization, it starts to die. Make it your goal to be better each and every day, in some small way. Remember the Japanese concept of Kaizen. Small daily improvements eventually result in huge advantages.

8. Take things a day at a time.

No matter how difficult your situation is, you can get through it if you don't look too far into the future, and focus on the present moment. You can get through anything one day at a time.

9. Measure everything of significance.

I swear this is true. Anything that is measured and watched, improves.

10. Anything that is not managed will deteriorate.

If you want to uncover problems you don't know about, take a few moments and look closely at the areas you haven't examined for a while. I guarantee you problems will be there.

11. Pay attention to your competitors, but pay more attention to what you're doing.

When you look at your competitors, remember that everything looks perfect at a distance. Even the planet Earth, if you get far enough into space, looks like a peaceful place.

12. Never let anybody push you around.

In our society, with our laws and even playing field, you have just as much right to what you're doing as anyone else, provided that what you're doing is legal.

13. Never expect life to be fair.

Life isn't fair. You make your own breaks. You'll be doing good if the only meaning fair has to you, is something that you pay when you get on a bus (i.e., fare).

14. Solve your own problems.

You'll find that by coming up with your own solutions, you'll develop a competitive edge. Masura Ibuka, the co-founder of SONY, said it best: "You never succeed in technology, business, or anything by following the others." There's also an old saying that I remind myself of frequently. It goes like this: "A wise man keeps his own counsel."

15. Don't take yourself too seriously.

Lighten up. Often, at least half of what we accomplish is due to luck. None of us are in control as much as we like to think we are.

16. There's always a reason to smile.

Find it. After all, you're really lucky just to be alive. Life is short. More and more, I agree with my little brother. He always reminds me: "We're not here for a long time, we're here for a good time!"

CHAPTER 70

10 WAYS TO KEEP CUSTOMERS HAPPY

It's not a very profound thought to state that one of the main things you can do to have a profitable business is to keep your customers happy; however, based on how many companies have unhappy customers this must be a more profound thought than at first blush. I remember a cover story in *Time* magazine a few years ago that said that customer service in America has gotten so poor that even mediocre service stands out as good with customers. Superior service blows customers away as it is so rare.

Below are some of the ways I have learned to keep customers happy during my 35+ year career:

1. **First focus on making your employees happy.** Unhappy employees are incapable of giving great customer service. If you want to have your employees give great customer service make sure that you are doing everything within reason to keep them happy.

2. **Offer guarantees.** When I bought my current company I commissioned a marketing firm to do a study to see what my customers wanted the most. While the survey was being done I asked our salespeople while and, unsurprisingly, they said our customers mostly wanted a low price. However, when the survey was done, our customers said that on-time deliveries were the most important thing to them. Price was #3. Now we offer a credit of 10% of the purchase amount, to be used on their next purchase, if we are more than one hour late versus our promised delivery time. As most salespeople say that their company has great service I have felt that most customers roll their eyes when they hear that. We put our money where our mouth is and not surprisingly, none of our competitors have

matched our guarantee because none of them can offer our great service.

3. **Provide a human touch.** If you are like me you, it tries your patience when you call a company and have to keep pressing keys on your phone or use multiple voice commands to get to a human being. In our company, the first voice you hear when you call is a human being. Yes, we use voicemail, but an automated attendant does not answer our phones.

4. **Return calls and e-mails the same day.** We strive to respond to all calls and e-mails the same day. I say "strive" because we aren't always able to do so if a call or e-mail comes in late in the day, but if we don't respond the same day we do so first thing the next morning. All calls and e-mails should be *responded to* within 24 hours and all issues should be *resolved* within 48 hours.

5. **Be punctual.** You and your employees should be on time, and preferably a little early for all customer meetings. If something happens that is going to make you late there is no excuse for not calling to let your customer know when to expect you, given the proliferation of mobile phones these days.

6. **Deliver bad news fast**. Good news doesn't spoil but bad news, unlike fine wine and cheese, does not improve with time. It only gets worse. If you have bad news for a customer do not procrastinate about delivering it. If you deliver bad news quickly you will usually get the news to your contact before he or she hears it from within their company. Plus, by delivering bad news first, you get to put your spin on it instead of the customer hearing it elsewhere and getting all worked up prior to calling you.

7. **Look professional.** When I started out in business in the mid-70s I wore a suit (not a sport coat and tie) every day. Being raised by a father who was a Marine, I also was trained to shine my shoes every day. I sent my shirts out to be laundered and I had my suits cleaned and pressed regularly. Today," business casual" dress is the order of the day. However, many people have pushed the boundaries of business casual dress and I see people who call on me that look like they slept on a park bench the night before our meeting. Even if business casual dress is

the standard for your industry there is no excuse for not looking sharp.

8. **Handle complaints quickly and professionally.** I learned many years ago that you can't begin to solve a customer's problem until you allow him or her the time to totally vent about the issue. Once they have vented, ask if there is anything else they need to tell you before you respond. Then respond by first asking, "What would you like me to do?" Many times a customer will tell you that they don't want anything other than to make you aware of the problem. Other times they will ask for credit or some other concession. Unless the request is well beyond the bounds of reasonableness, grant the request. Always consider the lifetime value of a customer during complaint resolution and you will find that you will rarely fail to grant the customer's request. Fast and professional complaint resolution builds customers for life.

9. **Invoice your customers correctly.** I have found that most late paid invoices are due to invoicing problems on our end, not the customer being a deadbeat. Sometimes we fail to send the invoice to the correct address (if the customer has multiple offices) or we forget to put the customer's purchase order number on our invoice. Other times we fail to bill a customer as per our quotation or we don't provide the requested proof of delivery. Invoicing your customers properly will not only get you paid quicker but will reduce friction between you and your customers.

10. **Say "Thank you".** I picked up a habit from one of my mentors early in my career. Whenever he and I were out and he saw customer, even across the room, he would make it a point to go over and say, "Thank you for your business". It amazes me that I meet with key suppliers regularly and rarely hear any of them say, "Thank you for your business". Make it a point to thank your customers for their business any time you see them. No one gets tired of being thanked, and as most people rarely get thanked, your company stands out.

CHAPTER 71

INTERVIEW QUESTIONS TO ASK AND AVOID

I always get nervous when a new manager makes his or her first hire. Even some experienced managers ask illegal questions of applicants. Over the years I have compiled a list of legal and illegal questions.

Below is a list of interview questions to ask and avoid. Be sure to consult with a labor lawyer in your state before passing this list on to your associates as labor laws vary by state.

AGE

> Instead of:
   When did you graduate?
   When do you intend to retire?
> Ask:
   Are you old enough to do this type of work?
   Can you supply transcripts of your education?

DISABILITY/PHYSICAL

> Instead of:
   Do you have a disability?
   Have you ever filed a workers compensation claim?
   Do you have a history of drug or alcohol abuse?
   How much do you weigh?
> Ask
   After reviewing the job description, "Can you do the duties listed in the job description, with or without accommodation?"
   If a worker has an obvious disability or reveals a hidden disability, you may ask the person to describe or demonstrate how the applicant would perform job duties.

SEX/MARITAL STATUS

> Instead of:

Are you married?
When do you plan to start a family?
Do you have children?
Do you have child care arranged?

> Ask:

Are you available to travel frequently?
Can you work overtime with no notice?
Can you work evenings and weekends?
When we check references/do a background check, are there other names we should look under?
Explain the hours of the business and ask if the applicant will be available to work any of these days or hours.

RACE

> Instead of:

Do you consider yourself to be part of any minority group?

> Ask:

There are no appropriate race related questions.

RELIGION

> Instead of:

Do you attend church
What church do you attend?
Does your religion prevent you from working on certain days or certain holidays?

> Ask:

Explain the hours of the business and ask if the applicant will be available to work any of these days or hours.

NATIONAL ORIGIN/CITIZENSHIP

> Instead of:

Are you a citizen of the US?
What country are you from?
Where is your accent from?
What nationality is your last name?
When does your visa expire?

> Ask:

If you are hired, are you able to provide documentation to prove that you are eligible to work in the US?

FINANCIAL STATUS

> Instead of:

Do you own a home/car?
Have you ever filed for bankruptcy?
Are you subject to any garnishments or child support orders?

> Ask:

Will you sign a form authorizing us to perform a credit check?

MILITARY

> Instead of:

Please provide the status of your military discharge.
Will you miss work to perform military service?

> Ask:

What experience did you gain in the uniformed service that is relevant to the job you would be doing?

ARRESTS AND CONVICTIONS

> Instead of:

Have you ever been arrested?

> Ask:

Have you ever been convicted of a crime? (You must qualify this question by stating that a conviction will not automatically disqualify a candidate).

CHAPTER 72

QUESTIONS THAT MAY BE ASKED DURING INTERVIEWS AND LAWFUL REASONS FOR NOT HIRING A PARTICULAR PERSON

My last post was on interview questions to ask and avoid. This post is a follow up to that and concentrates on questions that may be asked during interviews as well as lawful reasons for not hiring someone. Again, I am not a lawyer, and laws vary from state to state so be sure to consult with your labor law counsel before taking my advice.

QUESTIONS THAT MAY BE ASKED DURING INTERVIEWS

- Questions related to applicants ability to perform the requirements of the job.

- What research have you done on our company and industry?

- What is the best thing you have heard about our company? The worst thing?

- What skills do you bring us and how can you put them to work here?

- Give me an example of a complex problem you solved.

- What do you look for in a job?

- What are your short term and long term goals?

- How long would you stay with us?

- Why should we hire you?

- What are your strengths? Weaknesses?

- Describe the ideal co-worker. Supervisor.

- When we contact your last supervisor, what will (s)he say about you?

LAWFUL REASONS FOR NOT HIRING A PARTICULAR PERSON

- Applicant does not have the necessary education or training for the position.
- Lack of requisite skills for the position.
- Lack of required licensing or certifications.
- Unsatisfactory prior work history / references.
- Fails drug screen.
- Poor interpersonal skills.
- Personal hygiene.
- Applicant unable to work the required hours.
- Inconsistent, inaccurate, or fraudulent statements made by applicant on job application or during interview.
- Physically unable, with reasonable accommodation, to perform the essential duties of the position.
- Simply not the best applicant.

Hiring is the single most important thing that any supervisor does. Resist the temptation to cut corners and it will pay off for you.

CHAPTER 73

KEEP YOUR COOL WHEN COLLECTING MONEY

How can you collect money from slow paying customers without blowing up at them and losing your cool? Here are some things I've learned during my 35+ years of working with customers to obtain payment.

- **Be nice, but also firm.** Threaten gently. Let the client know the consequences of not paying on time or not sending a payment at all. Working in the terms "my collections agency" or "my lawyer" early on is a great way to light fires, which is not the best practice. Again, you have to be polite and gentle because being too defensive or aggressive can cause a fight, and a client is more likely to fight you on everything if you aren't polite. At the same time, don't be a pushover. Be reasonable with time limits, but let the client know that you are prepared to call in outside help if he or she cannot produce the payment. Keeping the client abreast of options and consequences allows him or her to understand the severity of the situation.

- **Offer non-paying clients a payment plan.** This serves as an alternative method to show the customer you are willing to compromise in order to get paid. I remind the client that we held up our end of the agreement and produced the work they requested, and would "appreciate" if they could do the same. I learned early on that just because you have payment terms of "net 30 days" does not mean people will pay you in 30 days. You have to call them, send them a new invoice and/or proof of delivery, and you frequently have to call them again. It is difficult being an amiable supplier one day and a tough-talking credit collector two months later.

- **Stop giving credit to anyone who asks.** Most companies do have credit cards. If you are selling something that is being resold, or providing a regular service, you probably need to extend credit to be competitive. For a small company with a limited staff, this will add one more burden that is easy to neglect, especially when you are hungry for sales. The only thing worse is spending a lot of time "trying" to collect money. An experienced business owner knows that the job is not done when the product is shipped or the service delivered, it's when you get paid and the check clears the bank.

- **Other Easy Payment Options**. Let them know that they can call you to make a payment over the phone with a credit card or debit card. This is a good option. Provide them with your website address if you have a feature that will allow them to pay their account online. Check by phone is also more being used more often now. Customers can fax or e-mail a copy of their check to you which you can process online through a secured website. In most cases you will receive the funds within 24-48 hours.

- **Build a good relationship**. Communicate immediately with a past due customer via an invoice copy and a computer generated message. Follow this up with a phone call. Creating a good relationship with the account payable person is very beneficial. Get to know your customer's accounts payable team personally. If they like you, it is possible you will get paid first. Keep detailed collections notes of all promises made and follow up strongly if there ever is a broken promise.

- **Listen**. Having a plan prior to making a collection call is crucial. Remember that the person is probably embarrassed, stressed, and will likely become defensive when you ask him or her to pay. Being prepared for this will put you ahead of the game. A little patience and understanding goes a long way. When customers are explaining to you why they have not paid or cannot pay, keep quiet and listen. No matter how much you want to interrupt, give them a chance to explain. Sometimes they will calm down just because you listened to them and they were able to vent. When they are done, address the problem and offer a solution—or a couple, if you can.

Collecting past due accounts is not for the faint of heart. There are people who are short of money, people who just don't like to pay, and people who are going broke. It is not always easy to tell the difference. There are people who will not pay unless you keep calling them. They most likely have a long list of creditors beyond you that they are not paying. The creditor who engages them the most will probably be the one that gets paid first. In this case, patience is not a virtue, it is a liability. In some cases, it is not worth doing business with them. But it can be worth it. Don't give up on those people who pay slowly. Keep reminding them of their obligation and find a way to make it simple for them to pay up. Be patient to a point, but don't let them slide!

CHAPTER 74

WHEN TO FIRE?

One of the toughest decisions a manager has to make is whether or not to fire someone who reports to him or her. During my career I have found that most managers wait too long to fire a clearly substandard performer. I saw one survey that showed that the average manager waited more than one year longer than they should have before terminating a weak employee. Yes, it's not fun (unless you're a sadist) to terminate people but I have found through experience that it's not the people you fire that make your life miserable, it's the people you don't. I have never once awakened the morning after terminating someone and regretted it. The only thing I have regretted was not doing it sooner.

Let's take a look at when I think you should terminate someone:

- **Stealing.** If I have airtight proof that someone has stolen from our company I terminate that person immediately. In my opinion, there are no second chances for stealing. I have found that if a person will steal from you once they will steal from you again. I also feel that if you don't terminate a thief you are setting a precedent that you may regret. If you fire one person for stealing but not another you are leaving yourself open to a possible discrimination lawsuit. (And yes, I prosecute thieves 100% of the time if I have a strong case. That sends out a strong message to the rest of your employees.)

- **Substance abuse.** If I have an employee that is using illegal drugs on the job or who is obviously impaired from alcohol during work hours I also terminate immediately. What someone does at night or on the weekend doesn't concern me unless it affects their job performance or violates the law (such as truck drivers who are subject to DOT regulations banning the use of illegal drugs.)

- **Criminal activity on the job.** If someone is selling drugs or other contraband on the job he or she is terminated immediately. I have found that if an employee will engage in illegal activity on the job they are probably doing other illegal things such as collusion or theft as well. Criminals rarely limit their illegal activities to only one area.

- **Theft or collusion.** If I have conclusive proof that an employee has been helping himself to merchandise from one of our stores or if an employee is engaged in theft via collusion with a customer or any other outside parties I also terminate immediately. Again, I want to send a strong message to the remainder of our employees that theft or collusion will not be tolerated, not even once.

- **Insubordination.** If an employee repeatedly refuses to obey a direct order from a superior I terminate the employee, provided that the supervisor's request was reasonable and consistent with what other employees are asked to do. Over the years I have had employees who have a problem with authority and who think that obeying the orders of a supervisor is optional. I'm a big believer in the chain of command and I think it's critical that supervisors be supported as they perform the sometimes unsavory task of management.

- **Negative attitudes**. One of the benefits of being in business in South Carolina, a right to work state that is only 3% unionized, is that you can terminate an employee for any reason or no reason. One reason that I have terminated many people over the years is a bad attitude. I have found that a bad attitude is more contagious than the Ebola virus. If you have one bad apple that is trying to spoil the rest of the barrel I believe you have to remove the bad apple. I don't terminate people with negative attitudes the first time they exhibit a bad attitude because everyone has a bad day; however, employees who constantly exhibit negative behavior are counseled and if the behavior continues after the counseling they're terminated.

This is not an all-inclusive list of the reasons I terminate people but these are the most common ones. I have found that I constantly need to challenge managers that report to me to terminate their poor performers. Some managers just don't have the stomach for termination and other managers are busy and don't want to go through the hiring process.

CHAPTER 75
HOW TO FIRE

My last post was on when to fire an employee. This post is on how to terminate one of your direct reports with dignity, while also limiting your exposure to a wrongful dismissal lawsuit. Once you have made the decision to terminate a poor performer I suggest you move quickly with the termination, but not so quickly that you violate the law or leave yourself open to a wrongful dismissal suit. You should also be aware that not only can your company be sued for wrongful dismissal but you, as the terminating manager, can also be sued personally. Now that I have your attention, here are my tips on how to fire.

- **Review the dismissal in advance with your labor lawyer or your labor law consultant.** We have a labor law consultant on retainer for just $90 per month. That is less than one phone call to a good labor lawyer. The labor law consulting firm we use has been in business for over 30 years and has an outstanding reputation in our part of the country. Our retainer entitles us to unlimited consultation on labor law issues. Even after over 35 years in business, I almost always find I have overlooked one or two key things after I talk to our consultant. If you can't find a good labor law consulting firm in your area then you should review all terminations with a labor lawyer prior to the termination. *Even an expensive lawyer's fee is less than a wrongful dismissal settlement or judgment.*

- **Decide on a severance package.** Unless I terminate someone for theft, repeated insubordination, or some other serious offense, I offer a severance package to the person being terminated. There are several reasons why I offer a severance package. First off, it's the humane thing to do and I have to look at myself in the mirror every morning when I shave. I try to treat other people the way I want to be treated. Second, a fair severance package can salvage a relationship with the person being terminated and you never know when your paths will cross again. Third, your remaining associates take note of how you treat people you're terminating. Humane treatment of people being separated from your company scores points with your other employees and may keep some of them from looking for another job if they feel that departing associates are being treated shabbily.

- **Be aware of discrimination laws.** Most business owners I talk with aren't aware that anyone over 40 is protected by a different set of labor laws. When we terminate someone over the age of 40, unless they are being terminated for a serious offense, we offer a severance package to the terminated employee in return for signing a full legal release. In the state where we are headquartered (South Carolina) employees over the age of 40 need to be given up to 20 days to decide whether to sign the release, and they have seven days after they sign the release where they can rescind the agreement. While you may not want to offer a severance plan to someone over 40 that you are terminating for poor performance, I submit that it is worth the peace of mind that you get when someone over 40 signs a legal release. The cost of an age discrimination lawsuit is generally much more than the cost of a fair severance plan. You also need to be aware of other protected classes. Sex, race, and religion are other protected classes as well. *Most people are surprised to know that there are no federal laws against discrimination for sexual orientation (but some states do forbid discrimination based on sexual orientation).*

- **Terminate in private.** I know that most labor lawyers and labor law consultants recommend that you have a witness with you during the termination but I have found that it only adds to the embarrassment for the person being terminated if you have an HR representative or another manager present for the termination. I have done it both ways and I have found that it has been much less embarrassing to the person being terminated if only two of us are in the room during the termination and I've not regretted it yet.

- **Terminate in person.** Recently the Wall Street Journal did a story on Carol Bartz, the CEO of Yahoo, being terminated over the telephone. Terminating her over the phone only made a bad situation worse and made her a lifelong enemy of the company. She immediately sent out an e-mail to all of Yahoo's employees stating, "I am very sad to tell you that I've just been fired over the phone by Yahoo's chairman of the board," she wrote. This made the company look cruel and heartless to every employee. There are times when you can't terminate in person such as when you have a remote employee who works several states away. If you set up a special appointment with a person who works remotely they almost always know why you are coming to see them and it only makes the situation worse. I have learned this the hard way. Years ago I called a remote employee who I only saw quarterly and said I wanted to see him in two days. He said to me, "You're coming to fire me aren't you? If so, save yourself the price of the airline ticket and just fire me now." I took his advice and did so. As I was prepared for the termination already I immediately launched into my severance offer. He and I are still friends as I treated him well with the severance package.

- **Offer outplacement.** For salaried positions I have found that offering an outplacement package also helps salvage the relationship with the person being terminated. If you can help your former employee get a new job quickly that not only can salvage the relationship with that person, but your other associates don't have survivor's guilt. Most outplacement packages are not very expensive and I have found them to be effective in most cases. I also have found that I sometimes end up having to do business with someone I previously terminated. It makes future business dealings much easier if the person you terminated has no animosity towards you.

- **Always terminate quickly.** Once you begin the termination you should try to conclude it within five or 10 minutes. If you have your severance offer ready it doesn't take long to go over the high points of it and hand it to the person you're terminating. Also, if you're asking for a legal release you should go over that briefly and leave it with the person being terminated as well. Do not engage in a debate. Be polite but brief.

- **Meet the terminated associate after normal business hours to clean out her desk in private.** I think it's cruel and embarrassing to march a terminated associate from your office or a conference room to her office or workstation and watch her put her personal effects in a box and then walk her out of the office in full view of all of her coworkers. I think it is much more humane to conclude the termination and then set a time to meet the terminated associate in the evening or over the weekend so that she can remove her personal effects in private. Again, the idea is to mitigate the embarrassment of the termination as much is possible.

Chapter 76

Succession Planning

When I talk with other business owners and ask if they have a succession plan I rarely hear a "yes". Most agree that succession planning is important to do but they just haven't "found" the time to do it. You may have heard the old expression, "No one plans to fail but most people fail to plan". This adage appears to be especially true when it comes to succession planning. Most people find out that they should have done a succession plan the hard way; after a tragedy or after a key employee walks out unannounced. Don't let this happen to you. Here are a few tips on doing a succession plan:

- **Do a plan and update it annually**. If you don't currently have a succession plan, start with you as the owner. Who replaces you if you die suddenly? Put this in writing so your heirs and partners (If you have any) know exactly who you think should succeed you...and why. Then do a succession plan for each of your direct reports. Ask them who they recommend as their replacement and then see how it matches up with your choice. Keep in mind that insecure managers will probably name someone who clearly isn't up to replacing them as they are worried that you asked for this information because you plan on firing them. You can learn a lot about the quality of your management team by who they recommend as their replacements. Generally, A players recommend other A players but B players tend to recommend C players as A or B players threaten them.

- **Review the plan with your board and management team.** This exercise not only makes it clear as to who should succeed whom but it also surfaces weak links on your team. If you don't have anyone on your team who can replace you or a key team member you should start looking for someone to add to your team to shore up this weakness. Also, you and your board can agree on succession issues in a calm and rational manner,

220

not when "under the gun" after a tragedy. Succession planning also helps you identify up and comers who, while "stars", need additional education or exposure before they can take on more responsibility.

- **Review your personal plans with your estate lawyer and accountant.** If you are the owner or a partner you should also review your succession plan with your estate lawyer and accountant as your plans may trigger high value transfers of ownership interests that can cause significant estate tax liabilities. Owners need to consider their liquid assets and insurance to ensure they are sufficient to offset such taxes. I have seen many businesses have to be sold by a widow or other heirs due to a lack of succession planning resulting in insufficient cash on hand to pay estate taxes. It's really sad to see a family business have to be sold, sometimes after several generations of ownership, due to the lack of planning by the principals.

Business succession planning is critical to the long term health and viability of your business. If you have been procrastinating in this area I hope this post will spur you to action. It may save your company.

CHAPTER 77

HOW PROFESSIONAL IS YOUR SALES TEAM?

During good times you can get away with a less than professional sales team; however, during the challenging times we are presently experiencing you need to bring your "A game" if your company is going to survive. How professional is your sales team? Here are a few things to evaluate about your sales force.

1. **Telephone use.** Are <u>all</u> calls from customers returned promptly? All calls preferably should be returned the same day, but no longer than 24 hours from receipt. Do your associates answer the phone professionally and cheerfully or does it sound like they're being interrupted when they answer the phone? If they don't answer the phone is their voicemail greeting professional and does it contain information about how to reach someone else who can help them if they aren't available? Do they change their voicemail greeting when on vacation so that the customer who is calling for them knows to ask for someone else?

2. **Prompt response to e-mails.** All e-mails should be responded to within four hours and all e-mails should be responded to before the end of the day even if you have to respond from home that night. Even if your response simply states that you are looking into the situation, you need to respond and set an expectation level for resolution to the issue or question.

3. **Following up.** It's amazing to me that many of the salespeople who call on me never follow up after the original call. It's a total waste of the cost of the original call if follow-up isn't done promptly. Recently I needed to have the driveway and parking area restriped at one of our branches. I contacted five companies that had been referred to me by friends. Only two of them even bothered to return my call. Then, only one of them got me a quote. I had to contact five other companies so that I

could get two other quotes, as I never buy anything without getting at least three quotes. I thought we were supposed to be in a recession! Why did I have to make 10 phone calls to get three quotes?

4. **Projecting a positive attitude.** Do your salespeople complain to their customers about how tough business is or do they share good news with their customers and project an upbeat persona? I don't care how challenging the economy is; your customers don't want to listen to your salespeople whine and complain. Go on some sales calls with several of your salespeople. If they complain about the economy to their customers in front of you imagine what they say behind your back.

5. **Pricing and negotiating.** Are your salespeople trying to beat your competition on price or do they try to get a premium for your products based on superior service, deeper inventory, faster delivery, greater product knowledge, and other factors? Have your salespeople been trained in the art of negotiating? It's amazing to me how many so-called "professional salespeople" have never had any training in negotiations. I always enjoy negotiating with salespeople who clearly have never been properly trained in the art of negotiating. I routinely take them to the cleaners even though I feel bad for them that they have been sent into battle by their employers without the proper weapons.

6. **Sales training.** Has your sales force been professionally trained or have they just been thrown to the wolves? When I used to do sales training I would ask the people in the room to raise their hand if they had ever been to a sales training class before. Generally, around 90% of the attendees had never been to *any* formal sales training classes. They learned from another salesperson "who's been around a while" but usually that person has never had any professional training either. I know times are tough but if you think education is expensive, try ignorance. It's a lot more expensive.

How does your sales force stack up against the above? If you know for a fact that your sales team excels in all of the above areas I assure you that you are in a distinct minority and you are probably cleaning your competition's clock.

CHAPTER 78

ARE YOUR SALESPEOPLE PROS OR AMATEURS?

My previous post talked about professionalism of salespeople. Below is a list of things that professional salespeople do. If your salespeople aren't doing most of these things they aren't pros, they are amateurs, and this kind of economy calls for pros. If one or more of your salespeople don't do most of the below things you should seriously consider additional training or even replacing them.

- **Reconfirm appointments.** Only amateurs drive or fly to a customer site only to find out the customer forgot about the appointment. Do all of your salespeople reconfirm their appointments a day prior or, if they are flying out of town, the day before leaving on their trip? My experience has been that a lot of customers forget about appointments so if your salespeople are flying to see a customer it can be very expensive if the customer isn't there when they arrive.

- **Call if you're going to be late.** Nothing bothers me more than a salesperson who shows up late to a meeting with me without calling me to let me know he or she is going to be late. To make matters worse, most of the time, they don't even apologize for being late. It seems like most people these days think that being late is acceptable. Ensure your salespeople call if they are going to be late.

- **Plan sales calls in advance.** A pro goes into every sales call with a written plan of objectives to achieve on that call. Amateurs just wing it. If you're like me, you can tell when you're dealing with a pro who has planned in advance for a meeting versus an amateur who is just winging it. What do your salespeople do?

- **Thank you notes.** I almost never get a thank you note from people who call on me. Once in a blue moon I will get a follow-up e-mail but it has been years since I have gotten a handwritten thank you note. While an e-mail "thank you" is better than nothing, a handwritten thank you note stands out and identifies you as a pro. (This isn't done after every call, but should be done after an initial call or after a big order.) Do your salespeople do this?

- **Use CRM.** Customer relationship management software is used by almost all pros. There are standalone CRM packages such as ACT and GoldMine and CRM modules are part of most ERP systems these days. There are also hosted CRM packages such as Salesforce.com. CRM software allows you to keep notes on what was discussed on previous calls, has a section for personal information about each customer that you can work into your sales calls and gives you a purchase history that you should review before every call. You should also take a few minutes to update your CRM system after every call or at night. Do your salespeople religiously use CRM software?

- **Rank accounts.** All accounts are not created equal but most salespeople treat accounts equally. If they treat accounts equally your best accounts don't get enough of their time and your worst accounts get too much of their time. I recommend the ABC ranking system. Their A accounts are high-volume, good pay accounts with great growth prospects and they should be seen weekly. B accounts have average volume and average pay records. They should be seen monthly. C accounts are low volume and slow pay and your salespeople should never call on them. If they call your salespeople they should return their phone calls promptly but they shouldn't waste their valuable time (and your money) calling on them in person. If your salespeople use this ranking system, or a similar one, I guarantee you that their sales volume will increase.

- **Personal growth.** Do your salespeople read books on sales and business, are they active in trade groups, do they go to sales training seminars, do they join sales and marketing groups and other things that help them grow as professional salespeople? If they aren't doing these things they are amateurs.

- **Send presents.** Pros do little things like sending baby presents, wedding presents, flowers after the death of the loved one of a customer, and similar things. They don't have to be expensive but just the mere fact that they do them will make them stand out as a pro. In fact, it's better that the presents not be expensive because if they are it may look like they are trying to bribe your customers.

- **Pass on some sales.** It's hard for any salesperson to turn down an order but you gain a lot of credibility with your customers when you turn down an order when what the customer is trying to buy isn't really the best solution to the problem. When you turn down an order and steer a customer to a competitor you stand out as a pro. Do your sales reps ever pass on a sale?

- **Ask for referrals.** Pros always ask for referrals from customers. Happy customers are more than willing to give your salespeople the names of friends of theirs that may be interested in your services. However, most amateur salespeople never even ask for referrals. Do your salespeople consistently ask for referrals?

- **Reference letter book.** I used to ask happy customers to write a reference letter for me on their letterhead. I would then put all of the reference letters in a binder with plastic sleeves so that the letters didn't get soiled. My book had over 100 reference letters and whenever I made a prospect call I would always take the reference letter book along with me and share it with my prospects. Invariably, my prospects would see multiple companies they knew that were happy with me and that helped me close more than one deal. Do your salespeople have reference letter books?

- **Be active in associations.** Pros are active in trade associations, amateurs are just on the membership list, if that. I found that I got a lot more out of trade associations than I put into them if I served on committees, chaired membership drives, went to most, or all, of the meetings, and went to the annual convention. Customers who are active in trade associations tend to buy from suppliers who support the trade association with their time and money. Are your salespeople active in trade associations?

Measure your salespeople against the preceding list. If they aren't doing most of the above have them start doing them and watch your sales take off.

Chapter 79
My Biggest Mistakes

I have made a lot of mistakes in my career but I learned a long time ago that the only thing worse than learning from a mistake... is **not** learning from a mistake. I always feel good anytime I can save someone else from learning something the hard way. Below is a list of some of my biggest mistakes. I hope I can save you from learning them the hard way.

- **Not firing fast enough.** I have mentioned this in previous posts but it bears repetition. I have never regretted firing someone but I have almost always regretted not firing him or her sooner. No matter how painful it is to fire someone and to find their replacement, once your gut tells you that you have the wrong person in a position and you have nowhere else you can put him, terminate him. However, be sure to do it with dignity and respect.

- **Not firing someone for disloyalty or theft.** I have caught people being disloyal or stealing and given them a second chance. I have always regretted it. My experience has been that if someone will be disloyal or steal from you once, they will do it again. Get rid of him the first time and save yourself a lot of heartache.

- **Hiring a warm body.** Sometimes you have a position open and are having a hard time filling it. Don't compromise and hire a warm body. Until you have a candidate who fully meets the position specification, don't fill the position. You are better off working overtime than cleaning up the messes created by someone who didn't fully meet the job description.

- **Skipping steps in the hiring process.** Again, when you have a position that needs to be filled ASAP resist the temptation to skip steps in the hiring process. For example, don't fail to do a background check, reference checks, drug screen, etc. Most of the time when I have skipped a step in the hiring process I have regretted it.

- **Not saving for a rainy day.** I once heard a speaker at a convention recommend to business owners that they put 10% of their annual earnings in a separate savings account for rainy day. I'm glad I listened to this advice, because if I hadn't done that I probably would already be a victim of the current recession. It's always good to have a rainy day fund, both personally and professionally.

- **Not having succession plans in place.** Good sports teams always have a lot of "bench strength". Your business should be no different. You should have a succession plan in place for all key positions and you should have people already on staff to be able to step into key positions as they come open.

- **Skimping on training.** It has been said that if you think education is expensive, try ignorance. Truer words have never been spoken. Don't skimp on training for your staff or for yourself.

- **Being lax on credit.** I have bought companies only to find that there were no credit applications on hand for **any** customers. Over the years, accounts were opened for customers without requiring the completion of a well-written credit agreement. I have probably seen more companies fail due to excessive bad debts than any other reason. Being strict on credit keeps you from having catastrophic losses and sends the poor credit accounts in your industry to your competition where they ding them instead of you.

- **Arguing with a customer.** The customer is always right... especially when he's wrong. No one ever won a fight with a customer. I don't care how "wrong" a customer is you will never win the argument. Not only will you lose that customer and make an enemy for life but that customer will tell everyone he knows his side of the story, and believe me it won't be flattering to you.

- **Not spelling names correctly.** When I was starting out in sales I sent a letter to a prospective large customer without verifying the spelling of his surname. His name was Craft and I spelled it Kraft. I got back a scathing letter informing me that if I couldn't even spell his name correctly how could he trust me to sell him millions of dollars' worth of products a year? The thought of that situation still makes me wince and it happened over thirty years ago.

- **Not reporting bad news immediately.** Fine wine gets better with time but bad news only gets worse. When something bad happens to you or your company report it to your stakeholders immediately. A few months ago we had a surprisingly bad month and I let our banker know at the end of the last day of the month even though I didn't have to report our results to him for 30 days. I immediately got back a reassuring e-mail stating that while he didn't like to hear our bad news he appreciated my telling him as soon as I knew it. Two months later he renewed our revolving line of credit.

- **Being overly optimistic with budgets.** I am an optimistic person by nature but I have found that being overly optimistic with budgets isn't smart. Banks set your loan covenants off of your budget in most cases so if you budget too aggressively you will end up with loan covenants that will be hard to meet. And in this type of economy the last thing you want to do is not meet your loan covenants.

- **Not cutting back fast enough at the start of a recession.** Most businesspeople don't want to start cutting expenses and laying off people at the first sign of a possible recession and I understand that. However, after three successive bad months you are probably looking at a recession and you need to cut deeply and quickly. If we hadn't laid off 35% of our employees in November of 2008 we wouldn't be in business today.

- **Not reassigning or terminating people who you have outgrown.** Some people who were fine when your business was doing $5 million a year are no longer capable of doing their job when your company is doing $50 million a year. You should try hard to find another position for those types of people in your business, but if you can't, you need to let them go. Yes, it's painful as you generally have gotten to know them and their families but it's more painful to let your business pay the price for retaining a person who has hit their ceiling.

- **Buying from too many suppliers.** Sometimes it's tempting to buy from every supplier with the latest hot product. However, my father taught me long ago that it's better to mean a lot to a few instead of a little bit to everyone. Plus you don't have to meet with as many suppliers. Try to buy from as few suppliers as possible and you will also have a lot more clout with those suppliers.

- **Trying to get the last nickel from every deal.** Drive a hard bargain but don't try to take the last nickel in every deal. Make sure that your supplier ends up with a profitable deal because unless the deal is mutually profitable it won't last for long and you will have to start the negotiating process all over again when the supplier you squeeze too tight stops doing business with you.

- **Improper delegation.** Delegating a task to a subordinate without giving clear directions on what needs to be done isn't delegating, it's dumping. Don't dump tasks on subordinates. Explain what needs to be done, and when it needs to be done, but resist the temptation to say "how" it should be done. Manage results, not technique. Your subordinates won't learn much from a task if you detail every step of how to get it done. Plus, by the time you finish detailing every step you could have done it yourself, thus defeating the benefit of delegation.

- **Not monitoring delegated tasks.** Especially when a new manager is first doing tasks you've delegated you should check in and see how the task is progressing. This way, if your associate didn't fully understand the task you can get him or her back on track before they get too far down the road in the wrong direction.

- **"Selling" your company during the interview process.** When I first became a manager and had to learn how to interview I had to be one of the worst ever. Instead of asking a small number of open-ended questions and listening/taking notes during the responses I spent most of the interview "selling" the candidate on our company before I had established that the candidate even fit our profile. Tip: When interviewing strive for a 25/75 mix, i.e. you shouldn't talk more than 25%

of the time and the candidate should speak approximately 75% of the time.

- **Jumping to conclusions during an interview**. Again, when I first started in management if I was interviewing a candidate with a similar background I tended to be less critical and spent too much time talking about our mutual background. Over time, I learned that I should keep an open mind until all of the questions on my list had been answered and the results were in from the background check and the testing we use.

- **Poor management of subordinates**. As I am not by nature a detail oriented person, when I first got into management, I tended to hire people and then "throw them to the wolves" instead of spending time training them and ensuring that they went to appropriate training classes. Your direct reports do not learn by osmosis. They learn by exposure, access to learning tools, and training classes. Don't skimp on any of these things with a new hire, no matter how busy you are.

- **Not doing monthly meetings.** I mentioned in one of my early posts that the legendary former CEO of Intel, Andy Grove, said that the most important management tool he employed in his career was the face-to-face monthly meeting. While I use e-mail heavily, I do a face-to-face meeting with each of my direct reports monthly. This gives them the opportunity to talk to me at length about not only business subjects, but personal ones. Having done monthly meetings for over 30 years I can unequivocally state that I agree with Andy Grove.

- **Not getting a new hire back on track at the first sign of poor performance.** Sometimes when we hire people and we see they aren't doing as well as we hoped we don't always intercede immediately. The natural tendency of many managers is to hope that, somehow, the new associate will get back on track on the room. Rarely does this work. When you see that a new hire, or someone you've just promoted, isn't performing as you expected, sit down with him and restate the objectives for the position and ask what you can do to help. Believe me; this is much less time-consuming than starting the hiring process all over again.

- **Skipping steps in the termination process.** When you've tried everything you can think of to salvage a struggling employee with no success, and you don't have any other options for this person in your company, then termination is inevitable. The only thing worse than having to terminate one of your reports is to bungle the termination. Always speak to a labor lawyer or a labor law consultant to review the planned termination to ensure that no important steps have been skipped and that you aren't asking for a wrongful termination lawsuit. Never fire in anger and never terminate someone hastily. If you do, sooner or later, you will likely regret it.

CHAPTER 80
LESSONS FROM MY MENTORS

I'm thankful to have had some outstanding mentors during my career. Starting with my father who I began working for after school when I was about 12 and continuing on to the present time I have been able to learn many things the easy way by having some great mentors. Here are a few of them and some of the many things I was fortunate enough to learn from them:

My father, Jim Sobeck.

- Anything worth doing is worth doing right.
- It's better to be one hour early than one minute late.
- Plan your work and work your plan.
- When doing an estimate always have someone else double check your work.
- There is no substitute for hard work. If you can't outsmart someone, outwork them.
- Always keep your word.
- Never jeopardize your reputation. You can always make more money but you can never get another reputation.

My first boss after college, John Evans.

- Always have a plan for a sales call. Never wing it.
- Selling is like a funnel. The more sales calls you dump in the wide end, the more sales come out the narrow end.

- Everyone likes to feel important. Try to find a way to make each of your customers feel important. It is different for each customer.

- Go after a few large accounts instead of a lot of small ones. It's a better use of your time and gives you a much greater payback.

My boss at Owens Corning, Jim McCauley.

- Use interview teams to get multiple perspectives on candidates.

- Never compromise when hiring. Wait until you find the perfect candidate.

- Hold first-class sales meetings so your salespeople feel special. They will then perform special too.

- Regularly hold sales contests to keep the competitive juices flowing through your sales force.

- Always dress sharp so you stand out from the competition.

Lanny Moore, a co-worker at BMA.

- Who's running your business, you or your employees? I bet you can do a better job.

- The battle is fought where the line is drawn. Draw it close in, especially when it comes to credit.

- People do what you inspect, not what you expect.

- If you don't have the time to do it right, when will you find the time to do it again?

- A business can only offer a customer price, service, and quality. The customer can pick any two. If you are the best at all three you will go broke.

- Turn dead stock into cash no matter what you get for it. Any amount of cash is better than letting dead stock gather dust.

- Come up with incentive plans for all employees. Everyone works harder when there is an incentive for them to.

Clarence Bauknight, my partner in several companies.

- Always do more "homework" than the person you are negotiating against. Then do several "dry runs" of the meeting or negotiation prior to the actual meeting so you are prepared for any and all variables.

- Do monthly meetings with each of your direct reports and have them send you a recap of what was discussed and any action items assigned.

- Never, ever give up. Keep trying until you succeed, no matter what the endeavor.

- Put "golden handcuffs" on great employees so they don't leave, or even worse, compete with you.

- Share the wealth. Don't keep it all for yourself.

- Recognize talent early and promote people before they are fully ready. Winners will rise to the challenge and stay fulfilled in their careers.

Bill Lee, a coworker at BMA.

- Be a lifelong learner. Never stop reading, going to seminars, listening to CDs, etc. There is no finish line.

- It's not the people you fire that make your life miserable, it's the ones you don't.

- Plan out every sales call. Have a list of anticipated objections and answers to each.

- Have a USP (unique selling proposition) to differentiate yourself from the competition.

- Create a reference letter book and use it to give credibility to your claims with prospects.

Michael Johnson, one of my bosses at BMA.

- In correspondence, multiply the "we's" and divide the "I's". In other words, instead of saying "I "in a letter say "we". It looks less egotistical and also stronger.

- Develop personal relationships with each of your direct reports... but don't get too close to where you can't be objective in managing them.

- Spend time and money on teambuilding. The stronger the team, the better the performance of the team.

Bud Stoner, another one of my bosses at BMA.

- Get engraved 3 x 5 notecards and send thank you notes to customers and coworkers regularly.

- Always reconfirm appointments, especially when traveling out of town.

- Send thank you letters for large orders and special favors.

- Always keep your office and car immaculate. It sends a strong message to all who come in contact with you.

Peter Drucker, the late Dean of management consultants, worldwide.

- It is more important to do the right thing than to do things right. Make sure you're not wasting your time doing the wrong thing perfectly.

- There are no bad people, only bad jobs. If you have to terminate someone it isn't their fault, it is yours. *You* put them in the wrong position.

- Effective leadership is not about making speeches or being liked; leadership is defined by results not attributes.

- The best way to predict the future is to create it.

- The purpose of a business is to create a customer.

- The most important thing in communication is hearing what isn't said.

Jim Collins, noted author of best-selling business books such as *Built to Last* and *Good to Great*.

- Get the wrong people off the bus and then put the right people on the bus. Don't bother coming up with a new strategy until you do this. Until you have the right people on the bus implementing a new strategy isn't going to work.

- Stay out of the limelight and let your people get all the credit.

- Good is the enemy of great. Many companies never become great because they think good is good enough.

- People are not your most important asset, the *right* people are.

- The moment you feel the need to manage someone, you've made a hiring mistake. The best people don't need to be managed. They need to be guided, lead, taught - but not managed.

Zig Ziglar, a legendary motivational speaker and sales trainer.

- To get what you want out of life, help other people get what they want.

- Set goals in writing and update them weekly.

- Spend 30-60 minutes talking with your spouse after dinner each evening instead of diving back into work.

- When someone tells you they need to think about your proposal more it means you haven't done a good enough job of explaining it.

- Being successful means having a balance of success stories across the many areas of your life. You can't truly be considered successful in your business life if your home life is in shambles.

- Money isn't the most important thing in life, but it's reasonably close to oxygen on the "gotta have it" scale.

- You were born to win, but to be a winner, you must plan to win, prepare to win, and expect to win.

- Your attitude, not your aptitude, will determine your altitude in life.

- People often say that motivation doesn't last. Well, neither does bathing - that's why we recommend it daily.

These are only some of the lessons I learned from these mentors. I also have had other mentors that are too numerous to list here. I have been very fortunate in my career to have had such great mentors. If you don't have at least one mentor, seek one out. You will be amazed at how much you will be able to learn from someone who has already achieved some or all of your goals.

Yes, you can have mentors you have never met. That's why I read so much. You can get great advice from the world's great thinkers just by buying their books. What are you waiting for?

Chapter 81
Cash Management

In a previous post I talked about cash flow management i.e. tips on generating the highest possible positive cash flow. In this post I'm going to talk about cash management. What's the difference? Cash flow management is doing things that enhance your positive cash flow. Cash management is managing the cash that you generate in your business so that you don't run out of cash.

Just as I have found that many managers and owners don't understand the difference between markup and margin, I have also found that many business people with whom I come in contact don't understand the difference between net income and cash. The best way to illustrate the difference between the two is to quote a professor I had in business school. He said, "Net income is nothing but an accounting term. You don't pay your bills with net income, you pay them with cash."

Over the years I have seen many companies go bankrupt even though they never reported a loss. How does a company file bankruptcy without reporting even a monthly loss? *You do so by running out of cash.* There are a lot of accounting tricks that can enable a business to report a monthly net profit while slowly running out of cash. The most common way of doing this is to abuse accrual accounting. I have seen a lot of companies capitalize expenses that should have been expensed in the month in which they were incurred, but instead, they capitalized the expense, thereby spreading the expense over a number of months or years instead of taking the income hit in the month in which the expense was incurred. Yes, things like a new corporate brochure that will last for two or three years should be capitalized and then amortized monthly over the life of the asset, but I have seen other things such as a large refund to a customer capitalized and then expensed monthly over a year so that the expense of this refund didn't negatively impact one month.

A lot of companies capitalize things that should be expensed when they are losing money. They do so to not report losses and/or to stay in compliance with loan covenants. Using "accounting tricks" such as this not only fails to comply with GAAP (generally accepted accounting principles) but, in some instances can be illegal, especially when done in public companies.

One of the most famous cases of a company that went bankrupt while never reporting a loss was the 1960's discount store chain, WT Grant. WT Grant was facing a lot of competition from a new competitor, Wal-Mart. Rather than face the music and make needed changes to compete with Wal-Mart the management of WT Grant began capitalizing expenses which should have been recognized all at once. While this allowed them to survive a bit longer than they should have, their demise was inevitable.

How do I recommend you manage cash? Well, in our company, I get a daily availability report that shows me how much credit we have available under our revolving line of credit. The report shows our availability at the beginning of the day, cash receipts received, invoices billed, checks written, and net availability both before and after accounting for checks written but not yet cleared through our bank.

If our cash gets tight we pass on taking prompt pay discounts and pay when the invoice is due, charge the payment to a credit card, negotiate extended terms with the vendor, sell unproductive assets, auction off dead stock, and/or accelerate collection efforts with our customers. We do whatever it takes so that we don't run out of cash.

It always amazes me when I meet with other business owners and ask them how they keep track of availability against their bank lines. The vast majority sheepishly admit that they don't have any good idea of how much availability they have, they just wait for the bank to call to tell them that they are overdrawn. I don't know about you, but if this were my system of cash management I would need to take sleeping pills every night.

CHAPTER 82

SELLING PRIVATE COMPANY STOCK

Over the years I have seen many business owners unwittingly break the law when they sold stock to key employees without getting experienced legal counsel involved. Many business owners are fortunate enough to have some extremely loyal employees who they want to reward by selling them stock in the company so they will have an equity interest and hopefully benefit when the company is sold or when they sell their stock back to the company at retirement. Sounds pretty simple, doesn't it? It isn't. If you are considering selling stock to some of your key managers keep the following in mind:

- **Sell to only financially secure accredited investors.** Securities laws carry severe penalties for business owners who sell stock to employees who are not "accredited investors". What is an accredited investor in the eyes of the law? An accredited investor is a person who has a net worth of at least $1 million, $200,000 in annual income individually, or $300,000 of annual income including their spouse. These requirements are to protect investors from being taken advantage of by sellers. How many of your employees meet the definition of accredited investors? Probably not many, if any.

- **Disclose information to the buyer.** Providing detailed financial information about your company to the buyer is the best thing you can do to protect yourself from a suit alleging that you took advantage of the buyer. Disclose everything that you can think of. The more you disclose the less your potential future liability.

- **Sell in large dollar increments.** The larger amount of stock you sell, the smaller your risk of being sued. Courts view buyers of large amounts of stock as more sophisticated than one of your employees who may only have bought $25,000 worth of stock from you and then later claims to have been taken advantage of. If you want to take some cash off the table and you sell several million dollars' worth of stock to, for example, a private equity fund, judges aren't going to view those types of firms as unsophisticated.

- **Require purchasers to hold shares for a year or longer.** This protects you from someone who is simply speculating in your stock. You may even have an employee who has been in contact with a competitor and is buying stock to resell to a competitor.

- **Require that purchasers can only sell their stock back to you.** If you do this you don't have to worry about your stock falling into unfriendly hands. Of course, you have to agree to buy the stock back at fair market value. Ascertaining fair market value can be tricky. One method I have seen that tends to be agreeable to most parties is that each party gets an independent appraisal by an appraiser of their choosing. If the appraisals are less than 10% apart the stock is bought back at the average of the two appraisal prices. If the appraisals are more than 10% apart a third appraiser is retained that is mutually agreed upon by both parties and the average of all three appraisals is used for the repurchase price.

Most business owners I talk with aren't aware of the laws regarding selling private company stock. Keep the above points in mind if you are ever going to sell any of your company stock and these tips might just save you from an expensive legal settlement.

CHAPTER 83
E-MAIL TIPS

Over the last decade the use of e-mail both for business and personal reasons has become ubiquitous. However, in my opinion, many people still use e-mail in a less than optimum fashion. E-mail used properly is a tremendous business tool and e-mail used improperly can be frustrating at a minimum, or career ending at worst. With nine locations of my current company, 15 direct reports, serving on three outside boards, (not to mention my personal e-mail) I usually get around 250 e-mails per day. Every IT person who looks at my Outlook folders and data files says I am among the heaviest users of e-mail they have ever seen. Given that, here are some tips I've accumulated in about 20 years of heavy e-mail use:

- **Make sure the subject of your e-mail accurately reflects the content of the e-mail.** This may seem obvious but I find that a lot of the e-mail I get either has no subject (drives me nuts) or the subject doesn't accurately reflect the content of the e-mail. Ensuring that the subject of the e-mail is indicative of the content not only helps you decide which e-mails to open first but makes finding e-mails much easier when you look for them in the future.

- **Change the subject line of an e-mail if you respond to an e-mail but change the subject.** Sometimes I send a person an e-mail and it causes them to think of something else and they just click reply without changing the subject line or starting a new e-mail and ask me about a totally different topic. If I need to find that e-mail in the future, it is extremely time-consuming because the subject line doesn't reflect the content.

- **Click "reply all" sparingly.** Yes, sometimes every person copied on the original e-mail needs to be kept apprised of the content of each and every future e-mail but that is exceedingly rare. Before clicking "reply all", think if each person copied re-

245

ally needs to get your reply. Also, before you say anything controversial via e-mail be doubly sure before clicking "reply all". See career ending e-mails above.

- **Use your e-mail program's spellcheck feature.** With the advent of spellchecking programs there is no excuse for misspelled words. Go to the "Options" area for your email program and check the following boxes: "Spellcheck all e-mail before sending", "Spellcheck upper case words", and "Check spelling in subject line". If you do that you will not send e-mails with misspelled words any longer (provided you use words in the right context).

- **Set up multiple e-mail signatures.** If you use Outlook take a few minutes to set up multiple e-mail signatures and then use the appropriate one for each e-mail you're responding to. I have found that my responses largely consist of, "OK. Thanks.", "Please update me on the status of this", "This is past due, please reply immediately", "Thank you for your interest in our company but we have no openings at present", and my formal business signature with my full name, title, phone numbers, and address. By taking the time to set up multiple signatures you can breeze through e-mails in a fraction of the time it takes to type each of those responses.

- **Set up folders in Outlook.** I have over 400 folders in Outlook and I drag e-mail I may need to refer to in the future into the appropriate folder. This may not seem like a profound thought to you, but I have seen many, many people who have several thousand e-mails in their inbox because they have never taken the time to set up folders. Setting up folders and then using them appropriately saves time and frustration when you need to refer to an old e-mail.

- **Set up multiple e-mail addresses.** I have my work e-mail address, a home e-mail address, an AOL address, a Gmail address, and a Hotmail address. I use various addresses with various types of people and companies. I especially use my AOL and Hotmail addresses when buying things from catalogs or signing up for newsletters so that e-mails from those parties don't clog up my work e-mail box. I check those addresses only periodically.

- **Blind copy yourself on e-mails on which you need to follow-up.** Unfortunately, only a few of the people that report to me complete tasks by the assigned due date. Because of this, when I send out an e-mail requesting a response by a certain date I blind copy myself. When I get my copy in my e-mail box I move it to "Tasks" in Outlook and select a follow-up due date, normally seven days hence. By doing this, when I check my tasks every morning, anyone who hasn't responded by the assigned due date shows as past due and gets a follow-up e-mail from me. The original e-mail is at the bottom of the task so I don't have to go to their folder, search for the appropriate e-mail, and resend it.

- **After three e-mails, pick up the phone or meet face-to-face.** I have found that after three e-mails on a subject you have generally reached the point of diminishing returns and it's better to either call the person you have been e-mailing or set up a face-to-face meeting. Otherwise, you build e-mail string several feet long and just get frustrated in the process.

CHAPTER 84

LEGENDARY CUSTOMER SERVICE

When I was growing up in a small town in the coal region of Pennsylvania in the late 50s through the mid-70s I was exposed to great customer service because everyone knew each other in my small town and customer service was how you differentiated your business from others. I remember going to the local hardware store with wood floors and bins full of nuts, bolts, nails, and other hardware items and being able to buy one nut or one bolt and the owner of the store would put it in a little brown bag and tell you that you didn't owe him anything. If you bought something that you didn't know how to install the owner of the store would walk you through the installation process and maybe even draw a diagram for you. Now if you go to Home Depot and you need just one nut or one bolt you have to buy a package of 50 or more and then, if you're like me, you use the self-service checkout lane. You don't even interact with a human being. And, in most cases, if you need quality advice on how to use the product you're buying, you're out of luck. Most of the big box stores are staffed largely with part-time people who don't know much at all about the products they're supposed to be selling.

How did this drastic change in customer service come about? There are a lot of theories and mine is that as the United States grew and became more transient, people started doing most of their business with people they didn't know and price became the big differentiator. In our company we have continued to use customer service as our main differentiator. On our website we state, "The answer is yes, now what was the question?" We also have an on-time delivery guarantee. If you ask for a delivery time and we are more than one hour late we give you a credit of 10% of that purchase amount off of your next purchase. As some of our sales are over $20,000 a 10% credit is a hefty penalty for being late. We also state on our website that we will make deliveries

24/7, even on holidays. Some of our concrete contractor customers have to pour concrete over a weekend because of rain being forecasted for the coming week and they have a contract that requires the job he finished by a certain date. When these kinds of situations arise we are more than happy to deliver at night or on a weekend as this differentiates us from our competition as I don't know of any of our competitors that are willing to do this.

We certainly aren't the best at customer service but I think were better than most. Here are some other examples of great customer service I have experienced:

- **Maui Jim sunglasses.** I am outdoors a lot and my eyes are sensitive to light. Over the years, I have found that Maui Jim sunglasses work best for me. Yes, they are expensive, but they have tremendous customer service, if needed. For example, the bridge on the nose of a pair of two-year-old sunglasses broke recently. They come with a lifetime guarantee so I went to their website and found that all I had to do was send the sunglasses in and pay a $10 fee for postage and handling. I got the sunglasses back in about 10 days and found that they had replaced one of the lenses at no charge. Their website said that it was $35 to replace a lens, and I had a small scratch on one of the lenses, but was too frugal to pay $35 for a lens replacement. Imagine how pleased I was when I got my glasses back, fully repaired, and with a note stating that they noticed one of the lenses was scratched and replaced it at no charge. Guess where I will always buy my sunglasses from now on?

- **Chophouse 47.** There is a steakhouse in my hometown called Chophouse 47. It is expensive but they have top-notch food coupled with world-class service. Here are two examples. One night my wife and I and another couple were driving to dinner when a massive thunderstorm broke out. I dropped my wife and the other couple off under the canopy outside of the front door. I parked my car and steeled myself for the run through the torrential downpour back to the restaurant entrance. Imagine how pleased I was when, as I was about to get out of the car, I saw our favorite waiter standing there with an umbrella and another one for me. Another example happened one night when my wife was not happy with an entrée she had never tried before. There was nothing wrong with it, she just didn't enjoy it. When we got our check my wife's entrée had been deleted. I pointed this out to our waiter and he said that as he noticed that my wife didn't enjoy it, he took it off of our bill. Guess where we go for every special occasion and where we tell our friends to go?

- **The Peppermill.** Recently a restaurant in our town called The Peppermill closed down after being sold to new owners. The original owners practiced tremendous customer service. For example, one night my mother was visiting from Pennsylvania and took ill after we ate our appetizers but before our entrées were served. I motioned for our waiter and told him to bring me a check as we needed to leave because my mother wasn't feeling well. I told him that even though we hadn't been served our entrées I expected to pay for them because we ordered them and they were probably almost done. A few minutes later the owner came over to our table and told me that our drinks, appetizers, and the entrées were on the house. He handed me a bag with all of our entrées boxed up. He said he was terribly sorry that my mother had taken ill and he didn't want to add insult to injury by having us pay for our dinner. We went back many times after that until the original owner sold out and the new owners destroyed the business by cheapening the quality of the food and lowering prices. The new owners thought that lower prices would bring in more customers but all it did was run off the customers who gladly paid for high-quality food and service in the past.

The book, *Customers for Life* urges business owners to look at the lifetime value of a customer, not just the value of one transaction. Businesses that take that view and look for ways to delight their customers with great customer service don't have to be as competitive on price and also create legions of loyal customers who tell their friends about your business. Even though we're in tough economic times, don't nickel and dime your customers and look for ways to provide customer service that doesn't just meet, but exceeds your customers' expectations. If you do this you will be around long after those who sell on price only are gone.

Chapter 85
Employing Family Members

Most of what I have read over the years about employing family members has been cautionary and negative, with good reason. My experience, however, has been almost overwhelmingly positive. When you are careful about hiring family members (yours or family members of your employees) you can get some of the best, most loyal, and most trustworthy employees anywhere. I think you have a greater chance of success in hiring when hiring one of your family members or a family member of a star employee versus hiring someone off the street that no one knows. That, to me, is the real crapshoot. There are, however, some guidelines which I think need to be adhered to:

- **Be forthright.** Make sure that the family member knows that there will be no free ride and that the family member will be expected to work harder than any other nonfamily member. Also let the family member know that he or she will be promptly terminated for poor performance. (And mean it.)

- **Do a background check.** Even when hiring my own son I adhered totally to our hiring guidelines, including having a complete background check run. How was I to know that he didn't get into some trouble while away at college that I didn't find out about?

- **Interview a family member just like anyone else.** Again, even with my own son, I didn't skip any steps in our interviewing process. He took the intelligence test and all of the personality profiles that anyone else has to complete. The results didn't surprise me but they could have.

- **Employment elsewhere.** When hiring your own child I believe that he or she should work somewhere else after college for at least three years and be promoted at least once before working in your company. By working somewhere else they will gain experience which may very well benefit your company, and by getting promoted at least once it will boost their self-esteem and show them that they can get promoted without being a family member.

- **Use an outside consultant.** Before hiring my son he and I met separately and then jointly with an industrial psychologist. I didn't want to find out the hard way that my son would have a problem working for me and I wanted his eyes opened by a trained psychologist about what it would be like reporting to me. We did one session each separately and one joint session and after the psychologist told both of us that he felt very comfortable that we could work successfully together we then did two follow up sessions 90 days apart after he started. After two sessions my son suggested that we stop doing them as he felt they weren't needed.

- **Make family members work in a variety of positions.** My son has worked in our warehouses, gotten forklift certified, worked on the sales counter, and made deliveries in addition to his original position as IT manager. He now understands more about how we operate and earned the respect of his co-workers; things crucial to his future success.

- **Make family members adhere to the same rules as everyone else.** My son has the same benefits as everyone else and adheres to all the rules in our handbook, including vacation. He also gets an annual performance review. In all respects he is treated like every other employee.

- **Have a clear delineation of responsibilities and a job description.** In my case, my son is our controller and IT manager. He started off as our IT manager but when the construction industry went into a deep recession I asked him if he could also be our controller. His willingness to do this, and his competence in the position, saved us a significant amount of money. I don't stick my nose into the accounting or the IT side of the business and he has little interest in sales, marketing, real estate, and logistics, which is my area of expertise.

- **Have a compensation committee set his/her pay.** My son's pay and title is set by the compensation committee of our board. This also keeps him and I from having what could be tense conversations about pay and benefits. I also think it meant more to my son when the chairman of our compensation committee told him that, after eight years working in our company, he was being promoted to Vice-President of Finance and Administration.

I know that in many instances hiring family members doesn't work, but if a family member is hired and managed properly I have found you can beat the odds and benefit immensely.

CHAPTER 86

INCENTIVE COMPENSATION PLANS

There are two schools of thought (at least) regarding incentive compensation plans. I have heard HR professionals rail against incentive compensation. Some say that you shouldn't have to bribe your employees to get their job done and some even say that a bonus plan is an insult to people who have been carefully chosen and take pride in their job. I am in the other school of thought. In over 30 years in management I have never had anyone be insulted by a bonus check and I certainly have never had anyone turn one down. I have also seen people (myself included) work nights, weekends, and holidays to earn a bonus. I can't think of one example where someone has done the same without the prospect of a bonus or a large commission check.

In the capitalist society in which we live, incentive compensation has rarely failed to get results for me. Here are a few tips to getting the most out of an incentive compensation plan:

- **Don't expect one thing while paying for another.** I have seen companies give poorly thought out incentive plans to employees that only made the situation worse. For example, I once saw a credit manager get a bonus plan that offered significant monthly bonuses for reductions in collection days (DSO). This credit manager "turned the screws" on the customers with the largest past-due balances, threatened legal action, and used other techniques which dramatically reduced this company's collection days. However, it also dramatically reduced the company's sales in the following months. **Be very careful to tailor each compensation plan to get _exactly_ the type of behavior you want.**

- **Bonuses should be lifestyle altering.** Generally speaking, you won't get significant additional effort from an employee whose bonus plan isn't lifestyle altering. A bonus plan that pays $5000 will get significant extra effort from someone making $25,000 a year but generally won't get you a lot of extra effort from someone making $150,000 per year. I have found that a bonus plan should yield at least 10% of base pay for lower and middle management employees and 20-50% of base salary for upper management. For CEOs I have seen plans that pay out 100% of base salary in some instances.

- **Tailor the bonus payout to the person receiving the bonus.** By this I mean most people respond well to cash but people in some higher-level positions may respond better to an exotic trip such as an all-expense paid trip for two to Hawaii or some other highly desirable location, including First Class airfare, and cash for spending on incidentals.

- **Don't have all plans pay out annually.** For middle and upper management an annual bonus plan works best but for blue-collar positions plans that pay out quarterly or even monthly may work better as many of the people in those positions live from paycheck to paycheck and they may leave prior to an annual payout because of necessity.

- **Must be present to win.** All bonus plans should require that the person getting the bonus be on board at the time of the bonus payout. You would not want to make a sizable bonus payout to someone who is no longer with your company, would you? (Or, even worse, can you imagine paying a large bonus to someone who is competing with you at the time you paid the bonus?)

- **Double up and double down.** For middle and upper management I advocate a bonus plan that pays out 2:1 on the upside and downside. For example, if your company's VP of Sales delivers 120% of your sales budget give him a bonus of 140% of his bonus target. Conversely, delivering only 80% of budget would result in only a 60% payout. I also advocate no bonus payout for less than 75% of budget achievement.

CHAPTER 87
LEASING VS. PURCHASING

I got an e-mail from a reader asking whether I prefer leasing versus purchasing and if I had a rule of thumb for making the lease versus purchase decision. Most people I know make this a very complicated decision-making process but I have a standard rule of thumb that I apply. It is: I purchase things that appreciate and I lease things that depreciate. Yes, that is a rather simplistic view of a complicated decision but I have found that, even after extensive financial analysis the smart thing to do is to lease things that depreciate and purchase things that appreciate. My thinking is, why expend precious cash on an asset that is going to depreciate, perhaps even down to zero, over time? A good example of this is purchasing trucks. Even the best cared for truck is going to be worth nothing at some point. Why purchase a truck when you can get a full-service lease and replace your trucks every 3-5 years with brand-new ones? In our business we have a fleet of tandem axle trucks with mounted forklifts that cost around $150,000 brand-new. We have ten of these trucks so if I had purchased them I would have expended over $1.5 million. Instead, I have a full-service lease that covers everything except fuel. The lease includes tires, oil changes, transmissions, the hydraulic systems - everything. And, if a truck breaks down they tow the truck and at no charge to us they provide a loaner truck at no cost. Our lease even includes free washes at their facility so our trucks always look sharp.

A hidden benefit is we always have a new looking fleet and our trucks don't get so many miles on them that they start breaking down and our customers deliveries get delayed. Yes, I realize I am paying more money over time by paying for a full-service lease but this frees up cash for financing inventory and receivables and I can buy the trucks at a fraction of the original cost when the lease is up. As we know whether a truck has been problem free or a lemon we get a great deal on a used truck and we know what we're getting.

We also lease forklifts, computer servers and network gear, phone systems, and even security cameras and monitors at all of our locations. If I had paid cash for all of these things, including the trucks mentioned above, I would have expended over $2 million in cash over the last five years. As the last few years have been extremely challenging in the building supply business I would probably be out of business if I hadn't preserved this cash by leasing.

Yes, I had to keep paying leases for some idle vehicles over the last few years. However, if I owned the vehicles I probably still wouldn't have sold them because used delivery trucks are worth less than half of what they were worth at auctions prior to the construction downturn. For example, I know a person who bought a tandem axle truck with a truck mounted forklift at auction for $29,000 when that truck costs about $150,000 just three years ago. Friends of mine in the building supply business who own their own vehicles and now have excess vehicles due to the downturn in business have "mothballed" the trucks they aren't using because they refuse to "give them away" at an auction. This, to me, is the worst of both worlds. They expended cash they wish they had back now for trucks they can't afford to sell because of the huge loss they would take which would lower their already meager profits, if they are even profitable at all.

Is my rule of thumb perfect? No, I'm certain it isn't. However, it has worked for me and I'm still in business to talk about it.

CHAPTER 88

OPEN BOOK MANAGEMENT

Most of my career has been with private companies but I worked for a public company early in my career and was a shareholder in private company that went public. Public companies have no choice but to share their financials with their shareholders; and employees and other interested parties of public companies have access to financial statements as well.

After leaving a public company early in my career I was fortunate enough to become a shareholder in a very progressive private company that shared monthly financials with all of their employees. So I am used to always sharing information and I was surprised when I found out that most private companies don't share financials with their employees. There are a lot of reasons for this. Some owners don't want their employees to know how well they are doing because they are afraid they will ask for a raise. Other owners don't want their employees to know how poorly they are doing because they're afraid people will start jumping ship.

I am of the school of sharing financials with your employees. Despite the above concerns I have found that it's hard to get your employees to do the right thing if they don't see the impact of it on the bottom line. I have had other business owners tell me that I'm crazy to do this and that my employees could share my financials with my competitors. That doesn't bother me in the least. One of my mentors who had the most impact in my life used to share his financial statements even with competitors when he would speak at trade association meetings. I asked him once why he had no concerns about sharing his financial statements with his competition. He told me, "I don't care if they see my financials because they don't have my employees so they can't produce the results I produce." He went on to say that he also wanted his competitors to see how high his gross margin was so that they might raise their prices!

In over 30 years of sharing financials with my employees I have never had a problem from doing this. Quite the contrary, I have had employees tell me that my profit is a lot less than they imagined and that now they fully understand why we need to do everything we can to maximize our gross margin and lower our expenses. Now, after I send out financial statements each month I often get e-mails or calls questioning items on the income statement and asking other questions about our financials. Sharing financials has been nothing but positive for me.

If you haven't been sharing financial statements with your employees and want to start, Jack Stack has written a legendary book called *Open Book Management*. I suggest you read this before you start sharing your financial information with your employees. It will give you a lot of tips about how to get started and what to avoid.

CHAPTER 89

PERFORMANCE APPRAISALS

I realize that in certain circles doing employee appraisals is considered "old school". Some human resource professionals say that appraisals are a thing of the past and that they aren't worth the time to do them. I disagree. I believe that a well thought out and well executed appraisal is an important management tool.

In our company we do two types of appraisals: a 90 day appraisal for new employees and an annual appraisal for longer-term Associates. The first part of our appraisal process is having the employee complete our self-evaluation form. The self-evaluation form is slightly different for a 90 day appraisal than for a regular appraisal. In the 90 day self-evaluation form we ask about practices that we might implement that the new employee may have learned at a former employer. We don't feel we have cornered the market on good ideas so we ask new employees to share with us any things that the employee may feel was done better at a company for whom they have previously worked. The self-evaluation form for existing employees obviously doesn't contain those questions.

Once I review the self-evaluation form I set the date for the review meeting and then complete our appraisal form. At the review meeting I always begin the process by reviewing the self-evaluation form submitted by the employee and discussing it in depth. I always look for disconnects between how the employee thinks he is doing versus how I think he's doing. For example, if an employee thinks he's doing an outstanding job and I think he is barely meeting our minimum standards, that sparks an in-depth discussion.

I also note whether the employee appears to have completed the form in five minutes or has put a lot of thought into completing the form. I have seen some people complete the form largely with one word answers and others with multiple paragraphs for each question. I am obviously more impressed with an employee who has put a lot of thought into completing the self-evaluation form.

Before moving on to our appraisal form I also ask the person I am reviewing to review me as a supervisor. I ask for likes and dislikes and suggestions on how I can be a better supervisor. I find this disarms a lot of people as most of those who report to me say that they have never had a supervisor ask how they are doing as a manager and how they might improve. I also find that by asking such questions it puts the person being reviewed at ease and results in more of a two-way dialogue than me just sitting in judgment of the person I'm reviewing.

After this discussion we turn to our appraisal form. Our form consists of a numerical (1-5) assessment of the various skill sets necessary for the position the employee holds. Next, there is a section that includes the employee's goals from the last review and how they did against their goals. We take great pains to ensure that the goals listed on the appraisal form are both specific and measurable. That not only focuses the employee better but avoids disagreements as to whether the employee met a subjective goal. If the goal is specific and measurable, how they did against the goal isn't up for debate.

The next section of our review form is only used when reviewing people who manage other people. That has five sections measuring how the manager is doing as a supervisor. I have noticed that most review forms don't have a managerial assessment section. Discussing how supervisors did their management duties also leads to some interesting discussions.

The next section of our review form is the reviewer's subjective assessment of the person they are reviewing. While goals should be specific and measurable, not everything that an employee does can be measured. This section allows for subjective comments such as, "is a real team player", "regularly volunteers for distasteful jobs", etc.

The final section of our review form establishes goals for the next 12 months. Again, the goals must be both specific and measurable. When doing the appraisal we discuss the goals set for the next year and are willing to adjust them if it isn't mutually agreed that the goals are doable. While we want our goals to be a bit of a stretch we want them to be attainable because if they aren't they serve as a demotivator.

After the review is done I suggest that you review the goals for the next year at least quarterly during your monthly meetings with the people who report to you. If you don't know what I mean by a monthly meeting check out my previous blog post on this subject. There is nothing worse than not discussing goals for an entire year and then expressing concern when they aren't hit.

One final comment about appraisals: I recommend not linking pay increases to appraisals. Most companies give raises (unless there is a salary freeze in place) in conjunction with the annual review. I recommend that you de-link the salary review from the performance review. The reason for this is it's hard for an employee who has just gotten a great review to understand why they aren't getting a large raise. During tough times you may only be able to afford a modest raise for an outstanding performer. If your salary review is conducted at a different time than the performance review it's much easier to explain a small raise to a key employee. Also, during downturns if you can't afford to give out raises then you simply don't schedule a salary review until the salary freeze gets lifted.

I agree that appraisals should not be done if they are done poorly because a slipshod review is a waste of time for both the manager and the employee. However, a properly done review can help improve both performance and morale.

CHAPTER 90

WHAT <u>NOT</u> TO DO ON A JOB INTERVIEW

In over 35 years of hiring I have pretty much seen it all when it comes to what not to do on a job interview. Here are some of the things you absolutely should not do when interviewing with me for a job:

- **Show up late.** One of the greatest truisms in life is, "You never get a second chance to make a first impression". Showing up late if you are interviewing with me almost guarantees you won't get the job. If you can't show up on time for a job interview how can you possibly be counted on to show up on time for customer meetings? I understand that sometimes being late is unavoidable due to an accident on the highway, getting lost, etc. However, if something comes up that is going to make you late need to call and say that you are going to be late. Don't just waltz in 30 minutes late and expect to get a job offer from me.

- **Dress inappropriately.** We are in the building supply business so I don't expect people to come for an interview wearing a coat and tie. On the other hand, I don't expect people to come to an interview with me wearing dirty, torn clothes or inappropriate clothing such as a tank top. If you are interviewing for a truck driver position, blue jeans and work boots are appropriate. However, if you are interviewing for a job in our accounting department then blue jeans and work boots are inappropriate. Use good judgment. One of the things I look for during an interview is good judgment. Just like speed in football, you can't teach it. You have it or you don't.

- **Ask stupid questions.** I once had a person interviewing for a sales position ask me if we do random drug tests. How stupid is that? I asked him why that was important to him and he said, "I smoke a little weed now and then; is that a problem?" Based on that statement I think he smokes weed more than just now and then. Want to guess if he got the job?

- **Bring up pay and benefits at the beginning of the interview.** If someone starts asking me about pay and benefits at the beginning of the interview I question their judgment. It is only appropriate to ask about wages and benefits after it has been determined that you are a good fit for the position. And, even then, let the interviewer bring up the subject.

- **Talk incessantly.** I don't know about you, but I don't care for people who, when you ask them what time it is, tell you the history of watchmaking. I like people that give concise and appropriate answers to my questions. Listen to the question and then give the shortest possible response that fully answers the question.

- **Don't research the company you are interviewing with.** One of my standard interview questions is, "Tell me what you know about our company." Some candidates amaze me with the amount of information they have gleaned from the Internet and/or mutual acquaintances about our company. Other candidates tell me they don't know anything about our organization, and worse yet, some people try to BS me and aren't even in the ballpark. You should never go on a job interview without researching the company you're interviewing with, and the person interviewing you. I had a recent meeting with a large potential client and was amazed to see what I was able to find out about him over the Internet. I was able to find out what fraternity he was in during college (from his Facebook page), what country club be belongs to (his club newsletter is online and mentioned he had a recent hole-in-one), his golf handicap (his golf club posts handicaps online), charitable organizations whose board's he was on (he was mentioned in their online annual reports), his home address (from www.411.com) and then I looked up the value of his home on www.zillow.com, and even where he likes to vacation (from his Twitter account). This information allowed me to make a lot of small talk with him and helped me get the deal. In fact, we talked about his hobbies for 90% of the meeting.

- **Check your phone during the interview.** Yes, I have had candidates look down at their phone during interviews with me and one even asked me if he could respond to a text message from his girlfriend in the middle of the interview. I am 57 but I doubt I am so out of touch with reality that this is an acceptable practice among the younger generation of hiring managers. Not only should you not check your phone during an interview but you should not even bring it into the interview with you. Leave it in your car unless your wife is nine months pregnant and she could go into labor at any minute.

- **Chew gum.** Again, I must be a real relic but I can't believe anyone with half a brain would think it would be appropriate to pop gum during an interview. I even had someone once try to hand me her chewed gum and ask me to throw it away for her. I'm not making this up!

- **Talk negatively about your current or past employers.** It always amazes me that people think I want to hear them bad-mouth their current employer or a past one. Don't they realize that I know that if they will complain about their current or past employer they will do that when talking about our company? If you have an ax to grind about your current employer, or any employer from your past, keep it to yourself no matter how true your complaints may be. This will not help you during a job interview with me or most other employers.

- **Make unrealistic salary demands.** I actually had a 25-year-old who was applying for an outside sales position tell me that he, "Wouldn't get off the couch" for less than $90,000 a year. I suggest that, when interviewing, you let the interviewer bring up the subject of salary and if it is below your expectations say so in a courteous way, not like the 25-year-old referenced above. (The interview with that person ended about 30 seconds after he made that statement.)

If you keep the above tips in mind you will fare better than most of the people that interview with me.

CHAPTER 91
INVENTORY CYCLE COUNTS

In any business with inventory, a sad fact of life is that you have to physically count it at least once a year to see if you actually have what your computer says you have. No one likes to do it, but it has to be done. Believe it or not, I still know people who only count their inventory one time a year. Thus, one day year they are either very happy or very upset. Most of the time it's the latter. I could never live in suspense for a year wondering whether we have a major inventory shortage at one of our eight locations, and I don't want to require our managers to have to count their entire inventory several times a year, so we do cycle counts.

What is a cycle count? Cycle counting entails counting just a portion of your inventory on a regular basis so that over the course of a year you will have counted either all of your inventory or the roughly 20% of your inventory that makes up about 80% of your sales.

The two main methods for cycle counting are "the ranking method" and "the geographic method". The ranking method is where you rank your inventory from fastest to slowest moving and then, on a regular basis, count the fastest moving items that make up 80% or so of your sales. Generally, if you are going to have inventory shrink it will most likely be among your fastest moving items because that's where you have the most item velocity, thus you will have the greatest opportunity for errors or theft. (As you can't sell your dead stock, your customers don't want it either and aren't going to offer your people cash under the table for it.)

The geographic method is where you start at one end of your warehouse and count a certain number of products each day as you work your way to the back of your warehouse. I don't recommend this method because you will, in my opinion, waste a lot of time counting slow moving items and dead stock. That's not where most of your problems will be, if you have any problems.

Our auditors have seen that our inventory variances are so minimal (most of the time we have an inventory pick up—see my prior post on this) that they don't make us do a full inventory of any of our locations unless their test sample shows a variance outside of their tolerance range. When that happens the offending location(s) gets to come in on a weekend and count every single item inventory. No one wants to do that so they take great pains with their cycle counts throughout the year so they don't have to give up a weekend to count their location's entire inventory.

No one wants to spend New Year's Day counting inventory so if you haven't already tried cycle counting talk to your auditors about it and see if they will agree to let you skip counting your entire inventory if you do regular cycle counts and don't have major variances.

Chapter 92

Does Your Company have a Social Networking Policy?

As social networks like Facebook and Twitter are growing like kudzu does here in the South (for you Yankees, kudzu is a vine that was imported from Japan over one hundred years ago to contain soil erosion and now it is all over the South and can't be killed) have you added a social networking policy to your employee handbook or as a standalone policy? If you don't, you should. Already there have been several high profile cases where employees were terminated for revealing company secrets over social media, disparaging company officials on Facebook, and other transgressions via social media. In most cases if the company didn't have a social media policy in place the jury found for the defendant.

Below is our policy. Feel free to use it.

SOCIAL MEDIA POLICY

[Company Name] takes no position on an employee's decision to start or maintain a blog or participate in other social networking activities. However, it is the right and duty of the company to protect itself from unauthorized disclosure of information. Therefore, the following policy addressing Company-authorized as well as personal social networking applies to all Company employees.

GENERAL PROVISIONS

Use of social networking media and technology include but are not limited to video or wiki postings, sites such as Facebook and Twitter, chat rooms, personal blogs or other similar forms of online journals, diaries or personal information postings not affiliated with [Company

Name].

Unless specifically instructed, employees are not authorized and therefore restricted to speak on behalf of [Company Name]. Employees may not publicly discuss confidential information regarding clients, products, employees or any work-related matters, outside company-authorized communications. Employees are expected to protect the privacy of [Company Name] and its employees and clients and are prohibited from disclosing personal employee and nonemployee information and any other proprietary and nonpublic information to which employees have access. Such information includes but is not limited to customer information, trade secrets, financial information and strategic business plans.

EMPLOYER MONITORING

Employees are cautioned that they should have no expectation of privacy while using the Internet. Postings can be reviewed by anyone. [Company Name] reserves the right to monitor comments or discussions about the Company, its employees, clients and the industry, including products and competitors, posted on the Internet by anyone, including employees. [Company Name] reserves the right to use search tools and software to monitor forums such as blogs and other types of personal journals, diaries, personal and business discussion forums, and social networking sites; and to use content management tools to monitor, review or block content originating from the Company that is not in the best interest of [Company Name].

Employees are advised that they should have no expectation of privacy while using company facilities, hardware, software, or other equipment or for any purpose, including authorized social networking.

REPORTING VIOLATIONS

[Company Name] requests and strongly urges employees to report any violations or possible or perceived violations to their immediate supervisor or the HR department. Violations include, but are not limited to, discussion of the Company or its employees and clients, any discussion of proprietary information and any unlawful activity related to blog-ging or social networking.

DISCIPLINE FOR VIOLATIONS

Violation of the company's social networking policy will result in dis-ciplinary action up to and including immediate termination. Discipline or termination will be determined based on the nature and factors of any blog or social networking post. [Company Name] reserves the right to take legal action where necessary against employees who en-gage in prohibited or unlawful conduct.

RULES AND GUIDELINES

Only authorized employees can prepare, post, and modify content on the Company's web site or any Company social networking location, such as a Facebook page. If there is ever question about the appropri-ateness of information to be posted, discuss the content with your manager or the HR Department.

All employees must identify themselves as employees of [Company Name] when posting comments or responses on a Company spon-sored blog or social networking site.

Any copyrighted information where written reprint information has not been obtained in advance cannot be posted on Company's web site, blog or social networking location.

When social networking, blogging or using other forms of web-based forums, the Company must ensure that use of these communications maintains our brand identity, integrity and reputation while minimizing actual or potential legal risks, whether used inside or outside the work-place.

PERSONAL BLOGS

[Company Name] respects the right of employees to write blogs and use social networking sites as a medium of self-expression and public conversation and does not wish to discourage employees from self-publishing and self-expression. However, employees are expected to follow the guidelines and policies set forth to provide a clear line between you as the individual and you as the employee.

Bloggers and commenters are personally responsible for their commentary on blogs and social networking sites. Bloggers and commenters can be held personally liable for commentary that is considered defamatory, obscene, proprietary, or libelous by any offended party, not just the Company.

Employees cannot use employer-owned equipment, including computers, company-licensed software or other electronic equipment, nor facilities or company time, to conduct personal blogging or social networking activities.

Employees cannot use blogs or social networking sites to harass, threaten, discriminate or disparage employees or anyone associated with or doing business with Company.

If you choose to identify yourself as a Company employee, please understand that some readers may view you as a spokesperson for [Company Name]. Because of this possibility, we ask that you state that your views expressed in your blog or social networking area are your own and not those of the company, nor of any person or organization affiliated or doing business with [Company Name].

Employees cannot post on personal blogs or other sites the Company trademark or logo or that of any business with a connection to [Company Name]. Employees cannot post company-privileged information, including copyrighted information, company-issued documents, or employee information.

Employees cannot post on personal blogs or social networking sites photographs of other employees, clients, vendors or suppliers, nor can employees post photographs of persons engaged in company business or at company events.

Employees cannot post on personal blogs and social networking sites any advertisements or photographs of company products, nor sell company products and services.

Employees cannot link from a personal blog or social networking site to [Company Name]'s internal or external web site.

If contacted by the media or press about a personal post that relates to Company business, employees are required to speak with their manager before responding.

Finally, keep in mind that information posted on a blog or social networking site is considered to be in the public domain, regardless of any personal security settings. Therefore, anything posted by an employee may be treated as if it had been stated face-to-face to the management of the Company. As a result, any improper postings or comments can be considered a violation of this policy that may result in discipline up to and including termination of employment.

If you have any questions relating to this policy, your personal blog or social networking, ask your manager or the Human Resources Department.

I HAVE READ AND UNDERSTAND THE COMPANY'S SOCIAL NETWORKING POLICY.

_____ / _____

Employee Signature / Date

Don't wait until you have a major problem. If you don't have a social media policy implement one now!

CHAPTER 93

TEN THINGS
TOP SALESPEOPLE DO

Most people think top salespeople are born, not made. I am proof that's not the case. When I started high school I was tall, skinny, and shy. I'm still tall but that's where the comparison ends. I learned to be a top salesperson in every company I have been with by consistently doing the following ten things.

1. **Plan every sales call.** I have a written plan for each sales call I make. I review my CRM system, note what was discussed the last time we met, review any personal topics that came up, and list my objectives for this call. It never ceases to amaze me that most salespeople have only a vague idea of a plan for their sales calls, if any. Most are what I call "industrial tourists"; i.e., a company pays them to drive (or worse, fly) around "visiting" customers, and the occasional prospect, buying lunches, playing golf, or similar things. Most salespeople don't have a written "game plan" for every call. They just wing it and hope for the best.

2. **Have a written plan to grow your top ten accounts.** When I was in sales I always had a plan to add to my sales to my top accounts. Marketing 101 teaches you it's easier to sell more to your top accounts who already know and like you than to prospect for new accounts, so you should always have a plan to sell more to your top customers. No one gets 100% of the business from any account so always be planning how to grow sales to your best customers.

3. **Review your "value add" frequently with customers.** I am always looking for "value adds" I can use to get more business from my customers. A value add could be providing labor along with your products to take this headache away from your customer, selling products pre-assembled, customizing prod-

ucts, providing financing, etc. Without a "value add" you are often times reduced to selling on price.

4. **Prospect for new business even though you are doing well.** Most salespeople don't prospect until their business falls off dramatically. Not prospecting for business when you're doing well is like not buying life insurance until after you've had a heart attack. Top salespeople are always prospecting and preparing for a rainy day.

5. **Begin your day with a list of things that you need to do that are both urgent and important.** Most people either fritter their day away doing "fun" tasks or they take care of the urgent at the expense of the important. Make a list of things that you need to do that are both urgent and important and stick to that list, at least for the morning. I move on to other things on my "to do" list in the afternoon but I reserve the morning for tasks that are both urgent and important.

6. **Become a serious student of the selling profession.** When I do seminars on selling I always begin by asking who has ever been to a seminar on selling before. Almost always only a smattering of hands go up. Next I ask how many have ever had a golf lesson, shooting lesson, swimming lesson, or any other type of lesson related to a leisure pursuit. You guessed it! Almost every hand in the room goes up. If you sell for a living and don't regularly go to seminars, read books, and listen to recorded programs on the art of selling you aren't serious about selling as a career.

7. **Build strong personal and professional relationships with customers.** The best way to keep your competition from taking your best customers away from you isn't by constantly lowering your price. It is by taking the time to build strong personal and professional relationships with your customers. By this I mean socializing with key customers and joining professional groups to which they belong and then being active in those groups. If you do those two things you make it infinitely harder for your competitor to take your key customers away from you.

8. **Don't waste your time on customers who pay slow, constantly complain, and who buy little of what you sell.** As a

professional salesperson, time is money and you need to spend your precious time in pursuit of big volume, good pay, and professional accounts that can buy millions of dollars from you over the years.

9. **Develop your personal brand.** By this I mean what are you known for in your market? How have you "branded" yourself? What do you do to set yourself apart from your competition? I used to do my own newsletter back in the days when I had to type it myself, take it to a copy shop, and mail it out. It wasn't great but no one else I competed with did a newsletter so I won by default. In today's world with e-mail and other technology tools, doing your own newsletter is much easier. This is just one idea. What else can you do to set yourself apart from the competition?

10. **Outwork the competition.** When I was in sales I started earlier and quit later than anyone else I knew of with whom I competed. When I couldn't get an appointment with a workaholic who was always "too busy" to see me I would get his attention by asking for an appointment at 6 AM or on a Saturday. Workaholics were always impressed when I would propose appointments at such odd times. Back before cell phones I gave my customers my home phone number and encourage them to call me 24/7 whenever they needed *anything*. I'm always amazed when a salesperson who calls on me doesn't return a call from me on Friday afternoon until Monday morning and then gives me the excuse that they turn their cell phone off over the weekend. You can be sure I never bother them again... with an order, or anything else.

In summary, selling isn't hard, but properly done, it is hard work. Always keep in mind the old adage, "There is never a traffic jam on the extra mile". The type of customers you want to sell will recognize that you are doing some or all of the above and, if you do it consistently, it will pay off. Take it from this tall, formerly skinny and shy guy.

CHAPTER 94

E-MAIL TIPS

Email use is now the norm in most every business in America and around the world. You would think that with the heavy use of e-mail people would learn how to use it effectively by now. I still cringe about half of the time when I get e-mail because of misspelled words, run-on sentences, lack of capitalization, poor grammar, and the one that drives me the craziest: the ubiquitous use of "reply all".

Here are a few tips that will help you be a more effective user of electronic mail:

1. **Turn on your automatic spell checker.** Every e-mail program I have ever seen has an option to "check spelling before sending". However, most people must not be aware of this and only occasionally manually run the spell checker before sending an e-mail. Just doing this one thing will make your e-mail look much more professional. If you use the most popular e-mail software, Microsoft Outlook, all you have to do is go to File, Options, Mail, and check the box that says, "Always check spelling before spending".

2. **Fill in the subject line.** Believe it or not, I still get e-mails every day with the subject line blank. As I get over 200 e-mails per day I ignore the ones with empty subject lines until I have responded to e-mails where the subject line grabs my attention. Also, spend a few seconds thinking about what to put in the subject line so that it accurately reflects your message and interests the reader enough to read your e-mail before others.

3. **If you change the subject when you reply to someone, change what is in the subject line.** Several times a day I get an e-mail that has absolutely nothing to do with the subject of the e-mail. This is because some people get an e-mail from me and it reminds them that they wanted to ask me something so they click on reply, totally change the subject, but fail to change

the subject line. This is really a problem when you try to search for a subject and the e-mail you're looking for is under a subject line that has no relationship to the body of the message.

4. **Explain why you forwarded an e-mail.** I regularly get e-mails forwarded to me with absolutely no message as to why the sender forwarded it to me. It is a pet peeve of mine when the sender won't take five seconds to explain why an e-mail has been forwarded to me. I am not a mind reader so if you forward an e-mail to me please explain why and let me know if action is required. Otherwise don't be surprised if you don't hear back from me.

5. **Give a due date.** When I send an e-mail to someone in our company where I am requesting a specific action I always include a due date. Otherwise, when I don't hear back for a week or two I am told that since no due date was given it mustn't have been too important. Better yet, put the due date in the subject line directly after the subject. Then there is no excuse for not getting a response by the desired date.

6. **Tailor your vocabulary to match the vocabulary of the recipient.** By this I mean, in our building supply business, when I send an e-mail to a customer that I know only has a high school education I avoid using unusual words that the recipient either won't understand or will feel demeaned by. Also, avoid using business grammar from the 1960s such as, "attached, please find", "pursuant to your correspondence of x-date", and the like. Not only is this superfluous verbiage but, again, it will make most readers feel like you are talking down to them.

7. **Follow-up on your e-mails if you don't hear back in seven days.** I find that when I send an e-mail to solicit business, ask for a favor, or simply when I send an e-mail to someone who doesn't know me, the vast majority of the time the original e-mail is ignored. I always blind copy myself on each e-mail of importance and then drag it into tasks in Outlook and set a reminder date seven days after the date I send the e-mail. If, in seven days, I get no response to my e-mail I send a simple follow-up mail asking, "Did you get this?" Over 50% of the time I then get a response. I think that busy people ignore e-mails from people with whom they are not familiar but when they

see a follow-up e-mail they know they are dealing with a professional, not an amateur, and they then respond.

8. **Be sparing in your use of "reply all".** Most of the time, after two or three emails all of the people copied on the original e-mail don't need to be copied any longer. Only copy those who really need to know what's in follow-on e-mails. If some of the people originally copied miss being copied on future e-mails they will let you know. (Don't hold your breath waiting for this.)

9. **After three to five e-mails stop using e-mail.** E-mail is great for quick answers and simple questions but once the email string has gotten three to five deep pick up the phone or go see the person you've been e-mailing. You will resolve the situation much sooner this way.

If you use most or all of the above tips I bet you will find that your e-mail productivity increases significantly.

Chapter 95
Lessons from Six Sigma

If you aren't familiar with the term, Six Sigma, it is a set of business management practices originally developed by Motorola in 1986. It achieved widespread notoriety after Jack Welch implemented it throughout General Electric during his tenure as CEO. Six Sigma is designed to improve the quality of products or processes by identifying and eliminating defects in products or processes. A Six Sigma process is one in which 99.99966% of the defects or errors are removed from business processes. The thinking is if you can produce near-perfect products or have near-perfect interactions with your customers, your sales and profits will correspondingly increase.

What are some of the major principles of a Six Sigma that you can apply in your business?

1. **Base your management decisions on long-term goals, not short-term goals, even at the expense of short-term profits.** This is easier said than done, especially if you are a public company. This is hard to stick to but thousands of companies have proven that it works. It pushes you to have a strategic plan that you adhere to, sometimes at the expense of short-term profits.

2. **Create continuous process flow so that problems are surfaced.** When you look at each of your business processes and break them down into components it is easier to find and fix problems. For example, take a process such as inventory receiving and break it down into each of its components starting with the original purchase order through the inventory put away process. Examine each step of the process and identify parts of the process that breakdown on occasion, and change the processes to make them more bulletproof.

3. **Use "pull systems" to avoid overproduction.** If you manufacture products, minimize work in process and inventory, cre-

ating a "just-in-time" environment. How much inventory do you have sitting around in your warehouses or on the plant floor tying up cash and gathering dust? You also eliminate inventory that becomes obsolete and needs to be disposed of, thereby hurting profits.

4. **Work to level out the workload and production instead of a stop/start approach.** This can be difficult for any business with last-minute customer demands, but what about the other processes in your business? Keep in mind that stop or wait time is waste.

5. **Build a culture that stops to fix problems to get quality right the first time.** In many companies there is such pressure to produce products quickly, or make deliveries quickly, that quality takes a backseat. Train your associates to understand that they are empowered to stop what they are doing when there is a problem and fix it before proceeding.

6. **Standardized tasks are the foundation for continuous improvement and employee empowerment.** Use Standard Operating Procedures (SOP's) throughout your business and standardize them to best practices. Standard procedures help employees know it is expected to ensure consistency.

7. **Grow leaders who thoroughly understand the work, live the philosophy, and teach it to others.** Train, recognize, and promote those who buy into the system and adhere to it 100% of the time. Also look for people who can teach it to others.

8. **Respect your extended network of partners and suppliers by challenging them and helping them improve.** Set targets, goals, and objectives for your suppliers. What is the net effect if they improve their products, which ultimately improves your customer's satisfaction?

9. **Get personally involved in the processes so you thoroughly understand each situation.** Get out of your office and get on the shop floor or the loading dock so that you personally understand the problems your associates are facing firsthand. It also does wonders for morale when your associates see that you are getting personally involved.

10. **Make decisions slowly, thoroughly consider all options, and implement decisions quickly.** Do your homework, be detailed and focused, then get it done quickly. Do not allow the implementation of a great idea to lose momentum due to a slow pace of getting it done. Wherever you see a potential for value, go after it and save money fast.

11. **Become a learning organization through relentless reflection and continuous improvement.** Constantly be looking at your business for ways to improve both processes and people. Break your business down into individual processes, or have someone do it for you, then drive out waste with passion to find extra value.

If you're having problems with quality which is hurting your bottom line and leading to unhappy customers you ought to consider at least learning more about Six Sigma even if you don't fully implement it in your business. What do you have to lose except for customer complaints?

CHAPTER 96

CONVERTING SUSPECTS TO PROSPECTS

During my career I have noted that most salespeople waste a lot of their time by not properly qualifying their sales prospects. How does one separate *suspects* from *prospects*? I have found that there are four hurdles you need to ensure that a suspect clears before you spend any significant time with them. The four hurdles are:

- **Need.** Does the prospect truly need your product? You should ask a few well-chosen questions to ascertain whether the prospect truly needs your product or service. If they don't really *need* your product or service, move on. Some prospects just like to chat and will waste your precious time if you let them so be sure to determine that they really need your product or service before you make any further calls on them.

- **Authority.** There is nothing worse than spending a lot of time on a prospect only to find that the person you have been romancing doesn't have the authority to make the purchase. You have to be careful about how you determine whether the person you are calling on has the authority to make the purchase because you don't want to make him an enemy. I have found that asking, "Will anyone else be involved in making the purchasing decision? If so, can we invite him to sit in with us?" works most of the time.

- **Timeframe.** When talking with a prospect ask probing questions that will tell you if the prospect's timeframe for making purchase is now. If not find out when the purchase will be made and follow-up closer to that date.

- **Ability to pay.** It always amazes me that salespeople will spend time calling on a suspect without checking with their company's credit department to see if the potential prospect has acceptable credit. It's extremely frustrating to salespeople (and sales managers) to spend weeks or even months trying to get a sale only to have the credit department shoot it down. Don't waste your time calling on suspects until you have found out that your credit department will allow you to accept an order from them.

Time is the most precious commodity for all salespeople but my experience has been that most salespeople end up wasting a lot of time by not ensuring that their suspects have cleared the above four hurdles. If you aren't already ensuring that your suspects can clear the hurdles noted above try doing this and let me know your results. I bet you that your sales will pick up significantly.

CHAPTER 97
THE SECRET OF SALES SUCCESS

Most sales trainers overly complicate the sales process. They teach techniques such as probing questions, trial closes, assumptive closes, and many, many other ways to make a sale. While these techniques have their place in selling, the true secret of sales success is building relationships with your customers. All things being even near equal, customers buy from people they like better than other people calling on them. Even if your initial quote is high, if the customer likes you and wants to do business with you, you will get "last look". Many times your customer will even show or e-mail you your competitors quote because they want to buy from you. In over 35 years of selling when I have been given last look I can count the number of orders I have lost on one hand...with fingers left over.

How do you get customers to like you more than the competition? Here are some techniques I have seen work over the years:

- **Eat breakfast and lunch with a customer daily.** One of our top sales people eats both breakfast and lunch with customers every day. Sometimes he even eats breakfast twice, with two different customers. "Why does he do that", you may ask? Well, sometimes he calls or e-mails a customer and asks him to meet him for breakfast the following day but doesn't hear back from him for several hours so he asks someone else and they accept. Then, the customer he asked first finally calls back and says that he can meet for breakfast. So, our salesperson has one breakfast at 7 AM and a second one at a different restaurant at 8 AM. This isn't quite as tricky as dating two girls at once but you still don't want to get caught at it so you should eat at different restaurants.

- **Entertain.** Find out what your key customers like to do at night and on weekends and then do it with them. It's just that simple. If you have a customer that likes to fish, take him fish-ing. If you like a customer who loves country music you and your wife should take him and his wife to dinner and a show. If you have a customer that likes to hunt, take that customer hunting. It really is that simple. Even if you don't have an expense account you should still entertain to the extent that you can afford to. I think golf is the best way to entertain. With warming up, golf, and lunch or drinks afterward you will spend five or six hours with your customer and *really* get to know him or her.

- **Send cards and presents.** You should send your key customers birthday cards, baby presents, graduation presents for their children, and the like. They don't have to be expensive, and it's actually better if they aren't because then they look like bribes. A simple, thoughtful gift or card goes a long way in building relationships.

- **Get involved with their causes.** If you have a customer who is deeply involved with the Wounded Warrior Project, the Red Cross, United Way, or another worthwhile cause you should get involved with these groups as well. Not only will you spend more time with your key customers but they will appreciate that both of you have a shared cause.

- **The Mackay 66.** Harvey Mackay wrote a classic book of business advice in 1988 called *Swim with the Sharks without Being Eaten Alive*. In the book he touts the Mackay 66. This is a list of 66 questions (www.harveymackay.com/pdfs/mackay66.pdf) for you to get the answers to regarding each of your key accounts. You obviously can't get the answer to all 66 questions on one sales call or it will look like an interrogation. Keep the list with you and answer a few questions on each call. Over time you will know more about your key accounts than anyone else calling on them and that will result in a deeper relationship and more sales.

As I said at the outset of this post, most sales trainers overly complicate the sales process. If you aren't already doing some or all of the above try doing it and I guarantee you will see your sales zoom.

CHAPTER 98

LASTING LESSONS FROM BUSINESS SCHOOL

Early on in my career I was fortunate that one of my first employers gave me the opportunity to go to the Executive Management Program at the University of Pennsylvania's Wharton School and I learned many things that have served me well throughout my entire career. Here are some of the top lessons I learned at Wharton:

- **No one plans to fail but most people fail to plan.** I never cease to be amazed when I find that a company that I interact with doesn't have a strategic plan or even a budget. As another friend has said many times, "If you don't know where you're going, any road will take you there". Take the time to plan and budget. It always seems worse than it actually is. In a previous post I mentioned the one-page strategic plan we use in our company. If you didn't see that post here is a link to it.

- **It's all about people.** I would rather have an inferior company with a mediocre product and a great team than the inverse. I have seen great people take a less than stellar product and make it a winner and I have also seen an inferior team destroy a great product or company. If you surround yourself with great people then managing is easy and going to work is fun. If you don't, work becomes drudgery.

- **Invest in education.** A lot of companies don't spend any appreciable money on educating their employees. A lot of times I hear, "It's too expensive" or "We can't spare him or her". My standard comeback to that is, "If you think education is expensive, try ignorance". Ignorance is a hell of a lot more expensive.

- **You cannot improve that which you do not measure.** The mid-20th century quality expert, W. Edwards Deming first coined that phrase and it is as true today as it was then. If you want to improve something (quality, fill rates, response times, etc.) you need to measure it and better yet, post the charts publicly or on your company intranet.

- **It's all about cash.** Many companies manage for profits not cash. Through accrual accounting you can post a profit while you're going broke. Never forget that you pay your bills with cash, not profits. Manage the business to generate cash because there is nothing worse than not being able to make payroll or pay a key supplier because you're out of cash.

- **Invest in technology.** Early in my career, I had a mentor who taught me to spend money on leading-edge technology because, as he pointed out, computers don't get pregnant, they don't go on strike, they don't ask for a raise, and most importantly, they don't join unions. In my current company there were eight people in the accounting office when we bought it and there are now three. Oh, and by the way, sales have almost tripled since we bought the company 10 years and two recessions ago.

I learned a lot of other things in business school but these are the main lessons that come to mind.

CHAPTER 99

BUILDING A COMPANY THAT'S "BUILT TO LAST"

Most of the people I know that own companies don't seem to realize that companies have personalities just like human beings. However, most companies with which I am familiar have ended up with a "personality" by default. These companies become known for certain things without having planned for the company to have been known for those things. By this I mean some companies are known for being fun to do business with, some are known for being difficult to work with, some are envied for how happy their employees seem to be, some are known for being difficult to deal with, etc. However, I only know a few companies that consciously set out to create the persona for which they are known.

If you were going to build a company and consciously strive to be known for certain things what would they be? In our case we have consciously tried to build a strong, efficient, profitable, and fun company. How do you build a strong, efficient, profitable, and fun company? Below are some of the things that we have consciously attempted to do:

- **Be very selective in our hiring.** Experience has taught me that we can't change the people we hire so we better be very careful to hire the right type of people. As mentioned in previous posts, we do extensive interviewing, background checks, and psychological assessments to make sure that we are hiring the right type of person that will fit in with our culture. If you do this properly you are a long way down the road towards building a successful company where high achievers want to work.

- **Put aside money for a "rainy day".** If we had not done this in our company we would not still be in business over four years after the construction industry began a near free-fall. If you have reserves you don't have to do things such as pay your suppliers late; miss payrolls; lie to suppliers, customers, and your employees; and most of all you don't have to touch the third rail of business which is to not remit to the government taxes you have collected on their behalf. Not remitting taxes to Uncle Sam is sheer insanity and should never, ever be done.

- **Automate.** One of the biggest parts of creating an efficient company is to automate as many tasks as possible. Any time you can automate a manual process you decrease the chance of a mistake being made, you need a smaller staff, and you eliminate jobs that are drudgery for people to do and that only make them unhappy.

- **Treat people with respect.** You would think I wouldn't need to say this but I am still amazed when I visit with fellow business owners and I see and hear how some of them treat their employees. I go out of my way to say "please" and "thank you" but I see other business owners that bark orders and treat their employees like indentured servants. I pointed this out to one owner only to have him tell me, "I pay them well so why should I have to say please to get them to do something"?

- **Treat everyone the same.** We do not have two benefit plans; one for management and one for the rank-and-file. Believe it or not, a lot of companies that I interact with have a gold-plated benefit plan for management and a bare-bones plan for everyone else. Not only do I think this is wrong, but once the word gets out about this morale is destroyed forever. I also hate reserved parking spots, especially those with canopies over them. I know of one company that cut everyone's pay during the recession and then the owner and his son each got a new Mercedes. Gee, I wonder why their employees hate them?

- **Avoid layers of management.** The more layers of management in a company, the further away management is from customers and employees. Plus, information gets filtered as it bubbles up from the bottom to the top and in many cases by the time it gets to senior management it bears little resemblance to what really happened. You also save a lot of money by not having layers of middle management. It was harder to have a lean organization before e-mail and cell phones but advances in technology have allowed us to have a very flat organization that is very responsive to customers and employees.

- **Deal with problems quickly.** Problems, unlike fine wine, don't get better with age. Whether it is a customer problem or an employee problem, deal with it as fast as possible, provided that you are comfortable that you have the facts straight. If you have a culture of dealing with problems quickly your company will stick out versus your competitors because most companies take too long to resolve problems and by the time they do the customer or employee relationship is irreparably harmed.

- **Create a culture of accountability.** If you build an organization where people are accountable and do what they say they're going to do, when they say they're going to do it, your job will be so much easier. Conversely, if you tolerate excuses and missed deadlines both you and your employees are going to be miserable.

- **Take extra good care of your top performers.** Early in my career one of my mentors told me that he would rather have one $100,000 a year person than two $50,000 a year people. It seemed odd to me that he wanted to pay an employee that much money back in 1979 until he explained to me that one person worth $100,000 a year generally does the work of three or more people, you only have fringe benefits to pay on one person, and someone that well-paid rarely leaves you because jobs that pay that much ($200,000-$300,000 in today's dollars) aren't readily available.

- **Give recognition where recognition is due.** A handwritten note sent to a top performer at home, a dozen roses sent to a top salesperson's wife to thank her for tolerating the long hours her husband worked to have a big month, handwritten birthday and Christmas cards, $100 bills (or more), taking an entire department out for lunch, and other tokens of recognition go a long way. You don't always have to give someone a five or six figure bonus check for them to feel appreciated.

- **Have fun.** This is last but not the least of the things I recommend you do to build a solid company. Keep it light around the company, don't always be serious, and look for ways to have fun with your co-workers. If you create a fun environment it won't feel so much like "work".

CHAPTER 100

HOW TO KEEP YOUR COMPANY OUT OF COURT

It's a sad fact of life these days that we live in a very litigious society. We read in newspapers and see on television every day a vast number of lawsuits for real and imagined grievances. Given the propensity of people and companies filing lawsuits for just about any reason, how do you keep your company out of court? Here are some of the ways we have managed to stay out of court over the years:

- **Create a culture of not breaking laws.** I have been fortunate that early in my career my mentors stressed the importance of operating within the law. It never ceases to amaze me how many people don't. For example, I have acquired companies that were paying every single employee on salary, in blatant violation of wage and hour laws. Amazingly, very few of these companies ever had a complaint lodged against them for doing this. If you do break wage and hour laws you are liable for treble damages on the unpaid overtime.

- **Pay your taxes and fees.** A prominent business leader in my hometown went to jail for tax evasion a few years ago in his early 70s. I can't imagine how horrible it had to be for his family to visit him in prison at that age. Prison is terrible at any age but I imagine it is even worse when you are elderly. Plus, his once sterling reputation has been forever destroyed. You especially need to make sure that you never fail to pay the taxes you withhold from your employee's paychecks. Failing to do this can land you behind bars. I have seen companies in desperate straits not remit payroll withholding taxes and end up regretting it. I would let my company go under before I would ever fail to pass through payroll taxes to the government.

- **Obey rules and regulations.** One company that I acquired had drivers that were driving large trucks without the proper commercial driver's license. To me, that is sheer insanity. If one of those drivers hit a minivan with a mom and four kids the resultant judgment would have broken the company. I just don't understand why people run that risk.

- **Do background checks.** Many business owners with whom I come in contact don't do a background check before hiring a new employee. Given that you can get a complete background check immediately, over the Internet, for less than $100, I can't understand why anyone would hire someone without getting a full background check. Not only does this keep you from hiring criminals but this could keep you out of jail because if an employee who was hired without a background check killed another one of your employees the financial settlement could destroy your company, not to mention living with that guilt the rest of your life.

- **Improper interview questions.** I have found that many companies allow managers who have never been educated about what you can and can't ask on an interview conducting interviews with prospective employees. I have interviewed people who have shared with me inappropriate questions they were asked on prior interviews and it can be appalling. Again, in our litigious society this is unnecessarily leaving you and your company open to a damaging lawsuit.

- **Not having an employee handbook.** A good employee handbook can also save you money and/or keep you out of jail. Key topics such as sexual harassment, proper work rules, safety guidelines, overtime rules, and other important subjects are all part of a well-written employee handbook. Absent an employee handbook your employees will just wing it and that can get you in a lot of trouble. Also, make sure that you have each employee sign a form acknowledging that they have received and read your handbook and keep that in their personnel file in case they ever bring an action against you and claim that they were never told your work rules.

- **Failure to do employee reviews and warning notices.** If you terminate someone for poor performance but have never given him or her an annual review documenting the poor performance you are leaving yourself wide open to a lawsuit. In between annual reviews you should also document subpar behavior with written warning notices. If you have a solid system of doing annual reviews and giving written warnings for poor performance you can avoid costly settlements from wrongful discrimination or discrimination suits. Absent those things you are leaving yourself wide open to a large settlement.

- **Failure to investigate employee complaints.** If you have an abusive supervisor who is violating the rules in your employee handbook and you ignore those complaints you are again begging for trouble. You are actually better off to not have an employee handbook than to have one that you do not enforce. Each and every complaint lodged against a supervisor or a coworker needs to be fully and thoroughly investigated and discussed with your attorney unless you look good in stripes.

- **Not telling the truth to government officials.** Sometimes, even the best run company ends up being accused of violating the law or committing a crime. We've all seen plenty of examples of the cover up being worse than the crime. Anytime you are contacted by a government official you need to instruct all affected employees to tell the whole truth and you are to do the same yourself.

The above is not a complete list of how to stay out of court but experience has shown me that it's a good start.

Chapter 101
How to get Appointments

One of the most frustrating parts of being in sales is trying to get an appointment with a person who doesn't want to meet with you. Before I get into techniques that have worked for me let's examine why some buyers refuse to meet with salespeople from companies with which they are currently not doing business. As I have done a fair amount of buying in my career and as I have asked this question of a lot of my customers here are some of the reasons I haven't agreed to meet with new salespeople as well as some of the reasons customers of mine have told me they duck potential new suppliers:

- **No time.** A lot of buyers are extremely busy, especially in this era of downsizing, and simply don't want to make the time to meet with a potential new supplier.

- **No interest.** Some buyers believe that they are very aware of all of the offerings available to them and they don't think it's a good use of their time to listen to a sales rep for product they have already deemed inadequate.

- **Personal relationships.** Some buyers have developed very close personal relationships with their suppliers and they don't want to jeopardize the relationship. Sometimes I have found, after several wasted years that the person I was trying to meet buys from a relative. I wish someone has just told me that.

- **Bad prior experience with your company.** Many times you will be trying to get an appointment with a buyer who has had a bad experience with your company in the past. This is a tough situation but it can be overcome with persistence and selling skills. I will do a post on how to overcome past problems next week.

- **Kickbacks.** In my over 35 year career I have only been asked for a kickback a few times. However, I have felt, but couldn't prove, that I couldn't get an appointment with a buyer because he or she was getting a kickback from a competitor. One of the times I was directly solicited for kickback a buyer who wasn't an owner of the company I was calling on told me that to get his business I would have to pay for a furnished apartment where he could meet with his girlfriend at lunchtime. I refused and never called on this person again.

- **Your product is too expensive.** Some buyers purchase on price only so if you represent a product sold at a premium price most buyers who are doing business with a lower-priced competitor of yours will refuse to meet with you.

The above is not an all-inclusive list of reasons why buyers won't meet with you but it's fairly comprehensive. I think it's helpful to know what you're up against when you're having trouble getting an appointment so you can formulate strategy to secure an appointment.

Given the above how do you get an appointment with someone who doesn't want to meet with you? Here are some of the things that have worked for me over the years.

A referral from someone your prospect respects. I have found this to be the best way to get in front of a prospect who has been ducking me. I ask around to my other customers until I find several who know the prospect and, if I have a good relationship with them, they will call the prospect on my behalf and recommend that he or she meet with me. When you can get *several* of your customers to call one of your prospects with which they have a close relationship you will almost always be able to get an appointment.

- **Request an appointment via e-mail.** I have found that most busy people hate phone calls as they are intrusive but I, and my top salespeople, have found that a well-written e-mail can get you an appointment. Your e-mail needs to be brief and well-written enough to grab the prospect's attention. For example, one of our top salespeople sends an e-mail to out-of-town project managers doing a job in his area requesting a brief appointment. He researches which products are specified on the job and then points out the products that we distribute that are going to be used on the project. He also mentions other similar jobs we have supplied. His e-mails almost always result in an appointment... and better yet, orders.

- **Call early or late.** If a prospect doesn't respond to your e-mail and you can't get past his or her assistant, call early or late when the assistant isn't there. Most busy people come in early and stay late and their assistant is usually there only during traditional business hours. I have called busy people at 6:30 AM and they were so shocked and impressed that a salesperson would be calling that early that I was granted an appointment.

- **Request an early morning appointment.** When I get to a prospect but they tell me they're too busy to meet with me I ask if I can meet them at 6 or 6:30 AM before their phones start ringing. Again, most busy people are surprised that any salesperson would ask for a meeting so early (as most buyers think salespeople are lazy) but this has worked for me several times. I make sure to show up a bit early and bring coffee and donuts with me. Several of these early morning appointments ended up stretching on for hours.

- **Send an unusual sized package.** When none of the above has worked for me I have had some success putting a letter inside box the size of a microwave oven and sending it via Federal Express. Everyone signs for a package of that size because they think they are getting some sort of gift. When they see my letter inside some prospects (but not all) are impressed with my ingenuity and give me a call and agree to an initial meeting.

- **Send part of a gift.** One friend of mine had a lot of success sending large prospects a glass case with a stand that would hold a football. A letter was sent with the glass case explaining that my friend had a football signed by all living Super Bowl winning quarterbacks that goes inside the case and he will be happy to deliver it if he can get an appointment. He said this was expensive (about $500) but it almost always worked. Obviously, you should only do this with prospects that have the ability to buy a lot from you.

- **Pay for the appointment.** What do I mean by this? On a few occasions nothing I did worked and I couldn't get an appointment with some very lucrative prospects. In those cases I would show up at their office and tell the receptionist or assistant who had previously told me several times that the buyer wouldn't see me that I would pay $1000 for 15 minutes of the buyer's time. I asked that the receptionist or assistant tell "Mr. Busy" that I know that "time is money" so I was willing to pay $1000 for 15 minutes of his time. I said that I would leave after 15 minutes if the buyer said I wasted his time. If the buyer is interested and asks me to stay then I get the thousand dollars back. I never once had a prospect keep the thousand dollars. Again, I think this worked because it was so novel and imaginative. One of the people I did this with remains a close personal friend. We often laugh about how I finally got an appointment with him.

CHAPTER 102

HOW TO OVERCOME A CUSTOMER'S PRIOR BAD EXPERIENCE WITH YOUR COMPANY

One of the most daunting tasks for any salesperson is trying to repair a relationship with a customer when one of your predecessors did something that totally turned the customer off on your company. Anyone who has ever been in sales has heard a customer say something like, "You have some nerve coming in my office after what your company did to me back in 1999". During my career I never cease to be amazed about how long some customers hold a grudge over something (real or imagined) done to them by someone else from your company, sometimes many, many years ago. Overcoming a grudge that has been held for a long time is extremely challenging, but not impossible. I have been able to overcome most, but not all, past grudges by doing some or all of the below things:

- **Referral.** If you have a happy customer that knows the grudge holder very well ask that customer to call on your behalf and vouch for you. If you can get a customer that is a friend of the person you are trying to sell after a past mishap, a referral, or better yet several, can get you back in the door.

- **A credit good on the first order.** I have given a former customer a $500 credit good on their first order as an apology for past missteps and as a peace offering. This has worked for me more often than not. One time a former customer used the credit on a $5500 order, the first sale we made to him in over 20 years. That was the best $500 I ever spent. I got a nice order, and better yet, resumed selling a customer others in our company had given up on. That customer ended up buying over $80,000 from us over the next twelve months.

- **A sincere apology.** If you are able to get in front of the aggrieved party a sincere apology can also work. I have said things like, "Mr. Jones, I understand that my predecessor made some serious mistakes in handling your account and beyond apologizing on behalf of my company, all I can say is that if you give me a chance you will see that I am different." I then make a point of handing the customer my business card and I point out that my office, home, and mobile numbers are all on the card and that he or she can call me 24/7 with any problems in the future. It's amazing how far a sincere, heartfelt apology will get you.

- **Ask for a small order to prove your worth.** I have asked customers that haven't bought from us in years to give me even a small order just to test me as to how I service my accounts. I had one customer give me a $150 order after months of begging for an order. I ensured that he received his shipment without any hitches, and exactly when I said he would. He was so impressed with the amount of care I exhibited on a small order that his next order was $7000. We are still selling that customer six years later.

- **Persistence.** When all else fails, be persistent. Persistence doesn't work with all types of customers but I have found that, generally speaking, the type of customer that I want to sell is a fair person and is impressed with persistence. If you refuse to take no for an answer (without being a pest) you can wear down even the most bitter former customer.

CHAPTER 103

MISTAKES TO AVOID
WHEN SELLING YOUR COMPANY

Even though the economy is still weak many business owners who did the right things to survive "The Great Recession" have had enough of being an entrepreneur and are selling out. There has been a recent rash of sales of companies, some of which have been in business for three generations. Having gone through three downturns in my career I understand the temptation to "chuck it all" and sell out. Having bought five companies in my career I have seen a lot of sellers make mistakes that cost them a lot of money. Here are the main mistakes to avoid when selling your company:

- **Not using professional advisors.** The owners of most of the companies I have purchased didn't use professional advisors. They used their accountant from Rotary and a lawyer they play golf with. As your business is probably the biggest asset you will ever sell, hire the best transactional lawyer and accountant you can find and also use a middle market investment banking firm or business broker. There are a lot of rookie mistakes that first-time sellers make and, I know from experience, they sometimes leave millions on the table.

- **Asking too much for your company.** Another reason to use professional help is that most sellers have an unrealistic idea about the value of their company. Most small business owners view their company as their "baby" and it's just as hard to admit you have an ugly baby as it is to admit that your company isn't worth what you wish it was. Professional advisors will show you "comps" so you can see what similar companies have sold for so you can sign off on an asking price that your advisors realistically can get for you.

- **Trying to hide major problems.** If a potential buyer uncovers a major problem that you have clearly hidden it can kill the whole deal. As a buyer, anytime I found a problem that I was certain was hidden from me on purpose I got worried that I would not find several other major hidden issues so I walked away from the deal. All businesses have problems and some have major problems. When selling a company the best way to deal with a major problem is to be upfront about it, explain it, and forget about it. You will score points with the buyer for not trying to hide it.

- **Letting it be known that your company is for sale.** If you are going to have professionals "shop" your company make sure that they do it discreetly so that your employees and competitors don't find out. This is easier said than done but I have done many deals that stayed secret until the day of the closing when we announced it. If your employees find out the company is for sale some of them will start jumping ship because they will be afraid they are going to be laid off by the buyer. This can be highly disruptive, and even fatal, to your company. Also, if your competitors know that you are selling out and you are in an industry where customers cannot tolerate any disruption in the supply chain your competition will tell your customers that the sale of your company is going to cause late deliveries and other problems and this can cost you much needed sales, or even some customers. Stress to your advisors that they are not to shop your company to anyone you have not signed off on.

- **Not getting a signed nondisclosure agreement from potential buyers.** Believe it or not, I have dealt with sellers who were representing themselves who didn't even make me sign a confidentiality agreement before letting me review their books and meet their key employees. Don't show anything more than a one-page executive summary to a potential purchaser without a signed confidentiality agreement. I have found that most confidentiality agreements don't have a "no hire" clause. What this means is the confidentiality agreement should have a clause prohibiting the potential buyer from hiring any of your employees for a period of at least three years. You don't want an insincere buyer to see your books, meet your key people, not go through with the deal, and then hire some of your best performers.

- **Negotiating with only one buyer.** It never ceases to amaze me when someone sells their company to the first person that approaches them without talking to other companies. One friend of mine was excited about receiving an offer of $12 million for his company. He had no debt so the full $12 million would go to him, at least until the government took their cut. I urged him to use a middle-market investment banker to prepare an offering memorandum (a.k.a. "book") and shop the company to a few prescreened buyers that were acceptable to the seller. Instead of taking the $12 million offer he ended up selling out for $28 million. He paid the investment banking firm almost $1 million in fees, but as you might imagine, he said it was the best money he ever spent.

- **Not planning for the tax ramifications of the sale.** Again, if you've never sold a company before the tax implications of the sale of a closely held business can make your head spin. Professional advisors can significantly reduce the tax bite and pay for themselves several times over. Don't skimp on using experienced tax professionals.

- **Being too eager to sell.** Even if your business has no hidden problems you don't want to appear to be too eager to sell. A savvy buyer who meets an eager seller will not make his best offer as he will be able to deduce that you are anxious to sell. Again, by using professionals they will interface with the buyer and negotiate on your behalf. However, you will still be in many meetings with the buyers and you need to be careful to not look overly interested in selling out. It's best if you come up with excuses for selling such as, "My kids aren't interested in this business" "I want to sell before the capital gains tax rates increase", or similar statements. I know it's hard to believe but I have had sellers tell me that they were selling because they were tired of the business and just wanted to get out. Statements like that do not get you full price for your company.

- **Overstating the future prospects for your company.** I have never yet met a seller who didn't show me "hockey stick" projections for their business in the future. Most of the time the business for sale had modest past and present earnings but the forward projections accelerate to where, if you plot them on a graph, the past and future earnings trend line looks like a hockey stick. The vast majority of the time you will be dealing with a savvy buyer who won't believe such projections. When I have bought companies and seen such projections I immediately discount them. If you show future sales and earnings growth of more than 20% a year no buyer is going to believe them. Make your projections realistic and you will score points with the buyer because buyers rarely see realistic projections.

- **Not fully understanding all of the terms of the sale.** A lot of entrepreneurs are not detail people so they just sign a purchase and sale agreement without reading and understanding each and every word. Do this at your own peril. I have seen many, many sellers say after the deal was done say, "Oh, so that's what that paragraph meant." No matter how short your attention span, when you are selling your company, take as much time as necessary until you fully understand, and agree with, all of the terms of sale.

No matter how worn out you might be from the last four or five years, if you decide to sell, get the best advisors you can find and listen to them. Then stay deeply involved in the process and make sure that you understand every single word in the purchase and sale agreement. If you don't, be prepared to leave a substantial amount of money on the table.

Chapter 104
Positive Management

One of the great lessons that I got from Ken Blanchard's best-selling book, *The One Minute Manager*, was to "catch people doing things right" instead of focusing on catching your employees doing something wrong. It's much easier to reinforce an employee's strengths than it is to correct a weakness. Plus, as my friend and mentor, Bill Lee, is fond of saying, trying to change adult human behavior is like trying to teach a pig to sing. A, it can't and B, you only aggravate the pig when you try.

Here are some of the positive management techniques that have worked for me over the years:

- **Praise in public, give constructive feedback in private**. This may sound very basic but most of the managers I know don't always do this. Most employees never recover from being publicly criticized. Sometimes, in the heat of battle, it's hard to not "jump on" an employee who makes a serious mistake but you need to learn to control yourself so that you don't do this. If you do it that employee will never trust you again and most of the time he or she will start looking for new job because they feel like their careers over with you. When I give constructive feedback it is always behind closed doors and I always begin and end with positives and I sandwiched the constructive feedback in the middle. No one likes being told they did something wrong but if you do it right, and do it in private, it can be done without lasting damage.

- **Give the credit to your team, take the blame personally.** Your associates will be loyal to you if you let them get all the credit when something goes right in your area. Conversely, when something goes wrong, a good manager falls on his or her sword and takes all of the blame for their team. Managers who do this develop extremely loyal staffs that will walk over hot coals for them.

- **Set clear expectation levels.** I have seen more than one manager give very vague directions to their associates and then explode when things aren't done properly. When I was in the software business I learned the phrase, "It's exactly what I asked for, but not what I wanted." As a manager, give directives in writing and with much specificity as possible. If it's a major project meet with your staff and discuss your request in detail to make sure that they clearly understand the objectives before they start working on the task. It's extremely demoralizing to have your staff work on a project for several weeks or months only to have you say that it isn't what you wanted and they need to start over again. It's also a waste of precious resources to have to do something twice (or more).

- **Make sure you have your facts straight before you criticize someone.** More than once I have called someone into my office and started to express my disappointment in him or her about a project done wrong only to find out that I didn't have my facts straight. Before you ever criticize someone make sure that you fully understand the situation. Always ask for his or her side of the story before you begin to give feedback. You will be glad you did.

- **Be consistent.** Some managers strictly enforce company rules one day and then are lax the next day. No matter what kind of day you are having, be consistent when enforcing company policies and procedures. It's very dispiriting to your employees if one day you are "by the book" and the next day it's anything goes. If you are consistent it's much less stressful on your employees.

- **Don't play favorites.** Another managerial fault that destroys company morale is playing favorites. Most of us have seen this happen in the workplace during our careers. When one person can do no right and another person can do no wrong everyone walks on egg shells. Strive to treat everyone the same.

- **Have a policies and procedures manual.** When I bought my current company there was no policies and procedures manual. I think everyone was supposed to learn what to do by osmosis. Creating a policies and procedures manual is a time-consuming process but if you form a committee to work with you on it not only will you create a great document for people to refer to but as you hash out each of the policies and procedures with the committee you will improve how things are done around your company and get employee buy-in in the process.

- **Be timely**. Some managers give feedback immediately but others wait for months to give feedback. By then the employee, in many cases, can't even remember the transgression. Give feedback on a "real-time" basis and see if you don't find it will be much more effective.

- **Be kind.** Remember the old saying, "People don't care how much you know until they know how much you care." Sometimes an employee makes a mistake because they are distracted due to a serious problem at home, money problems, relationship problems, etc. When someone that reports to you makes a serious error always begin a feedback session by asking if something is wrong outside of the office that you should be aware of. Be careful not to pry but if you just ask an open-ended question you will be amazed what people tell you. If you are then sensitive to the issue it will go a long way towards building trust (and better performance) from that associate.

CHAPTER 105

WHY CUSTOMERS BUY FROM YOU

When I ask salespeople why their customers buy from them I get a variety of answers. I hear, "Because of my great service", "I know a lot about the products they buy", "I have called on them for a long time and they trust me", "Billy and I played football together in high school", "We go to church together", and the like. I have never once heard, "Because my price is lower than the other guy's". The truth is there are a lot of reasons why customers buy from you but one of the biggest reasons is that your customers (assuming that you sell a fair amount) like you more than they like someone else. Why they like you is normally a combination of the above.

What can you do to get more customers to like you more than the other guy? Here are a few things that have worked for me over the years:

- **Don't lie.** This may seem simplistic, but I have seen many salespeople ruin their career by lying to their customers. Don't lie about what your products do, don't lie about when you can deliver... don't lie about anything. If a customer catches you in a lie you may as well move on to another customer.

- **Have your customer's best interests at heart.** Many times in your career you will be confronted with a situation where a customer wants to give you an order for something you know isn't the best solution to their problem. Amateurs take the order. Pros turn it down and steer the customer to the company that has what they need. Passing on orders that aren't the best solution for your customers is one of the best ways to get a customer to like you more than the other guy.

- **Get your customers to trust you.** How do you get customers to trust you? That's simple; don't make claims about your product that aren't 100% true. If your customer sees over time that you're 100% accurate with what you say about your products it will take a lot for a competitor to take this customer away.

- **Get them to respect you.** Respect is similar to trust but different. Respect is pretty much the sum total of the above. Customers also respect winners. Don't ever beg for an order or ever do anything that could be in any way construed unethical. Once your customers respect you they will have little interest in talking to the competition.

- **You offer the best "value".** Amateurs try to get business by having a low price. Pros get business by having the best total value. Total value doesn't necessarily mean best price. It means that all things considered (price, service, quality, delivery time, credit terms, etc.) you offer a better value than the competition. Having the best total value isn't always apparent to the customer. That's where salesmanship comes in. It's incumbent upon you to sell your total value, not just your price.

CHAPTER 106

HOW TO GET REFERENCES WHEN HIRING

I am always surprised when someone hires a person that used to report to me and doesn't even make an attempt to get a reference from me. Yes, I know that a lot of companies refuse to give out information beyond date of hire, date of separation, and job title but you would think that some people would at least try to get a reference. I have found that if you can get five or six references on each candidate your decision as to whether or not to hire the candidate gets significantly easier. I'm aware that candidates give you their best references, but if their best references are lukewarm, doesn't that speak volumes about the candidate? On the other hand, if the references rave about the candidate (but not overly so to where it sounds like they were coached) that helps make the hiring decision much easier. Also, I ask for five business and five personal references and I call all of them and see who will talk to me. (I generally do this while driving when I have plenty of time.) Personal references are generally much more glowing than business references, and are usually not highly objective, but I have heard some great stories about candidates from their friends that have made the hiring decision a snap. For example, I once heard a story from personal reference about how a candidate pulled him out of a burning building. The story checked out with the candidate and I'm a sucker for hiring people that will lay down their lives for their friends. He turned out to be one of the best hires I ever made.

How do you get references in the litigious age we live in when most companies won't tell much? Below are a few things that have worked for me over the years:

- **Get cell phone numbers**. When you ask for references ask for the cell phone numbers of the references. Not only do you not have to talk to wives, children, switchboard operators, and HR managers, but many times you get directly to the person you were trying to reach and you catch them off guard before they put on their "corporate hat".

- **Get the references to lower their guard.** To lower the guard of references I usually say something like, "I have made the provisional decision to hire "Joe" and have a few questions for you about how I can help Joe achieve his full potential. That way, people think the decision has already been made and they'll either help you or, in some cases, through their words or their reaction, let you know that you're making a bad decision.

- **Use a release form.** We have a release form that releases the reference from any and all liability for giving information about our candidate. The release form is signed by the candidate and for some companies, that's enough for them to give you an accurate reference. However, some companies still revert to the old corporate line of not giving out information, even if you have a release form.

- **Ask for names and cell numbers of coworkers.** While many supervisors won't give you information about one of their former direct reports, most former coworkers have no such reservations. If you can talk to several former coworkers of your applicant you can also learn a lot of information. For example, one former coworker of an applicant of mine said to me, "I hear he has licked his cocaine problem, and if so, he should make a great employee for you. He did great for us until he got into coke." Seriously, someone said that to me.

- **Ask for customer references.** Do this especially when hiring for sales positions. However, many other positions come in contact with customers so if you are hiring for customer service, credit manager, or other positions that interact with customers, ask the applicant for customers he or she worked with in a previous position. Good applicants tend to make friends with many customers and are able to furnish you with their cell phone numbers. A customer reference is extremely important to me and if several customers rave about someone I'm interviewing that scores huge points with me.

In summary, don't skip the important hiring step of checking references. If you use the tips above you should be able to get several references that will make your hiring decision much easier and significantly increase your batting average.

Chapter 107

How to Ruin Your Career

Since graduating from college in 1976 and getting into management in 1978 I have seen a lot of young people succeed in business but I've seen a much larger number of people flounder or outright fail. There are only a few ways to succeed in business but there are a lot of ways to fail. Here are some of the ways I have seen people destroy their careers. Avoid these bad habits:

- **Not hitting due dates**. One of the surest ways to destroy your career with me is to develop the habit of not being on time. Whether it is turning assignments in late or getting to work late, if you develop the bad habit of being late this will kill your career at most companies. My father used to tell me it was better to be an hour early than one minute late. So many people think that being on time is optional anymore that you will stand out versus your peers if you are simply on time.

- **Excuse making.** My father also used to say, "There are two things in life: results and excuses. If you don't have the results, I don't want to hear the excuses". Most bosses don't want to hear excuses and if they hear them often enough your career will be short-lived. When you make a mistake, admit it. Don't make it worse by coming up with a long, drawn out, convoluted story to try to avoid taking the blame. When people who report to me do this they don't report to me for long.

- **Not responding to phone calls and emails on a timely basis.** Given that most of us now have cell phones, tablet computers, and laptops, there is no excuse for not responding to phone calls within four hours and not responding to emails within 24 hours. If you regularly make your boss follow-up with you because you didn't respond to a call or email on a timely basis you may as well start looking for a new job. In this tepid economy bosses have too many other options to put up with an employee who doesn't respond in a timely basis.

- **Telling a customer off.** I have overheard employees of mine telling a customer off when a customer irritated them. I don't know why anyone would think they have the right to tell a customer off but I have seen too many people do it over the years. As the legendary sales trainer and motivational speaker, Zig Ziglar, is fond of saying, "When you're tempted to tell off a customer remember that you can feed your ego or you can feed your family, you can't feed them both".

- **Not being prepared.** When I first was promoted into management from a sales job in New York I walked into my new boss' office in Dallas without a notepad. He looked up at me and told me to go get a notepad and never come to his office again without one. His point was that I should take notes on our conversations so that I don't forget what was said. Suffice it to say that I never walked into another meeting with a supervisor (or a customer) without a notepad.

- **Lying.** Nothing will end a career with me faster than lying to me. Once I feel like I can't believe every word someone that reports to me says, I have no use for them. Resist the temptation to shade the truth and always tell the truth, the whole truth, and nothing but the truth.

- **Not learning from mistakes.** Another saying I love is, "The only thing worse than learning from a mistake is *not* learning from a mistake". I don't mind if someone learns from a mistake as long as it's an honest mistake and it doesn't happen a second time. When someone repeatedly makes the same mistake that tells me that they are sloppy, stupid, or both. In any event, I have no use for them.

- **Not "doing your homework".** One of my longtime mentors stressed to me, and the other people who reported to him, that you never meet with a customer or supplier without "doing your homework" prior to the meeting. By this he meant that you should find out as much as possible about the person you're meeting with. This may mean looking up earnings reports from your public suppliers or looking in your computer system to see the sales trends with one of your customers before meeting with that customer. Better yet, have a CRM system and check it for the latest information on your account before you meet with them. When you just "wing it" at a meeting with a supplier or customer it rarely works out well.

There are a lot of other ways to get fired but these are the top ways to lose your job if you work with me.

CHAPTER 108

WHEN TO SAY *NO*

During my almost 40 years in the business world I have seen a lot of people derail their careers by not knowing how or when to say *no*. I know this may sound strange because conventional wisdom says that to get ahead in the business world you should say *yes* to your supervisor and to your customers. While that is generally the case, I have seen a lot of careers get torpedoed because someone said yes to a request when they should have said no.

Many times people get in trouble by taking on tasks for which they are ill-suited or for which they don't have the time to do properly. By trying to be perceived as a team player and taking on a task that they shouldn't have, I have seen more than one career damaged or even destroyed. I'm not saying that you should say no to requests from your manager or a key customer often but when the request is for more than you can reasonably deliver you're better off to nicely say no than to say yes and let down your supervisor or your customer.

When considering saying no, clarify the request being made of you to ensure that you fully understand it. What are you really being asked to do? How will success be measured, exactly what do you need to do to do the task properly? Do you have the proper experience to do the job? If you do all of the above and you conclude that you aren't the best person to do the job, and that you might fail at the task, explain this and politely decline.

Sometimes you have the proper skills to do the task but you still should decline it if you don't have the time to do the task *correctly* by the due date. I had a manager who once reported to me who tried to curry favor with me by saying yes to each and every task I assigned to him. This person thought that by accepting every task willingly that he would get ahead. Unfortunately, he took on more than he could do properly and after he made several major errors I had to terminate him. When I explained why I terminated him he was puzzled. He couldn't understand how saying yes to my every request could lead to his termination. I explained to him that he should have told me that he couldn't do the tasks properly rather than either doing them wrong, or late.

As mentioned above, if you decline a task presented to you by your supervisor you need to do so tactfully. Take the time to review all of the other tasks you currently are working on with your manager so that he or she can see that you are being prudent, not lazy.

Learning when to say *no* might just save your career!

CHAPTER 109

MY GREATEST LESSON FROM ZIG ZIGLAR

The recent passing of Zig Ziglar, noted motivational speaker and sales trainer has caused me to reflect on a great man who influenced my life in a huge way. Early in my selling career Bill Lee gave me some cassette tapes of Zig on the selling process. I found his ideas to be enlightening and his voice mesmerizing. Zig used his voice like a musical instrument and I could listen for hours even if he was reading the phone book. I quickly listened to every tape he ever made, read several of his books, and saw him live many times. However, one of the highlights of my life was spending five days with Zig and his family when he spoke to the family meeting of a business group of which I'm a member. He spoke every day of our meeting, on many topics. Even the young children were enthralled by his speaking style and his message. I fondly remember our son Thomas (who was 15 at the time) patiently waiting in line after one of Zig's presentations so Zig could autograph Thomas' copy of perhaps Zig's greatest book, *See You at the Top*.

While I learned many things from Zig that still benefit me today, the one that helped me the most is the tip he gave us about marriage. Zig, like me, was a workaholic by choice. He loved what he did and so work was fun for him. He said that he and his wife Jean ("the red head") would eat dinner and he would retreat to his study and work some more. Jean wasn't happy about that. After some discussion Zig suggested that after dinner he and Jean would leave the dishes sit and they would talk for a half hour or so and once they had talked about their days and any pressing issues, Zig would do the dishes while Jean relaxed and then, and only then, did Zig go to his study. He said this solved a long standing problem at home and he recommended it.

We started doing this in our home and we still do to this day. It has made Cindy much happier and I enjoy the chats after dinner as well. Try it in your home. I bet it works for you.

Chapter 110
The Key to Success

There have been hundreds, if not thousands, of books written about success and how to achieve it. I know this because I have read more than 100 myself. In the almost 40 years I have been in the business world full-time since graduating from college I have learned that the key to success is very simple: follow-up.

Over the years I have had hundreds of salespeople try to sell me something for one of my businesses, or personally, only to never hear from that person again. Not even once. That always amazes me. I recently needed a small home improvement job done at our home and called five companies that had half page or larger ads in the Yellow Pages in my hometown. In all five cases I got an answering machine or voicemail. (This is beside the point, but all of the recorded messages were amateurish, at best. Another tip: make sure that your company's answering machine or voicemail messages are professional.) Of the five messages that I left, exactly one company called me back. Why spend hundreds or even thousands of dollars a month on a Yellow Pages ad and then not return calls left on your answering machine? I can't fathom why people spend the money on a Yellow Pages ad and don't track the inquiries left on their answering machine to ensure that they are followed up on and to see their closing percentage.

Even though I have been a CEO for a long time I'm still very involved in selling. In fact, I once read that the job description of a CEO is, "best salesperson in the company". There are other definitions but I agree that this is the best job description for a CEO. If you can't sell your company to other people, and you are the CEO, you have a huge problem. But I digress. My point is that I'm involved in major accounts selling, selling banks on loaning us money, selling property owners on giving me a lower price on their property than the asking price, selling people on joining our company, etc. I'm sure you get my point. When I am "selling" I find that the vast majority of the people I'm contacting ignore my first call or email. However, when I follow-up I get to the person I'm trying to reach over 75% of the time. Why is that? My theory is that people are extremely busy these days and simply can't talk to every person who calls them or respond to every email they receive. However, when they are followed up with they can see that the person trying to reach them is a pro, not an amateur, and they respond. Unless it's a very large deal I don't follow up more than three times because then I think you're just being a pest. When you have contacted someone three times and they still won't respond to you they actually *are* responding to you through their silence.

My friend, Dan Adams, says it best: "The key to success is consistent persistence". If you want to be successful be consistent in your persistence. You will find that the following up will improve your closing rate no matter what you're trying to sell.

CHAPTER 111

THE KEY TO SUCCESS
FOR MANAGERS

In my last post I stated that the key to success is follow-up because, simple as it may sound, it has been my experience that the majority of people don't follow up most of the time. The same is true with most managers. I was lucky enough that one of my first mentors, when I was just 23, told me, "People do what you inspect, not what you expect". He felt so strongly about it that he even had a sign with that statement on it in his office.

I have found this to be true. In fact, I spend over two hours first thing every morning sending reminder emails to reports of mine who didn't respond by the due date I gave them. I do this via the Task function in Outlook. When I send an email to one of my associates I always blind copy myself and when I get my copy back in my inbox I transfer it to the Tasks function in Outlook. I generally set a follow-up date seven days hence unless I need a response sooner than that.

Another one of the secrets of effective managers is to never assign a task without also giving a due date. I learned the hard way that when I didn't give a due date and I followed up after a week or so I regularly heard, "You didn't tell me when you needed this". It has been my experience that I have to follow-up much less when I have given a due date and also, when someone doesn't respond by the due date, I have taken away their excuse that they didn't know the task was due. Also, once the people who respond to you learn that you are going to follow up 100% of the time if they don't respond by the due date you will find that the majority will start to respond by the due date. However, If one of my reports chronically misses due dates I terminate him or her. I don't have the time or temperament to be an adult babysitter. I also let it be known why he or she was terminated as the remainder of my associates get a strong message when I do this.

Yes, modern management theory states that Theory X managers follow up with their employees but that Theory Y managers realize that this makes their employees look like they aren't trusted and demoralizes them. I have tried both theories and I have found that with college-educated, white-collar workers, Theory Y works most of the time. However, with high school educated (or even lesser educated) blue-collar workers, Theory X is necessary.

If you aren't assigning due dates when you assign a task, and if you aren't following up 100% of the time, try it for a while and see if you and your associates don't become more effective and productive.

CHAPTER 112
CALENDAR INTEGRITY

One of the people I reported to early in my career was a former IBM executive who taught me the phrase, "calendar integrity". By this he meant that when you had an appointment at a certain time, a report due on a particular date, etc., then you needed to be on time for the appointment/turn in the report on time. Yes, this is a fancy phrase for "being on time" but I have always liked this phrase because of the implication that being on time has to do with your integrity.

Over the last several years I have found that the vast majority of people with whom I come in contact are late to meetings, late with reports, late to dinners, etc. To make matters worse, rarely do I ever get an apology from the person who is late. When I do mention that a person was late they look at me like it is wrong of me to expect them to be on time.

When I speak to college students I point out that one of the ways they can separate themselves from other college graduates is to have calendar integrity. I point out that it's so rare that it's a way they can stand out from the hordes of other college students trying to get jobs. I mention that I frequently have people show up late for job interviews and that if I see that someone can't even be on time for job interview, how can they possibly be on time to meetings and with reports after they are hired?

As we are living in the age of cell phones and smartphones there is no excuse for not calling to say that you are going to be late to a meeting or sending an email to ask for an extension on a due date for a report. Yes, there are unavoidable things that happen that legitimately cause one to be late to a meeting but there is no legitimate excuse for not calling to say you will be late. Also, as most of us are doing multiple jobs due to the weak economy it isn't always possible to be on time with a report. However, as soon as you see that you aren't going to be able to hit a due date you should contact the person to whom you report, and ask for an extension. When I am asked for an extension I almost never fail to grant.

As you seek to differentiate yourself from others throughout your career, practice calendar integrity. I bet it will help you get ahead.

CHAPTER 113
LEARNING FROM BAD EXAMPLES

In several past blog posts I mentioned many of the great bosses and mentors that I've had over the years. I've been very fortunate to have had some fantastic mentors who taught me a lot of things the easy way instead of my learning most things the hard way. Yes, I still made plenty of mistakes, but nowhere near as many as I would've made if I hadn't been fortunate enough to have had some great bosses and mentors along the way.

I'm also fortunate that I have only had two "jerk" bosses during my working years. One of my jerk bosses was a guy I reported to while I was working as a welder in a mobile home plant for one year during college. This boss was a total tyrant to everyone who reported to him but turned into an exemplary manager every time the owner of the mobile home plant came around. He was the most two-faced person I've ever reported to.

My other bad boss came later in my career, after college. He is now deceased, so in deference to the dead I won't give too many details about him as I know that some of my blog readers knew him. I will, however say, that he was an alcoholic who was drunk by noon every day and who was a total dictator. If you reported to him you soon learned to schedule a morning appointment through his secretary so that you could talk with him before he got drunk. All the people who reported to him begged his secretary for morning appointments because they all knew what it was like dealing with him in the afternoon.

The point of all this is I believe I learned more from these bad examples than I did from the great bosses I worked for. I vowed that I would never be like either of these bosses and that I would treat people with dignity and respect, unlike them.

Many years ago I heard the phrase, "No one is totally worthless; you can always serve as a bad example." These bosses sure proved the truth of this axiom. If you have a "jerk" boss ask yourself what things about this boss will you commit to never doing? Make a list and refer to it occasionally. If you're like me, you'll find that you learned a lot of great lessons about what not to do from a bad boss. Avoiding doing these things will help you be a good boss more than you can imagine.

What kind of boss are you? Are you a positive example or negative example? I hope you're a positive role model but if not, take solace in the fact that, "No one is totally worthless; you can always serve as a bad example."

CHAPTER 114
HOW NOT TO SELL ON PRICE

One of the biggest challenges for any business is dealing with customers who are price shoppers. The other big challenge is educating your salespeople on how to respond to requests for lower prices from their customers. Most salespeople who have not received the proper education in dealing with price objections take the path of least resistance and cut the price to get an order. My salespeople are no different. Yes, I have some unbelievable salespeople who know how to fend off requests for lower prices. However, I also have plenty of salespeople who cave in and give a lower price the first time a customer asks for it. Now, if you do not give your salespeople pricing authority they can't cut the price, but in today's fast-paced world I've found that we get a lot of orders because our salespeople don't have to request a price variance from one or two levels above them as with our largest competitor. I was on one sales call where the customer told me that we got the order because our salesperson responded to a price request immediately and our competitor took three days to respond after he got pricing approved by both his district manager and his regional manager.

There is no one correct way to handle pricing. You have to decide what works best for your business. However, if you do give pricing authority to your salespeople you need to ensure that they are properly educated and how to respond to requests for a lower price. One of the best books I've ever read on dealing with price objections was written in 1992 by Lawrence L. Steinmetz, Ph.D., a former professor of management at the Graduate School of Business at the University of Colorado The title of this book is, How to Make Your Prices Stick. I've read many books on selling and, specifically, on handling price objections but Larry's book, in my opinion, is the best.

Below is a review of Larry's book that I found on Amazon. I share it with you as I think the unnamed writer of the review really captured the essence and key lessons of this important book.

The title of this book is somewhat misleading because it does not indicate the full scope of what Steinmetz provides...and achieves. True, he suggests all manner of strategies and tactics to overcome sales resistance based almost entirely on price. (He correctly suggests that those who buy ONLY on price be avoided. More about that later.) However, I think this book's greater value is derived from Steinmetz's systematic and convincing repudiation of various self-defeating mindsets. For example, those who are so desperate to sell (and earn some money) that they make all manner of unnecessary concessions. In effect, they negotiate against themselves. (Steinmetz: "Business is a game of margins, not volume.") Here's another example. Those who fulfill what I call the "Self-Fulfilling Negative Prophecy":

This is NOT a sales manual. Rather, an extended dialogue between Steinmetz and those readers who are reasonably intelligent, very ambitious, highly energetic, eager to learn what they think they know but don't, not easily discouraged, and — most important of all — willing to consider vary carefully what Steinmetz suggests. He requires each reader to set aside their (probably cherished) assumptions about "salesmanship," most of them based on received wisdom that is either obsolete or never true in the first place. Is selling always a "numbers game"? No and Yes. No if the percentage is based on the number of sales made as a result of cold calls to everyone in the telephone directory whose last name begins with "J." Yes if the percentage is based on the number of sales made to carefully selected, pre-qualified prospects. True, there are differences between walk-in sales (e.g. at vehicle dealerships and department stores) and offsite sales (e.g. at the prospect's location). Even so, Steinmetz cites five "cases" (price, quality, service, competence of salesperson, and error-free delivery) which apply to both. I agree completely that "business is a game of margins, not volume." I am also convinced that re-orders (i.e. repeat customers), not merely orders, should be a primary objective. As Steinmetz explains, price may result in one order but quality, service, competence of salesperson, and error-free delivery create and then sustain long-term customer relationships.

Why avoid those who buy only on price? Steinmetz offers nine reasons:

1. Price-buyers take all of your sales time.

2. They do all the complaining.

3. They "forget" to pay you.

4. They tell your other customers how little they paid you.

5. They drive off your good customers.

6. They're not going to buy from you again anyhow.

7. They'll require you to "invest up" to supply their needs — and then they'll blackmail you for a better price.

8. They'll destroy the credibility of your price and your product in the eyes of your customers.

9. They will steal any ideas, designs, drawings, information, and knowledge they can get their hands on.

There are dozens of such checklists, step-by-step processes, reminders, dos and don'ts, cautions, and value affirmations throughout the book as well as hundreds of examples of real-world sales situations. Problems and complications are inevitable. Steinmetz identifies the most recurrent ones and explains how to resolve them. Implicit is Steinmetz's pride in what he views as the profession of sales. He is wholeheartedly committed to quality of product and service. He understands the importance of making prudent promises and then keeping every one of them. He has little (if any) patience with whiners, chiselers, corner cutters, liars, and hypocrites. He views providing service to customers as a privilege, indeed as a moral obligation.

Here in a single volume is a wealth of information and wisdom which Steinmetz has accumulated over a period of many years, presented with a non-nonsense writing style enlivened by his wry sense of humor. All of his advice is eminently practical and easily applicable to most sales situation. However, I presume to offer some advice of my own. Read and then re-read the book, highlighting or underlining whatever seems most relevant to your own situation. Then focus on your most urgent needs. That is to say, do not attempt to apply immediately everything you have learned. Experiment. Take a few prudent chances. Over time, I think you will achieve significant improvement of your skills and a stronger sense of pride in how you earn a living. One final point. Not all prospective customers are worthy of your attention and effort. Concentrate only on the ones who are.

If you are a salesperson, sales manager, or owner and you haven't read this book I urge you to order it (or the audio version) from Larry's website (www.pricingexpert.com/). I guarantee you won't regret it.

Chapter 115

Is Your Website Helping or Hurting Your Business?

When the World Wide Web took off after the IPO of Netscape in 1995 most (but even today) not all companies had a website created or did it themselves in the next few years following their IPO. Unfortunately, some of these first-generation websites are still in existence today and I think they are hurting the companies behind them because they give an old-fashioned or low-tech look to the company. When I was starting out in business in the 70's I would tell a prospective new supplier to send me some of their literature to review. Now everyone just asks for a link to the supplier's website and/or does a Google search on the company. When people look at your company's website does it portray your company in the best possible light? Or, do you look like a late 20th century dinosaur?

Here are a few things to check about your website to ensure that you are getting maximum effectiveness from it:

1. Does your homepage clearly communicate what your company does and how to contact you?

2. Do you list the USP's (unique selling propositions) for your company on your site so that prospective customers can see why you are better than your competition?

3. Do you offer useful content to those viewing your site or is it just blabber about how great you are?

4. Does your site list who your suppliers are and do you have active links to your supplier's websites?

5. Are the suppliers listed on your website still your main suppliers? Do you have any new suppliers you haven't added to your website?

6. Is your website optimized for top ranking in the various search engines that are used today? If you haven't had a professional do SEO (search engine optimization) you should have this done. It doesn't cost much and it can significantly increase your ranking when customers search on the products and services you provide.

7. Do you update the content on your website frequently? I'm always amused when I see content on some of my competitor's websites from three or four years ago. If you want people to go to your website frequently make sure that you refresh the content on a regular basis and that you make it valuable to your customers.

8. Is there a way for your customers to contact you from your website and is it easy to find? (Our toll-free number is in bold on our homepage.) Also, nothing runs a customer off faster than a contact form that requires 10 minutes to fill out.

9. Do you have a process in place to ensure that inquiries from your website are responded to within 24 hours, preferably sooner?

10. Do you have an employment section so that people looking for a job at your company can easily contact you?

11. Do you have the address/phone number of your location and a link to a map so customers can see where you are located? If you have more than one location do you have all of your locations listed, including map links?

12. If you're a business-to-business company that offers house credit is there a link to your credit application on your website?

13. If you are participating in social media (and you should be) do you have links to your Facebook, Twitter, LinkedIn, and other social media sites?

14. Do you use a service such as Google analytics to see how many people are visiting your site, your "bounce rate" (what percent of the visitors to your site only view the home page before moving on - a sure sign that your site is boring), and the average time a visitor spends on your site? There's also a wealth of other data available via Google analytics, and the best part is it's all free!

Remember the old adage, "You never get a second chance to make a first impression". These days your website is generally the first impression a prospective customer gets of your company. What kind of impression are you making?

CHAPTER 116

BUSINESS SCAMS TO WATCH OUT FOR

One thing I have learned from 40 years of being in the business world is that there are a lot of scammers out there who try to separate a business owner from his or her money on a daily basis. Just as people continue to fall for these letters from Kenya and other countries offering to share millions with you if you will help them get the money out of their country, or emails stating that you have inherited millions from an uncle you never met or heard of, there are plenty of business scams as well. Obviously a lot of people continue to take the bait or these criminals wouldn't continue to perpetrate these frauds.

Because of the prevalence of these scams, as well as for many other reasons, I learned long ago to sign all of our Accounts Payable checks. Over the years I have stopped more payments than I can count that had fooled our Accounts Payable department to the point where they had issued a check to the scammers and sent it to me for my signature. As I look carefully through the payables each week I pull these fraudulent invoices out and tear up the checks we have issued to these companies. One of the biggest pieces of advice I can give a small to medium business owner is not to delegate the signing of the checks to someone else. No one will scrutinize the payables as closely as the owner will. Plus, it discourages your employees from trying to issue checks to fraudulent companies they may have set up if they know that the owner looks at every invoice and check.

When I was in my 30s I was CEO of a computer systems company that sold both nationally and internationally. Right after taking over as CEO I started double checking behind our controller who had signed all of the checks (without the CEO reviewing them) for many years. Just in reviewing the first check run I pulled out four fraudulent invoices that were about to be paid. By reviewing all of our payables and signing the checks I have stopped more than fraud. I have also found invoices that were being paid too soon (as well as too late where we had missed the prompt pay discount), expense account abuse (I once saw where one of my employees gave a 100% tip to a waitress. He was obviously trying to impress her on my nickel.), and non-adherence to company handbook rules. I have found subscriptions to nonbusiness related magazines, payments to relatives for work done at outrageous rates, and much, much more.

There also are a lot of other scams that escape the scrutiny of some Accounts Payable personnel. Here are just a few of them:

- **Copier paper invoices.** This is one of the oldest business scams out there. A con artist creates a legitimate looking invoice for copier paper and sends it to thousands of companies whose addresses they get from list brokers. Just like lottery tickets, only a few of them hit, but it only takes a few to make thousands of dollars a month.

- **Printer cartridge invoices.** This is similar to the copier paper scam accept that sometimes these companies actually do provide cartridges. However, invariably, they are of inferior quality and many of them will actually destroy your printer and render your warranty invalid. They send the cartridges with an invoice so some accounts payable people figure the invoice is legitimate as the cartridges were received so someone there must have ordered them.

- **Yellow Pages scams.** We get several invoices a month that look like legitimate invoices for Yellow Page ads. Some of them are so realistic that I have to spend several minutes studying the invoice closely until I finally see some fine print that says, "This is not an invoice. This is a solicitation." Be on the lookout for these because most of them are extremely realistic looking.

- **Renewal of trademark invoices.** We have trademarked our logo and tagline and it is now time to renew the trademarks and I have gotten several invoices warning me that we will lose the rights to our trademarks if I don't remit to them ASAP.

Scam artists search the Federal Register and find the names of companies whose trademarks are expiring and send out extremely realistic and official looking invoices that lead you to believe they are from the federal trademark office. Again, if you look at these very closely you will generally find a statement similar to the one on the fake Yellow Pages invoices stating that it is a solicitation, not an invoice. Trust me, whichever law firm did your trademark filing will be certain to send you a renewal notice. Don't pay an invoice from anyone else.

- **Overseas orders.** Now that email is ubiquitous I, and others in my company, receive emails almost daily from scam artists purporting to be overseas contractors who are having a hard time finding the products we sell in some third world country. They list a large number of products that they need immediately and they even offer to have someone pick up the materials as they will take care of the overseas shipment. They always offer to pay with a credit card. When I first bought my current company the Internet was still in its infancy and a couple of my employees fell for this. The credit cards were initially approved but after the materials left our premises we would hear several days later that the card was fraudulent and the credit card company was not going to be paying us. A lot of business owners think that as long as a credit card is approved at the time of purchase they are out of the woods. This is not the case. Credit card companies reserve the right to reverse the charge if it turns out to be fraudulent. When I get an email asking us to provide materials for overseas jobs I respond that we only do so with payment in advance, via wire transfer. As you might imagine, I never hear back from them.

- **Better Business Bureau complaints.** We also get a fair number of emails purporting to be from the Better Business Bureau stating that a complaint has been made against our company and that we need to click on the attached link to read the complaint. If you click on the link, a virus infects your computer network and can do untold damage to your hardware, your software, and your data. Some hackers even gain access your bank account and write checks from it or wire transfer money to their untraceable overseas accounts. If anyone ever files a complaint against you with the Better Business

Bureau you will get a letter from them, not an email. I have verified this with the head of our local Better Business Bureau.

- **Patent trolling.** This is one of the newer scams. How it works is you get a very realistic and official looking notice from a software company stating that your company is using software that violates one of their patents. The letter demands that you purchase a license for their software or they will lock down your computer system. Believe it or not, some of these scammers (most of them based overseas) actually have the ability to lock down your computer system so none of your employees can use it. They gain access to your computer system when someone in your company clicks on a link in a spam email and opens up a Trojan horse that invades your computer system. This is another thing that, despite the numerous warnings, some people continue to do. Do not click on a link in any email from a person you do not know very well! If you get a letter alleging a patent violation turn it over to your local police department immediately.

As I said, this is not a complete list of all of the scams out there. New scams pop up every day. Whenever you're not sure about whether something is a scam go to www.scamwatch.com and search for information about the possible scam. This can save you a lot of time, money, and aggravation.

CHAPTER 117

HOW TO HIRE, MANAGE, AND RETAIN MILLENNIALS

"Millennials" are employees of aged 18 to 34 years old. For us baby boomers managers many of us have a hard time relating to millennials. I hear managers my age (58) constantly lament that, "they don't make them like they used to". Well, of course they don't, times change and so do people. I have had an easier time relating to millennials than most people my age because I was CEO of a software company for 15 years.

When I was first entering the job market in the late 70s it wasn't unusual to work for one company your entire career. That is no longer the case. Research has shown that millennials' average stay a company is two to five years. Company loyalty is not the strong suit of most millennials. Why is that? Well, it's my observation that millennials aren't loyal to their companies because their companies aren't loyal to them. The turbulent economy of the last several years has resulted in mass layoffs, restructurings, pay cuts, benefit cuts, and other things that don't engender loyalty in employees.

So, how do you motivate and retain millennials so that your investment in their training isn't wasted? Here are some things that have worked for me:

- **Training and conferences.** Millennials are more loyal to their profession than to their employer. However, if you help your millennial employees stay on top of their profession by sending them to conferences and training classes it will help you retain them.

- **The latest technology**. If you allow your millennial employees to upgrade the computer hardware and software they use when working for you to the latest and greatest it will improve your ability to retain them. Nothing turns a millennial off more than to make them use outdated technology. Conversely, if you allow them to constantly upgrade and work with the latest technology your chances of retaining them are increased significantly.

- **Flexible work hours.** Unless absolutely necessary, don't hold millennials to rigid work hours. Manage results, not technique. If they want to come in late and stay late, as long as it doesn't inconvenience coworkers or customers, why not?

- **Working from home.** If your millennials have tasks they can be done from home, let them work from home occasionally. Married millennials generally are in marriages were both the husband and wife work and if you allow your employees to work from home on occasion so they can watch a sick child or be there to let the cable repair man in, that will help endear them to you.

- **Dress code.** Don't require millennials to adhere to a 1950s dress code. That doesn't mean that they should be allowed to come to work slovenly but if you allow them to dress casually and comfortably not only will they stay with you longer but you will probably get more productivity from them.

- **Bringing pets to work.** This may not work in a doctor's office but our daughter works at an advertising agency where employees are allowed to bring their pets to work on Fridays. When our oldest son was first out of college he worked at a software company that allowed their employees to bring pets to work every day. If it won't disrupt your workplace too much, consider allowing pets to be brought to work.

- **Fun work environment.** A lot of companies now have foosball machines, pool tables, Ping-Pong tables, and the like available for employees to use on breaks or as stress relievers. Again, if your business is a law firm, this may not be right for you but it may work for many other types of companies.

- **Drinks, snacks, and meals.** A lot of software companies on the West Coast started the trend of providing free drinks, snacks, and meals as a way to keep employees at work instead of going out for lunch or leaving early for dinner. If you can afford it, this is a great way to retain millennials.

CHAPTER 118

HOW WE WERE SCAMMED

I find it ironic that less than a month after writing Chapter 116 on *Business Scams to Watch Out For,* our company was the victim of a scam not described in that chapter. It was a new one to me. I share the details with you to perhaps save your company from a similar fate.

The scam began when one of our outside salespeople received a fax from a company in a state in which we do not do business, asking for a quotation on a product that is readily available anywhere. Our salesperson faxed back pricing and, low and behold, received a purchase order without ever talking to the "customer" or negotiating the price. I was not informed of this as I would have definitely smelled a rat. No contractor buys something without at least a little haggling about the price. And no one I know does business with a new company solely via fax. Had I been informed of this at that time I would have killed the deal immediately. However, the downside of having nine locations is that I don't know everything that is going on at each of our branches.

Our salesperson got this new "customer" to fax in a completed credit application. Our credit manager faxed out credit reference forms to the three companies they listed as references and promptly got an extremely positive response from all three. This was warning sign number two. It normally takes several attempts to get a credit reference to complete our credit check form. When all three companies responded quickly, and with glowing reports on this prospective new customer, another red flag should have gone up. Again, I wasn't informed of this. (It now appears all three "credit references" were fake companies with fax numbers set up by the scammer.)

Our credit manager also pulled a D&B report on this company and, while it only had sparse information on this company, there was nothing negative about them and the D&B report said that they average paying their bills only two days past the due date. Based on their credit references and the D&B report our credit manager set them up with a $5000 credit line and this new "customer" made a $3000 purchase at a much higher than average gross margin. Red flag number three.

Less than a month later, and before the initial purchase was due, the customer faxed in another request for quotation. Our salesperson, thinking he had lucked into a sheep he could fleece, put an even higher gross margin on his second quote and, to his surprise; he received another PO via fax. His quotation was for almost $20,000 this time, at a 44% gross margin, in an industry where gross margins in the 20's are the norm. As this purchase would be over the customer's $5000 credit line, our salesperson spoke with our credit manager who, based on the previous false information obtained during the initial credit check, increased their credit line, and approved the sale.

When the initial purchase wasn't paid in 30 days our automated system sent a nice letter asking if the payment had been overlooked. At 45 days, our automated system sent a slightly more pointed letter asking for payment. At 60 days, our credit manager called this customer only to find that the phone line had been disconnected. At that point she did a Google search on their company name and found multiple companies complaining about having been scammed by this company. At that point her stomach sank and she informed me that it looked like we had been the victim of a scam.

We have since filed a complaint with the police department in the town listed on their credit application. The police told us that the FBI is involved as this company scammed over 700 companies out of over $20 million in merchandise across 35 states. Our cost for the merchandise we lost in this scam is almost $13,000. Yes, there is some chance that the FBI will find these people and recover our merchandise, but I'm not very hopeful of that.

We now have a new policy in our policy and procedures manual. It basically states that no one is to sell an out-of-town company unless we receive payment via wire transfer or a certified check, **prior to our shipping the materials**. I hope that by sharing this embarrassing episode it will save even one of you from the same painful experience.

CHAPTER 119

HOW TO GET AHEAD
IN A BIG COMPANY

When our middle child, Thomas, graduated from Georgia Tech a few years ago his first job was with a multi-billion dollar a year company. As I worked for a similar company early in my career and was fairly successful Thomas asked me for some tips on how to get ahead in a big company. Over the years several friends asked me for similar advice for their children. Below is what I told Thomas and what I still say today.

1. Arrive at least 15 minutes earlier than required and stay at least 15 minutes later than you have to. Establish a reputation as a hard worker quickly.

2. When someone asks for a volunteer in a meeting, especially for a dirty job, raise your hand. Most people just do enough to get by and look down at their shoes when volunteers are being solicited for dirty jobs.

3. Hitch your wagon to a star. By this I mean if it becomes apparent that someone in your division is a superstar and is above you on the org chart, let him or her know that you want to continue to work with them as they move up. Conversely, if you end up working with someone whose career is about to implode try to get a transfer away from that person as soon as possible.

4. Dress for the job you want, not the job you have. However, don't out dress your boss. If your boss dresses like a slob and you look like you stepped off of the cover of GQ he will try to get you fired.

5. Always go to work with freshly shined shoes. A lot of young people right out of college wear cheap shoes, and to make it worse, wear them to work all scuffed up. By a few pairs of good shoes, put cedar shoe trees in them nightly so that the

leather doesn't wrinkle, and wear a freshly polished pair every day. Also get a travel shoe shine kit and take it out of town with you on business trips. That way if your shoes get scuffed you can polish them in your hotel room.

6. Don't talk much in meetings when you're first starting out. Listen, take notes, and only speak when your opinion is solicited. No one likes to hear a loud mouth right out of college who thinks he already knows it all.

7. This also applies to day-to-day interactions. Listen much more than you talk. People respond very well to other people who at least consider their point of view. Before you share your opinions, or even facts, about an issue, listen to others, really consider their point of view and then, if appropriate, offer your opinion.

8. Under promise and over deliver. If you're asked when you can have a project done, add about 25% to your estimate and then if you deliver on time people think you're early.

9. Seek a mentor. Once you see who the superstars are that are one or two rungs above you, ask one of them to mentor you. Most people are flattered to be asked to be a mentor and you will learn a lot of things the easy way.

10. Take good notes in meetings. There's nothing worse than taking bad notes and ending up doing the wrong thing and then having to start all over again.

11. Have a good follow-up system and put every single task you need to do in it. **Don't ever be late with anything - be it a report, memo, or anything.**

This advice has been helpful to Thomas (who is now an analyst for a huge corporation) and many others. If you, or someone you know, works for a large company give these tips a try.

CHAPTER 120
TIPS ON INTERVIEWING FOR A JOB

A former coworker commented on one of my recent blog posts and asked if I would do a post on tips on interviewing for a new job. She said that her nephew was having trouble getting a job and she wanted a few tips. So, here is some advice on interviewing:

- **Dress slightly better than the job for which you are interviewing.** Try to find out how people dress for the position for which you are interviewing and dress slightly better than normal. I say slightly better because you don't want to show up for an interview for a forklift operator position dressed in a suit. Conversely, you don't want to show up for a job in a big company's accounting department dressed in blue jeans and work boots. You also don't want to show up the person you are interviewing with.

- **Arrive 15 minutes early for the interview.** This will allow for getting lost or being stuck in traffic. You have no idea how many times people show up late for an interview with me. Remember, you never get a second chance to make a first impression. Make sure your first impression is good by being early.

- **Make sure your shoes are polished.** I see many people show up for interviews dressed nicely but wearing scuffed or dirty shoes. My father used to say that getting all dressed up but wearing unpolished shoes was like driving a brand-new Cadillac with dirty hubcaps. I agree.

- **Make sure your fingernails are trimmed and clean.** Men should make sure that their nails are evenly trimmed and that there is no dirt under their nails. Women should also refrain from extremely long fingernails and those painted with unusual designs. Such fingernails give the impression that you don't work hard.

- **Your clothes should be clean and pressed.** I frequently interview people who are wearing clothes that look like they were slept in. Make sure your clothes are impeccably clean and not wrinkled.

- **Bring a copy of your resume.** Sometimes the interviewer can't immediately access a copy of your resume so bring on with you. Make sure it is printed on high-quality paper.

- **References.** Try to get references from former employers on their letterhead and bring copies with you to give to the person you are interviewing with. A handful of references from well-respected companies will definitely make you stand out.

- **Transcripts.** If you're a college graduate, bring a copy of your transcripts with you to share with the person interviewing you. (If your transcripts aren't good, forget this tip.)

- **Background checks.** Most companies will check your criminal record, your credit, and your driving record. If there are any negatives in any of these areas explain them to the interviewer so he or she doesn't see them on your background check without any explanation from you.

- **Drug tests.** Most employers also require a pre-employment drug screen. If you aren't certain that you can pass a drug screen don't bother interviewing until you can.

- **Research the company you're interviewing with.** In the Internet age there is no excuse for not researching the company you want to work for. There is a plethora of information on companies of all size on the Internet. Simply Google the company and then take notes. Mention some of the things you learned during the interview. That will impress the interviewer.

- **Clean up your social media.** If there are pictures of you doing bong hits, passed out, or doing anything else embarrassing, get such things off of your social media sites. Almost all employers will do a Google search of your name which in most cases will lead them to your social media sites.

- **Your email address.** If your email address is something like partymonster@gmail.com, change it to something more businesslike. You know what I mean.

- **Ask for the job.** At the end of the interview, if you are interested in the job, ask for it. A lot of employers are suckers for people who "ask for the order".

- **Offer to work for free.** In our current slow growth economy, if you offer to work for free for a short period of time (provided you can afford to do so) this may separate you from the other job candidates as the prospective employer will get a "free look" at you in a work environment.

- **Send a thank you note.** I estimate that less than 10% of the people I interview send me even a thank you email, much less a written thank you note. A written thank you note is another thing that will set you apart from the pack.

If you're looking for a job try the above tips and I guarantee they will help you.

CHAPTER 121
WHY YOU SHOULD BE
AN AUTODIDACT

Some of you may be wondering, "What's an autodidact?" For those of you not familiar with the word, an autodidact is a self-taught person. Why should you be an autodidact? Well, there are many reasons.

First, I have found that most of us in business didn't study business in school. For example, I was a government/pre-law major in college. I thought I wanted to be a lawyer ever since I watched Perry Mason on TV as a child. However, in my junior year of college a guy who was a few years ahead of me in high school graduated from law school and was hired as an assistant district attorney in my home county at a starting salary of $17,500. As I would have to pay for three years of law school myself and as, at that time, the cost was going to be around $30,000 I decided that I wasn't going to work and borrow $30,000 to make $17,500 a year to start. I got into sales and never looked back. However, as I didn't have a business education I had to learn about business if I wanted to move out of sales into management. I decided to learn on my own. I read books on business, I subscribed to business magazines such as *Forbes* and *Fortune*, I started reading The Wall Street Journal daily, I listened to business and sales tapes in my car while driving around my sales territory, and I went to seminars and conventions. I have never stopped doing these things.

Second, the business world changes at a rapid pace. If you're going to succeed in business you need to be either an autodidact or have the time and money to continue to take graduate courses at a university. If you aren't growing, you're dying. I know a lot of people my age who haven't read a business book since college. Some of these people ask me how I am able to blog on so many topics, and the answer is: because I'm in autodidact. There is no finish line.

Third, it will help you succeed in the business world if you stay on top of changes in the industry in which you make your living. If you can converse with customers on topics related to their business, or better yet, inform them of changes in their industry with which they are not yet familiar, that will endear you to your customers. Customers want to buy from people and companies that are progressive and changing with the times, not companies that are trying to hold back the tides. Being an autodidact is good for business.

Fourth, if you're in management, being a lifelong learner will help you attract and keep top people. Sharp people don't want to work for a dinosaur. I'm almost 60 years old now and when I interview bright young people it's palpable how surprised they are that I can converse on so many topics of the day. I remember when I was younger and interviewed with a person that is my present age and I couldn't wait for the interview to end because there was no way I was going to work for this guy.

Fifth, it will help you in your dealings with lenders. About two years ago, our current lender assigned a new banker to our account. At our first meeting I did a PowerPoint presentation of over 50 slides on our business. I showed the new banker where our business was in the past, where we were then, and where we were going. At the end of the presentation he told me it was the single best presentation he had ever gotten from a client. Shortly thereafter he increased our credit line. If you're a business owner and you rely on a sharp CFO to do presentations to your banker, you're making a mistake. If the banker thinks that the CFO is the brains of the operation, not you, you may find your loan being called in the future.

In closing, my favorite Bible passage is about being a lifelong learner. If you're not familiar with it, it is Ecclesiastes 11:6 and it states, "In the morning sow your seed, and at evening withhold not your hand, for you do not know which will prosper, this or that, or whether both alike will be good." In other words, don't stop learning as you grow older. It may be things you learned later in life that will make you successful rather than things you learned while you are in school.

Are you an autodidact? If not, I hope you will be shortly.

CHAPTER 122

MY TOP TEN
PRODUCTIVITY TIPS

It has been said that if you want something done, ask a busy man to do it. That's because most busy people (if they are successful) have created a system that allows them to be more productive than the average person despite being very busy. As I am CEO of a nine location building products distribution business, CEO of a real estate holding company, on the boards of four for profit companies and one nonprofit organization people frequently ask me how I get so much done. Below are my top ten productivity tips:

1. **"To- do" list.** I don't use a standard to-do list. After reading *First Things First* by Stephen Covey I created a four grid spreadsheet that I use as my time planner. The four grids are important and urgent, important but not urgent, not important and urgent, and not important and not urgent. I update the spreadsheet every day before I leave the office so I begin the following day organized and ready to go. I also look hard at the spreadsheet every day for things that I can delete or delegate. Also, by reviewing it every evening before leaving the office I'm not surprised to see my tasks for the next day.

2. **Work first on the "important and urgent" tasks**. Sometimes it's tempting to knock off some small easy tasks from your to-do list but if you want to be highly productive you need to force yourself to complete several items from the important and urgent quadrant each day before you complete any of the easy tasks.

3. **Set deadlines and start dates for tasks.** Once you have done that track them using the Outlook Task feature so that you don't forget due dates. Once I put the due date for a task into Outlook I don't have to remember it. It pops up when I need to begin working on the task.

4. **Follow-up on the things you delegate before they are due.** If you wait for a project to be delivered to you on the assigned due date you may end up disappointed because the person you delegate it to may have forgotten about it. I typically send a reminder halfway between the date I assigned a task and the due date to make sure that the task hasn't been forgotten.

5. **Handle things only once.** I don't get a lot of paper mail anymore but if I need to respond to something I get in the mail I try to respond to it immediately. If I can't I set up a task in Outlook and scan the paper into my computer and then file it in my "to be responded to" Outlook file folder. With emails I need to respond to I do the same thing as above.

6. **Block out time on your calendar to do key tasks.** If you have a major project to do block out some time on your calendar and when that time arrives, turn off your phone, close your door (if you have one) and buckle down on completing the task as soon as possible.

7. **Document everything.** I don't rely on my memory. After meetings I send an email to all the participants documenting what was discussed. That way if there is ever a disagreement about what was discussed in the meeting there is a written record to review. I do this even for phone calls if what was discussed is important.

8. **Disable your emails from popping up in Outlook and on your smart phone.** Before I did this I would be working on something and an email popping up would distract me because I would, many times, respond quickly to the new email instead of finishing that which I was working on.

9. **Avoid paper files.** I scan all important documents into my laptop computer so that no matter where I am in the world, if our attorney, accountant, insurance broker, etc. needs an important document I can forward it immediately rather than rooting through a file cabinet.

10. **Have an agenda for meetings.** If you are chairing a meeting provide an agenda ahead of time so that people can be prepared and so you can stay on schedule. Meetings without an agenda tend to wander aimlessly and accomplish very little. If you aren't chairing the meeting ask for an agenda and don't go to the meeting unless you get an agenda. Your time is valuable... don't waste it on a meeting without an agenda.

CHAPTER 123

MANAGING
SUPPLIER RELATIONSHIPS

Most businesspeople don't need to be told to cultivate relationships with their customers, especially their top customers; however, most business owners and managers I talk to aren't proactive in managing supplier relationships. Why should you cultivate relationships with your suppliers? After all, you are buying from them so why should you romance them?

Well, the answer is simple. Your top suppliers can significantly enhance your profitability...if they want to. How can they do this? One of the most important ways is getting you product to sell when their products are in short supply. Yes, for the last several years the weak economy hasn't caused many products to be in short supply. However, throughout my career I have seen many times when products were in short supply, or even on allocation. If you have a strong relationship with your key suppliers they can get you products to sell even when they are in short supply. Also, suppliers (if they want to) can do other things for you such as rebates, extended payment terms, and provide you with marketing support funds. Are you starting to get my drift?

How can you manage supplier relationships? Here are some of the things I have done over the years:

- **Quarterly meetings.** In our company we meet with our key vendors quarterly to discuss how our purchases stack up versus the previous quarter and the previous year to date. We discuss opportunities to increase our purchases and come up with action plans to make them happen. This is also a good forum for suppliers to have access to our top executives and pitch new products, discuss any declines in purchases of some of their products, and get feedback on their marketing programs. You should never meet with a key supplier for quarterly meeting without meeting with your team beforehand to discuss what is going to be said and who is going to play what role. Also, after the meeting you and your executive team should discuss what happened at the meeting and whether your objectives were achieved.

- **Get to know the C level people at each of your key suppliers.** When you know the CEO, COO, CFO, etc. you can get favors that lower-level people within the supplier's organization don't have the authority to grant. I once also got the CFO of a supplier of mine to loan my company $2 million to buy a competitor. I pitched the CFO on how buying the competitor would cause us to buy more from their company. I don't think he would have agreed had I not entertained him at The Masters golf tournament the previous year.

- **Entertain your key suppliers.** As mentioned above, I have taken many key suppliers to prestigious events such as the U.S. Open golf tournament, The Masters, highly rated private golf clubs, to dinner and to shows, etc. Not only do you build important relationships with your key suppliers but as most of your competitors who buy from the same suppliers don't entertain them you stand out in a class of your own. This comes in very handy when you need a favor.

- **Don't take the last nickel off the table.** I have seen too many suppliers "beat their suppliers up" for the last nickel in each and every negotiation. That is pennywise and pound foolish. Someday you may need a favor from that supplier and that will be their time to get even. In fact, when negotiating a large deal, I ask the supplier if they are still making money on the deal. I explain that I want them to make money when dealing with us because I know that we won't have a good, long-term relationship if they aren't making money off of us.

- **Discount your bills.** Throughout my career I have made it my practice to take prompt pay discounts. Not only does this add substantially to your bottom line, but when you need a favor from a supplier or when you need an especially good price, your chances of success are much higher if you pay your bills early rather than late.

- **Buy strategically.** A lot of business owners I know don't give much thought as to why they buy from certain suppliers. A mentor of mine once told me that he buys from two types of suppliers: those who can help him and those who can hurt him. The former is rather obvious but the latter type of supplier may need some explanation. Depending upon your business, there may be some suppliers you aren't particularly fond of but if you don't buy from them they will sell your customers direct or sell one of your competitors when you don't want that particular competitor to have that product line. Think about your reasons from buying from each supplier and deal with them accordingly.

- **Pursue suppliers you want to buy from but who won't sell to you.** In my business, building products distribution, there are a fair number of exclusive relationships. When a supplier who I want to buy from won't sell me I have often spent several years "pursuing" a vendor I really need to round out my product offering. We make it a point to contact each supplier who presently is offering exclusive to one of our competitors, at least once a year. Sometimes we find that they have "fallen out of love" with one of our competitors and they finally accept our overture. If you have a supplier you want to buy from but they are selling someone else, don't accept this as being "carved in stone" and pursue them over the long term. When we have done so we have ended up buying from that supplier more often than not.

If you aren't already cultivating your relationship with your key suppliers, and suppliers you want to do business with, I hope this has made you think about adopting a new attitude towards your suppliers.

EPILOGUE

The reason I wrote this book is because, over the years, many friends, and people I have served on many boards with, have said things like, "You should write a book", speaking of business lessons I've shared with them, so I did. Also, I wanted to "Pay it forward" as I have bene-fitted from tremendous wisdom shared with me by some brilliant men-tors. I also wanted to share lessons I learned the hard way in hopes of sparing someone else from the mistakes I made along the way.

If you have some experiences or insights you wish to share I would greatly appreciate your comments and reactions to the lessons present-ed here. Please feel free to email me at jrsobeck@gmail.com.

ABOUT THE AUTHOR

Jim Sobeck was born, raised, and educated in Pennsylvania. During his career he has been in sales, manufacturing, marketing, sales management, and first became a CEO at age 34. He has bought four companies during his career and did one start-up. He has been married to Cindy since 1978 and has three successful, happy adult children, and one grandchild.

Made in the USA
Charleston, SC
31 May 2014